MW01505227

Science Of Being

Teachings by Eugene Fersen

Published 2011 by

THE LIGHTBEARERS PUBLISHING, LLC

a division of

THE SCIENCE OF BEING WORLD CENTER

All rights to the information in this book are reserved
and protected by Copyright Law.

No part of this book may be reporoduced in any manner

whatsoever without the written permission of

THE LIGHTBEARERS PUBLISHING, LLC

or

The Lightbearers ~ Science Of Being ~ World Center N.G.

and its Next Generation AHLB'S.

©2011 THE LIGHTBEARERS PUBLISHING, LLC

www.ScienceOfBeing.com

SCIENCE OF BEING

SCIENCE·OF·BEING
BY
EVGENE·FERSEN

Copyright © 2011

THE LIGHTBEARERS PUBLISHING, LLC

The Lightbearers ~ Science Of Being ~ World Center N.G.

All rights reserved.

ISBN-13: 978-0615913087 (The Lightbearers Publishing, LLC)
ISBN-10: 0615913083

THIS·BOOK·OF·SCIENCE·
·IS·DEDICATED
TO·THE·AVTHOR·OF·ALL
·SCIENCE·
TO·HIS·GLORY·
&·FOR·THE·GOOD·of·HVMANITY
BY·HIS·LIGHTBEARER·

SCIENCE·OF·BEING

·INTRODUCTION·

Let those who read this book understand that its main objective is to bring Enlightenment to Humanity through Pure Knowledge aflame with Love, and its mission is to pave the way to Peace and Harmony and Power.

Though a book of Science, it is a friend of true Religions and Philosophies. They will find their fundamental tenets scientifically explained by the Science of Being, which will also show them that they are all brothers, because Truth is One, and is the Golden Thread on which are strung the varied pearls of Religions and Philosophies.

The day will come when Humanity will have outgrown its present concepts of Divinity, when Man will have lost his faith in teachings based on Faith alone, the day when utter despair will grip the heart of a World which has lost its God. Humanity will then discover through the Science this book teaches that God has always lived with men, yet they have not known Him.

 ·THE·AVTHOR·

TABLE OF CONTENTS

Baron Eugene Fersen

Baron Eugene Fersen was the eldest son of a Grand Duchess of Russia/Poland, known as Marie Olga Alexandrovna Medem of the Royal House of Medem and DeLacy—two of the oldest and most prominent of all bloodlines in the history of royalty— reaching back thousands of years. His mother knew before his birth that he was to be a guiding light for the people of this World; she called him *Svetozar*, meaning *The Lightbearer*, which he began penning publicly when he volunteered in the Russian Red Cross during the war. The Baron's mother saw to it that her son had the proper teachers and education that would assist and support the Absolute Eternal Aspects of his Soul so as to fulfill his divine destiny.

Baron Eugene was a direct descendent of Count Axel Fersen on his father's side and on his mother's, William The Conqueror. Eugene's uncle was Count Leo Tolstoy, the writer famously known for his renowned literary works *War and Peace* and *Anna Karenina*. Tolstoy was one of Gandhi's greatest influences and friend.

Baron Eugene came to the United States for his second lecture tour in 1904 to share his already popularized teachings and lessons known as *The Science Of Being*. From 1906 through 1921, Baron Eugene was investigated by the U.S. Government's Justice Department as a possible radical. He was teaching what the U.S. Government termed as 'radical religious thinking.' This investigation accelerated during World War I, 1914-1918. In late September of 1921, the United States Government closed their investigation. By early 1923, the U.S. Government allowed Baron Eugene to become an American Citizen and granted him free reign to publish through the American Press, his already renowned teachings.

Before Baron Eugene was sworn in as an American, the presiding judge cautioned him, that once he took the oath to become an American Citizen, he would no longer be able to take the polish royal throne he was born to. Henceforth, Baron Eugene was known as Eugene Fersen to the American public, as Teacher and Author. Eugene knew his divine purpose and mission was not to reign over Humankind from a throne but to assume a modest seat of service for the spiritual progress of all Humanity.

Eugene Fersen was intimately associated with the world's most eminent teachers, scientists and philosophers. Some of his most profound personal teachers were from the lineage of the Great Magi. Eugene Fersen, 'The Teacher of The Teachers,' launched in his time the greatest 'Human Potential Movement' that would later become the inspiration for what he called, the 'New Age.' From the late 1800s, Eugene's teachings taught or influenced many of the great historical teachers: Charles Haanel (The Master Key System), Dr. Hotema, Elizabeth Towne (Publisher of Nautilus Magazine), Wallace D. Wattles (The Science Of Getting Rich and The Science Of Being Well), Edgar Cayce, Annie Besant (Translator of the Bhagavad Gita, Theosophist, and Leader of Woman's Rights), Huna Max Freedom Long (great teacher of the Huna ways and teacher to the founders of the Course In Miracles), Charles Fillmore (Founder of The Unity Church), Samuel Clemens (author of Mark Twain), William Walker Atkinson (one of the three Initiates of the Kybalion), Nikola Tesla, Manly P. Hall, Jon Peniel and the list goes on. Rudolph Steiner himself was touched by Eugene's teachings and had him as a guest speaker/ teacher in the Steiner Schools whenever Eugene could be available. His exceptional and unsurpassed teachings continue to influence Humanity today.

Eugene Fersen taught anyone who had a genuine interest in the *Science Of Being*, the Truth, and the path to spiritual and human liberation. At the time of his parting into the Great Beyond in 1956, he had personally instructed well over 20,000 students and at that time more than 100,000 people worldwide had read or been exposed to the teachings of the *Science Of Being*. These teachings today are regarded as some of the most inspiring literary works in the study and education of Quantum Science, Spiritual Science, Human Enlightenment and the study of the Soul.

Eugene came to share with us the Truth of these wisdoms with the hope that Humankind would free themselves from the myths that held them hostage and bound them to an un-liberated existence here on Earth. He shared that there are still vast amounts of profound wisdoms that remain veiled from Humankind because the un-liberated subconscious mind had become resistant to comprehending those truths. Eugene knew and had faith that as humans enlightened their bodies and minds and raised their Spiritual Vibrations as they lived in the physical world, more would be revealed to them.

Eugene Fersen, 'The Teacher of the Teachers' gave to the world with an open heart, mind and spirit these profound truths, his life's purpose, and his *Seat-of-Power and Privilege*. He believed deeply that all of Humankind regardless of race, class, creed, gender or difference should have access to these great wisdoms that were once only privy to the rich and powerful. He acquired, as he lived, the manna all alchemists are looking for, the peak of spiritual attainment. In that state is where one's body, mind and spirit reach Its highest vibrational aspect of spiritual evolution while living in physical form; where one's Spirit becomes One with Its pure Soul.

Eugene Fersen's life purpose was to bring to Humankind the lost principles of their first Primal Ancestors so as to assist Humanity to complete their task to awaken, to the All-knowing latent scintillating star that resides within each of their Absolute Eternal Souls.

Science Of Being Lightbearers World Center © 2004

The Relative Heavenly Eternal Realm
Know Thyself And Thou Shalt Know All

When Eternal Soul, through Its use of Spiritual Energy benevolently chose Mind-fully to separate from the Graces of the Heavenly Eternal Realm and Its Superconscious oneness with the Great Principle – The Creator, a new "Bio-Neuro-Spiritual World," and a Solar System to support Its inhabitants, were artfully born in this Universe. These new systems were solely encrypted with all the wisdoms and Life Force Energy to support and nourish Soul's sophisticated yet subastral creation, as long as the skills to decipher and access the Nature of their algorithm designs was preserved within the lineage of Soul's Spirit as it lived in this new World.

Hence, the Souls that came forth from this phenomenon emerged in elemental form- crystallized vibrations as separate aspects of the One true Nature of their prior Divinity and began creating substance to support their mission; their purpose in a now material world. These now Earth bound Souls, backed with the help of "The Great Law;" and with the hope that Supreme Harmony would reign in their new world, believed they would achieve and prevail at their Earthly purpose and task to create a Heavenly Eternal physical world.

Souls that once inhabited the Eternal Realm aspired to experience the spiritual alchemy of a "Bio-Neuro-Spiritual World." There encoded and housed in these newly formed matter-bound Heavenly bodies, was their "Eternal Supreme DNA." These Souls outfitted with the profound aspects and abilities of their Supreme Eternal Nature encoded in their human DNA; backed with their divine intent, began to re-create collaboratively the nature of their divinity in this new world. Souls in the Eternal Heavenly Realm, the Realm of Harmony, never knew fear, aging, death, hunger, poverty, physical suffering, pride, hatred or lacked the power of Love - attraction.

In the Eternal Realm, the Universal Laws operate as one law and those laws are infinitely governed by three immutable forces called "The Great Law." But, here in the Relative Realm there would be altered aspects to the Universal Laws in relation to Soul made manifest in a physical world: First - that Soul, through the Eternal Force of Its Spiritual Energy would have access to and the use of Its Supreme Aspects of Creative Force so as to create what It desired at Mind's free will. Secondly - in the Earthly Realm, the Universal Laws that were once inseparable Eternal Forces became separate Eternal Aspects of their once united Heavenly Nature. And Thirdly – If Soul's Spiritual Vibrations are not in tune with the Supreme Nature of Eternal Harmony before reentering the Eternal Realm, then by way of the governing aspects of the Law of Attraction and the supporting virtues of the Law of Evolution, Soul would be drawn again to incarnate solely with the intent to liberate Its Spiritual Vibrations from the magnetic rhythms that bind Soul's Spirit to the material plane of existence.

As these Souls took root in the Relative Realm, they began to manifest and create life without a conscious understanding about there being a physical separation from their Divine Nature, the Universal Laws, their Creator or one from another. But this would change throughout their evolution. While these Souls forged and carved out their new world they simultaneously created energy-dynamic relationship with all that they had created through the Laws of Cause and Effect, the Law of Rhythm and the non-negotiable Immutable Laws of the Universe. They began to Love and worship the perishable instead of the Eternal and created Laws from untruths instead of embracing the Laws that once brought them Salvation, Preservation and Liberation.

Most Scintillating as a Brilliant Star was to be the prevailing aspect of the Eternal Mind made manifest. But, throughout time on the physical plane of existence, mind was deceived by Its own power and misplaced Its benevolent Truth, Divinity and Eternal plan. Spirit reuniting with Its Eternal Twin, Soul and awakening to Its Divinity, has become Humanity's age old quest for the unknown. To "Know Thy Self," as a living manifestation of the All Powerful living force of the Eternal and to make this Wisdom Law (Truth,) once again has now become Humankind's foremost aim and their mind's greatest challenge.

The choice to transcend the Physical Realm and return to the ways of the Eternal was a path never lost; there at the bridge to the Infinite is a gate that swings freely and at will between these Worlds. Still today it seems for Humankind, that there is yet a long road to travel before Liberation is realized and materialized on the Earth Plane; but with the help of The Great Law and the merciful aspects of the Law of Evolution and its loyal ally Hope, Humanity will prevail.

As more Light is shed on the Wisdom that is before me in the rare archival documents written and taught by The Teacher of The Teachers, Eugene Fersen, I have been shown that there has always been a proper scientific and spiritual term for our Earthly Realm. It seems over time, it has escaped Humanity's grasp to embrace and be-hold. Now that we have entered the "Sixth Race of Humanity," the race of the "New Age," where much Truth has been laid before the feet of Humankind, it is now suitable and a moral obligation to reveal what has been shown to me and from this day forward address this realm by its proper and All Powerful name, "The Relative Heavenly Eternal Realm."

I have come to fully understand, as I embrace my purpose, my Destiny as Acting Head Lightbearer for the Science of Being ~ Lightbearers World Center the "Why," I was chosen to hold the space of the Seat Of Inspiration for this generation – that I would in my time, carry out the most important virtue of its duty - to put forth the unpublished Wisdom left for me in print without reservation or withholding. I have intimately come to know the Baron Eugene Fersen by reading and being with his work since I was a child. I was taught by his words and by the actions of my Lightbearer Family, the deeper meaning of Truth and shown the depths and tenacity of Love. While Eugene lived, he eradicated the forces of the rhythms that bound the human Spirit to the polarities found in this World.

As I continue to unfold and put into print the rare archival information, I know without a shadow of a doubt that these teachings and other wisdoms still not yet revealed were never to be kept secret from Humanity. These unprincipled actions have created and supported a consumptive deterioration in the Evolution of Humankind. Eugene never referred to the Science Of Being Teachings as Esoteric or attributed their wisdoms to any one philosopher or teacher except for the Great Principle and for very good reason, as those statements worked against the Law – Truth. He taught The Science Of Being teachings freely, whenever one was ready to learn and wherever he was given the opportunity to speak about them; he did so with a devotional determination that was unwavering, until he went into the Great Beyond.

The Seat of Inspiration, the seat Eugene Fersen sat in, has been an immeasurable seat for me to behold; I do my best to honor my Destiny and purpose in a good way; with a great respect for All Life. For as many thumbprints that exist in human form and blueprints found in Nature, that's how many religions reside on our planet. The path that each Spirit must live to become One again with Its Eternal Soul and Its Creator is as unique as Its thumbprint. As I honor the incomparable you, I also honor your personal relationship with the Eternal and the path – the "Why," you must live so as to unearth your Divine Destiny and return to the gate that swings freely and at will between the worlds.

Written and Copyrighted by Laura Taylor-Jensen, Acting Head Lightbearer
The Lightbearers ~ Science of Being ~ World Center N.G.

SCIENCE-OF-BEING

Note To Readers

Welcome to this new reprinting of *"The Science of Being"* by Baron Eugene Fersen, published exclusively by The Lightbearers - Science of Being - World Center and The Lightbearers Publishing. The original book was published in 1923 with a very limited circulation. The contents of the original book brought a timeless inspirational message for the ages, along with extraordinary physical features, such as pure gold ink, India Bible paper, various covers of leathers, including snakeskin, and faux leather bindings and original graphic illustrations by Malcolm Thurburn, a well known Scottish artist of the period. Great effort has been taken in reproducing the original art clearly and accurately from the original printing and in maintaining the integrity of intent by Baron Eugene Fersen with the emphasis he placed on certain text by using all capital letters. You will notice in this reprinted edition there are places where all capital letters are in TIMES ROMAN or all capital letters are in PAPYRUS. When you see all capital letters in TIMES ROMAN that was the way it was in the original text, which represented emphasis of that text. When you see all capital letters in PAPYRUS that was the text originally printed in gold ink and was used to represent the Pure Mental Ray, which was and is to impress the importance of the message on the subconscious human mind.

The original *"Science of Being"* book also featured the imprint of swastikas in gold ink throughout the text and in the beginning of most paragraphs. This, of course, was done many years prior to the misuse of the swastika. This ancient symbol represents the Sacred Four Square Principle, which you will learn about in this book, and it also represents Immortal Everlasting Life! The Baron chose to charge each paragraph with Universal Life Energy, which that golden symbol imbued in the original text. We at The Lightbearers Publishing and at The Lightbearers - Science of Being - World Center feel and know the sacredness of this ancient spiritual symbol and wanted to share its original true meaning and the Baron's intent.

In the Light and With the Light of Love,
    The Lightbearers Publishing staff,
    and The Lightbearers - Science of Being - World Center

ABOUT THE COVER PHOTO

THE MORNING STAR
"The Picture with a Soul"

This picture is considered the masterpiece of Princess M. Eristoff, a renowned Russian artist, member of the French National Society of Fine Arts, in Paris, whose wonderfully living portraits and extraordinary mystic subjects have won high honors in the annual exhibits at the French "Salon." It was painted during the first years of the Great War, at the request of Baron Eugene Fersen, of Moscow, Russia, its present owner. It represents in allegorical form, the transition NOW in process in the evolution of Humanity.

Profound night envelopes the desolate earth. A few stars smoulder dully through the blanketing clouds, and intensify the oppressive gloom below. Across the dreary waste comes a Being clad in white, his serene countenance illumined by the light he bears before him, his eyes fixed upon Infinity and Eternity. And through his eyes Infinity and Eternity look out upon the world. The helmet that encircles his brow is as if carved from the deep blue of an untarnished firmament, and holds written in its gleams Determination and Inspiration from above. His simple garment of white is lustrous with Purity of Purpose. And the light cradled in his strong hands is the Morning Star, Herald of the New Day, whose approaching glory even now stains the remote horizon with a greenish glow of promise. A golden cross flames in the heart of the Star, standing united with it as the emblem of a New Era, in which Love purifies Mind, and Gentleness refines Energy. Broad are the shoulders of this Bearer of the Light – broad enough to carry the burden of the whole world – and bare are his strong limbs. No covering guard his feet from the sharp stones that strew his path, or blunt the keen fangs of heat and cold and storms; yet his steps do not falter; he moves tranquilly on, strong in the knowledge of his mission, dispelling the mists and obscurity by the radiant splendor of that Star. At the touch of his bruised foot springs forth bluebells, ringing joy to the hearts of men, and his blood waters a flowery trail for those who will follow. On the stone panel beneath his feet is engraved the great message he brings to the world. "Men of the Earth, Brothers in Eternity, arouse your souls! Awake! The hour so long waited for, the promised hour, has come. Over the dark firmament of suffering Humanity is rising the Morning Star, heralding the day when you will understand that man's most sacred duty is to be Man – that is, to manifest Life, Intelligence, Truth, and Love. There is no higher aim, no vaster problem, and those who realize this will break the fetters with which Ignorance and Fear have bound unconscious Humanity, will stand up free, and know themselves to be the Eternal Manifestation of the Unmanifest, Witnesses of the Great ALL, Sons of the Absolute, whom you call – God."

This realization brings to man powers before unknown, because so great. The four giants who serve Nature, the Elements, - Air, Fire, Earth, and Water – are laid prostrate at his feet, dominated by him.

The two aspects of the Star – Phosphorus, the Morning Star, the Star of Gladness, announcing to Humanity the glorious birth of a new day, and Hesperus, the Evening Star, the star of mystery and sadness, warning Humanity of the approaching darkness – unite to form henceforth a single Star. And on the side of Hesperus, a triangle, falling amid streaks of lightning, symbolizes Humanity's involution, while on the other side, the side of Light, is seen the flame of Love lifting the same human triangle back to the realm of Eternal Harmony. A dark swastika, protected by the fiery cross, adorns the left capital of the two pillars a further symbol of the same idea of involution, and is contrasted to the luminous swastika of evolution which burns from the shadow of the same cross on the right capital.

Malcolm Thurburn, the author of this mystical frame, is an English artist whose novel and original ideas, have created a great sensation in America and Europe. Both artists, Princess Eristoff and Malcolm Thurburn, have embodied their very souls in this picture, and thereby endowed it with an extraordinary appeal which mere technical perfection could never impart. The more one sees it, the more fascinating it grows, a living messenger to those who possess it, of wonderful times to come. It is a picture which brings blessings and harmony to the homes where it abides. And above all, it is a real companion, because it is A PICTURE WITH A SOUL.

Size of the actual picture is 16 x 34
and available at ScienceofBeing.com

LESSON ONE

SCIENCE·OF·BEING
FIRST·DAY

LESSON·ONE
THE·ABSOLVTE (SPIRIT)
THE·FIVE·ASPECTS·OF·THE·GREAT·PRINCIPLE

THE·FALL
THE·BEGINNING·OF·INVOLVTION
"LIKE·A·STAR·FALLING·FROM·HEAVEN
DID·HE·FALL·TO·EARTH"

CREATION — "LET·THERE·BE·LIGHT"
THE·EARTH·AS·FLAMING·NEBVLA
ELEMENT — FIRE — INVOLVTION
THROVGH·FIRE
COLOR — — GOLD·&·ORANGE

SCIENCE-OF-BEING
FIRST-DAY

> **·I·AM·ONE·**
> **VNITY·IS·THE**
> **LAW·OF·THE**
> **ABSOLVTE**

LESSON - ONE
THE·ABSOLVTE·(SPIRIT)

GREAT question – the greatest of all questions – has been asked by Humanity for countless ages, "Is there a God?" From the point of view of Religion, it is accepted on faith that there is a God, Divinity, Who is called the Father of Man and of the Universe. But human beings are not satisfied with believing on faith; they want to know, to have irrefutable proofs of the existence of Divinity. Therefore has it become the task of Science to investigate the matter and find an answer to this question, an answer which will satisfy the searching of the rational mind; and Science has solved the problem nobly.

Science-of-Being

卐 Through scientific investigation, it was discovered that there is a Universal Force, which may be termed Eternal Energy – Primal Energy – pervading the whole Universe, filling Infinite Space.

卐 If Primal Energy fills Infinite Space for one moment, it becomes at that moment one with Space; and if it is one with Space for one moment, it must be one with Space for Eternity, because there is no place where it can lose itself. Therefore, by logical reasoning, the Basic Energy of the Universe is found to be Infinite, and at the same time Eternal, has always been and always will be so. Through further investigation, it was discovered that Infinite Energy expresses itself in most admirable laws, sublime laws; that it shows the profoundest intelligence and logic, a self-consciousness expressed in the divinest terms; laws invariable, true to themselves, mathematically correct, and above all, harmonious and beautiful.

卐 As a result of all this reasoning, was discovered, through Its first Universal Manifestation as Primal Energy, That which has always existed, the Eternal Unmanifest called God, conscious of Its own power, law emitting, law abiding and most Harmonious. In other words, there is a Unit, a One, existing eternally, expressing Itself through Its Creation, the Universe, consciously governing it, sustaining it in a condition of Eternal Harmony, and loving it – for Harmony and Love are one. Harmony means Attraction. Love IS Attraction.

卐 Thus Science has discovered Divinity under another name. Therefore for the word "God," which would have been used in Religion or Philosophy, will be substituted a word having a deeper meaning, covering broader ground, - the word "Principle."

卐 The word Principle is not related especially to Divinity, but applies equally to every science, logic, activity and art, as the principle of music, the principle of mathematics, etc. The word Principle gives a clearer idea of the Great First Cause, of Divinity, than does the word "God." The word itself cannot be exhausted by its various definitions, and if instead of a few definitions, we should give ten thousand, the whole ground would not have been covered. Yet there are five words which characterize the word "Principle" in general,

LESSON - ONE

including Principle as applied to the Great First Cause (Divinity), The Great Principle.

Scientific Definition of the Word Principle

卐 "PRINCIPLE IS THAT WHICH CREATES, CONSTITUTES, GOVERNS, SUSTAINS AND CONTAINS ALL." These five words include all the various lesser definitions. What must Principle do first? First it must CREATE, because it cannot handle anything before it has created the very thing it has to handle. Thus the first activity of each principle, no matter if it is the principle of music or of mathematics or of anything else, must be creation. The principle of music creates notes, the principle of mathematics creates numbers, etc.

卐 But creation does not inevitably mean order. It maybe chaos. So that there should be order, it must CONSTITUTE, that is, assign to each phenomenon its proper place which it will keep eternally. With numbers, the activity of constitution demands that one is made 1, two is made 2, three is made 3, etc. and each has its proper place. Two can never lapse into three, or three can never become four, - they are all IMMUTABLE. It is only because they are what they are, eternally, immutably, that we can calculate at all mathematically. The most complicated, intricate calculations are possible only because each cipher has its place assigned, constituted in order out of chaos.

卐 What is the next activity of Principle? It must bring forth out of itself its laws – changeless laws – by which it GOVERNS that which it has created and that which it has put in order, constituted. These laws are then named. There are, for example, the laws of mathematics. Through the applications of these laws we attain the invariable result of our calculations. If we misapply the laws we make mistakes. This applies equally to music, to logic, etc.

卐 But the acts of creation, constitution and governing may be for but a moment. There is nothing in these three activities which ensures their continuance. After Principle has created, constituted and governed, it must SUSTAIN its very creation so as to make it permanent, eternal.

SCIENCE-OF-BEING

卐 And finally, if Principle creates everything there is out of itself, it must then CONTAIN within itself all its creation. It must be the father of its creation, It must be the circumference, from within which springs all creation; and since Principle from its own center creates all and becomes its own circumference, therefore, it is the center and circumference of all. PRINCIPLE IS ALL.

卐 So it is with the Great Principle, The Great First Cause, Whom we call Divinity, or God. FROM ETERNITY OUT OF ITSELF THE GREAT PRINCIPLE CREATED THE UNIVERSE, INCLUDING MAN AND EVERYTHING ELSE IN THE UNIVERSE. FROM ETERNITY IT ASSIGNED TO EACH CREATED THING ITS PROPER PLACE. Every blade of grass has its place, every star knows its course; and as long as all keep their places and perform their duties, the Law of Order in the Universe continues to operate. But if they should slip from their places or fail in their duties, there is chaos. The Law of Order and Harmony is transgressed.

卐 AFTER IT HAS ASSIGNED TO EVERYTHING ITS PROPER IDENTITY, ITS INDIVIDUALITY, IT ISSUES FROM ITSELF THE UNIVERSAL, CHANGELESS LAWS, WHICH THEN GOVERN THEM. Everything down to the smallest electron is governed by Its Laws – Laws as precise, as invariable, as mathematical as the laws of mathematics itself, for mathematics is part of Its Creation and is therefore subject to Its Laws. Nothing can be above or beyond these Laws, for they are a manifestation of the Eternal Activity of the Great Principle Itself.

卐 THE FOURTH ACTIVITY OF THE GREAT PRINCIPLE IS ITS POWER TO SUSTAIN. IT POURS OUT ALL LIFE AND ENERGY FROM ITSELF, AND SANCTIONS AND SUPPORTS ITS OWN LIFE, INTELLIGENCE, LAWS AND LOVE SO THAT THEY WILL EXIST WITH IT ETERNALLY. From It proceeds all.

卐 And lastly, as the mother-bird covers her fledglings with her wings, so the Great Principle enfolds all Creation within Its boundless protection and Love. IT CONTAINS THE WHOLE UNIVERSE and therefore may be said to be in a way greater than Its own Creation. Yet It is identical with

LESSON - ONE

Creation, for Creation is the exact counterpart of the Great Principle, the Eternal Unmanifest, of which we perceive but the Manifestation. No one has seen the Great Principle, the Unmanifest, at any time. We perceive and appreciate It only through Its manifest Laws. THE UNIVERSE IS THE MANIFESTATION AND THE SCIENTIFIC, ACTUAL PROOF OF THE EXISTENCE OF THE GREAT PRINCIPLE.

TO THIS PRESENT STATE OF HUMAN CONSCIOUSNESS, THE GREAT PRINCIPLE APPEARS IN FOUR DISTINCT ASPECTS –

LIFE

MIND

TRUTH

LOVE

卐 They are in a certain scientific order; they have been so eternally and cannot be changed. It has been said, "God is first Love." But one cannot love if one does not already live, and even Divinity Itself cannot reverse such a sequence. THE GREAT PRINCIPLE IS FIRST LIFE. It must first live and then It can think. It must first live and then It can express Truth, Law. It must first live and then It can love. THE FIRST ASPECT OF THE GREAT PRINCIPLE, THEREFORE, IS LIFE.

卐 What comes next? MIND. For Life must become conscious of itself, conscious of its own existence. If it were not conscious of itself, Life might be said not to exist completely; but it is able to say, "I think, therefore I am."

卐 Next must come TRUTH, LAW. The Self Conscious Life must be true to itself eternally, law-emitting, law-abiding, since it can only work harmoniously when it is true to itself.

卐 And finally, what must be last? It must be LOVE-HARMONY. For if Life were not capable of Love, of Harmony, it would be set against itself, repelling instead of attracting, self-hating and therefore self-destructive. Love and Harmony are synonymous terms. LOVE IS THE LAW AND ALSO THE FULFILLING OF THE LAW; it is Love alone that sets the seal of Eternity on all; it is Love alone that justifies Eternity and makes it what it should be, a blessing. Without Love, Eternity would be the most terrible hell imaginable, for it is only when we know that there will be Everlasting Harmony that we can face Eternity. And the only guarantee of Eternal Harmony lies in the fact that The Great Principle Itself must love eternally, in order to maintain throughout Eternity Its Own Existence. That is why we cling to Love to the very last, when all else, Life and Mind and Truth, have apparently failed us. LOVE IS NOT FIRST IN ORDER BUT IN IMPORTANCE. Whatever else may be achieved will be of no use without Love, for it is the beauty and radiance and joy of the Universe.

卐 These are the Four Aspects of the Great Principle. They are instantaneous and simultaneous, yet expressed in their logical order. This order cannot be changed; it is fundamental and scientific. Those Four Aspects of the Great Principle, as manifested in our lives, may be regarded as the four corners of a perfect square, and their mutual relations analyzed from a scientific point of view.

卐 Let us take the upper left corner, Life. What does Life face, if we pass a line across the square diagonally? We find Life facing Truth. What does this mean? It means that THE FIRST ETERNAL DUTY OF LIFE IS TO BE LIVED, that it must be true to itself. For if Life is not expressed through activity there is no hope possible for it. In order that there should be continued activity, energy manifested (thus making all else possible) Life must be true to its own mission, TO LIVE; for this reason it faces Truth.

卐 What has Life on its right side? It has Mind. The right side is always considered the dominant side, because it stands for the right. Therefore Life has Mind on its right side. This implies that LIFE MUST BE CONSCIOUS OF ITS OWN EXISTENCE, of its own operations, of its own duties, for if it were not self-conscious, it could not achieve all that is should achieve.

卐 Upon the left side, Life has Love. This means that Life must not only be constantly active, conscious of itself and it activities, but that in order to be eternal, IT MUST ALSO BE A LOVING AND HARMONIOUS LIFE. It is the left side which is the side of the heart, the organ, the symbol of Love.

LESSON · ONE

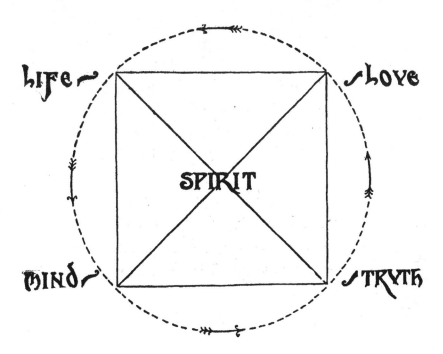

We come now to the lower left corner of the square, Mind, and draw a line across the square diagonally. What does Mind face? It faces Love. This means that the Minds eternal duty is to be expressed first in Love; it must interpret Harmony, for without this nothing would be good in its work. Therefore, Mind must always face Love. THIS IS THE GREAT LESSON THAT MIND HAS TO LEARN, THE LESSON OF LOVE.

What has Mind on its right side? It has Truth. This means that it must demonstrate Truth, because Mind had once perverted Truth in his own nature. It is said of Satan that he was a liar from the beginning; and yet Satan is Lucifer, is Mind. Therefore, THE NEXT LESSON THAT MIND MUST LEARN IS TO BE TRUE. Truth implies Law —a constant reminder to Mind to be law-abiding, for it was Mind also that first violated the Law.

And upon the left side, Mind has Life. It must express activity – MIND MUST BE OPERATING, THINKING. As that is a natural function for Mind, it becomes a secondary duty; hence Mind has Life on its left side.

SCIENCE-OF-BEING

卐 At the third corner of the square stands Truth. What does Truth face? It faces Life, for TRUTH MUST FIRST BE LIVED, Truth which is not lived is not Truth. For that reason, the first thing that Truth has always to face is its own expression, its manifestation.

卐 Law, the corollary of Truth, must be demonstrated, put into operation. The Laws of the Universe must be eternal and voicing themselves eternally, or the Universe would sink into chaos.

卐 And what stands upon the right side of Truth as its dominant power? Love. FOR TRUTH, LAW, MUST PROVE ITSELF TO BE ARDENT, COMPASSIONATE, TENDER, a law of harmony and beauty. It must be radiant and great-hearted, not the cold, dry truth of the intellect. It is the burning Truth of Love.

卐 On the left side of Truth stands Mind. It signifies that Truth must be expressed consciously; the Law must be intelligently formulated; but those functions being natural to Truth, Mind is placed on the left side of it.

卐 And finally to the fourth activity of The Great Principle. What does Love face? Love faces Mind. Love manifests itself last, but is the most sublime of the Four Aspects. IT IS A POWER SO GREAT, A GIFT SO PRECIOUS, THAT IT MUST NEVER BE WASTED OR MISUSED. IT MUST BE USED INTELLIGENTLY; FOR THAT REASON IT FACES MIND OR THE CAPACITY OF DISCRIMINATION. Jesus said: "Cast not your pearls before swine." Do not squander Love, the precious gift, on those who do not understand it. Jesus knew these laws, and the relation of these Aspects of the Great Principle to each other; therefore he warns us to be careful not to throw away this most wonderful treasure. SO LOVE MUST FIRST FACE MIND.

卐 What has Love upon its right sides? It has Life. This means that Love must be continually expressed in activity. IF WE DO NOT LIVE LOVE, THEN WE DO NOT LOVE.

卐 At its left side is Truth. Love must be true to itself. But Love IS always true to itself. Truth, Law, is a very secondary power for Love, because by its own harmonious nature it is always law-abiding, always true to itself.

LESSON - ONE

The Two greatest powers in the World, Love and Mind, are facing each other in the Square. They are the two manifestations, the first dual emanations of the great Principle of Divinity, - Christ and Lucifer. Love expresses Christ; Mind expresses Lucifer. Satan was once called Lucifer, The Carrier of Eternal Light; his Eternal Mate was Christ, the Anointed One. But Mind in his pride had fallen, AND CHRIST, LOVE, TO SAVE THE WORLD, ASSUMED THE ACTIVITIES WHICH HAD BELONGED TO LUCIFER AND BECAME BOTH IDEAL LOVE AND PERFECT MIND. Originally it was not so, and finally it will also not be so. There will come an adjustment, and the two counterparts will be re-united and become equal again.

Mind comes to us and leads us to Perfection, yet it cannot enter with us through the door of Perfections, of Heaven, for it is an exile from Heaven. For the time being it is shut out; and because it is seemingly separated from the Infinite Principle, it cannot grasp Infinity. It is only through Intuition and through emotion, especially of the higher self, that we can become One with the Great Principle, and rise into the highest vibrations, into the Infinite All. Mind can not bring us there. It is Love, the Christ in our nature, that part of us which has never fallen and which has remained perfect eternally, which ALONE CAN LEAD US BACK TO INFINITY. It is therefore our duty to work out of limitations imposed on us by Mind, the Lucifer principle in us, and to ATTUNE MIND TO THE CHRIST PRINCIPLE IN US; this redemption will unite again these two apparently diverse principles in Eternal Harmony.

Now if equal lines are drawn from the four corners of the square upwards to a common point, the figure produced will be a pyramid. And if we work harmoniously and simultaneously from the four corners, Life, Mind, Truth, and Love, and extend these to one point, that point will symbolize SPIRIT the Absolute, the All-inclusive Principle from which everything proceeds and to which it finally returns. The ancient Pyramid of the Egyptians, built so many centuries ago, meant this very thing. It meant Divinity working from the four-square Humanity, through Life, Mind, Truth and Love to Its own apex, Spirit.

SCIENCE·OF·BEING

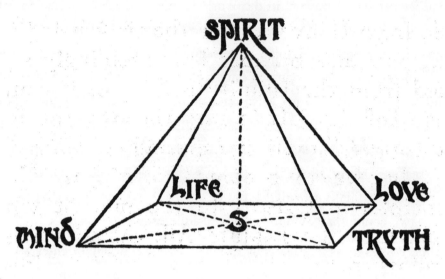

🔆 Geometrically it would be impossible to construct a perfect pyramid unless each side were equal to the others; the apex would never be reached if even on side failed in its proportions. So it is just as impossible from the point of view of the Absolute Law to reach Spirit, if any one of the Aspects of the Great Principle in us is at fault. THE FOUR SIDES MUST BE HARMONIOUSLY EQUAL; none must fail or dominate the others. We should not concern ourselves too much about reaching the apex, Spirit, if only we work conscientiously at harmonizing the four sides, for the Law itself will look after the results of our work.

🔆 We are building up the ground under ourselves in working out these four Aspects of the Great Principle, for EVERY TIME THAT WE PERFORM AN ACTION ENERGETICALLY, INTELLIGENTLY, ACCURATELY, AND LOVINGLY WE HAVE PLACED BENEATH OUR FEET A STRATUM THAT EXTENDS TO THE FOUR ANGLES OF OUR SQUARE. Thus we have risen by this much, and gradually, using every activity performed with energy, intelligence, accuracy and love, as a step upwards, we shall rise nearer and nearer to that point which is Spirit, and which is the final goal of all human endeavor. When we reach Spirit we do not ourselves know how we reached It. Nor do we need to know, for it works

LESSON - ONE

according to Law, and all we must do is to LET THE LAW WORK FOR US AND NOT CONCERN OURSELVES WITH THE FRUITS OF OUR ACTIONS. If the work is good, the result will be good, according to the law of Cause and Effect. It is all so simple, and yet human beings so little understand it and wonder why their progress is stopped. Some one says, "I am so loving, so generous, I am willing to give everything. Why can I not rise?" Perhaps one of his qualities is not developed, one of the corners of his pyramid not properly built.

卐 The problem is to find out which one of the corners is underdeveloped. Let us take, for instance, any one of the little daily actions which all of us have continually to perform in our lives – not something which we especially like to do, but just an ordinary action which has more the character of a duty than of pleasure – and let us analyze how we perform that action. If we do it energetically, the Life corner is strongly built. If we do it intelligently, the Mind corner is properly represented. If we do it accurately, the corner of Truth (Law) is also well balanced. And if we do it lovingly, the Love corner is then in harmony with the other three corners. But if we discover in the actions we analyze that some of those four qualities are too weak in comparison with the strong, all we have to do is to reinforce the weak characteristics in order that they should strike a proper balance with the strong. NOW BY ONE OF THOSE ORDINARY ACTIONS OF OURS WE CAN FIND OUT THE WHOLE OF OUR CHARACTER, just as by analyzing a drop of water taken from a pool we are able to discover all the qualities of the water of the whole pool. In correcting the weak sides in those little daily actions of ours, we will by and by improve our whole character and make it harmonious, thus properly building up our Life Pyramid. This will secure us a speedy progress in our individual evolution.

卐 THE POINT IS THE CONSUMMATION OF PERFECT HARMONY FROM ALL SIDES. From these four basic corners, from the so-called human square, we rise to the Divine Point. If we look down from above, we find the

SCIENCE-OF-BEING

Four Aspects, the Manifestation below; and if we look up form the Four we behold the one Point, Unity, the Great Principle, the Unmanifest, Spirit.

卐 And thus we have also the correlation of numbers; we have the number four of our human square and the number three of the Divine triangle represented in the side of the pyramid, four added to three making seven, a number of completeness. Besides that, by multiplying four and three, we have twelve, again a number of completeness, but manifesting it under a different aspect. Seven and twelve play a very important role in our present stage of Evolution.

卐 When we realize these Aspects of the Great Principle, our duty is naturally to manifest them in our lives, to live the Four Aspects. What does it mean TO LIVE LIFE? Of course we are all living. To live Life means much more than that. IT MEANS TO DO ALWAYS ONE'S DUTY AT THE RIGHT TIME. Now most human beings do not at all do their duty at the right time. They have no idea of the necessity of doing it at the right time. Imagine an orchestra playing; the duty of each musician, according to the laws of orchestration, is to sound his notes, to play his passage, at a certain time; and if he and his fellow musicians do it properly, we have beautiful and harmonious music. But if each musician were to play his notes a little earlier or a little later, what would happen? There would be discord. In a way man cannot play false, because all notes are true notes; but man can play false when he plays the right notes at the wrong time. This is the very thing we do when we individuals fail in our duties. We either do the right thing at the wrong moment, or else when the right moment comes we forget our obligations. The result for us is discord. The discord which we create in this way is the most detrimental, because if our actions are maladjusted and ill-timed, we start new causes which will have their results at a given time; and if the causes are started at the wrong time the effects also will come at the wrong time. Either way we plant the seeds of disharmony, and for that very reason so often we do not seem adjusted to our lives, and find that things continually happen to us in a disharmonious way. Our days are made up of a number of small events, some of which are seemingly important, some of no importance; but there is usually something that does not work properly, and the cause of it is an action hidden in the past. We had not performed our duty at the right time. We must always see if there is an obligation to meet, and we not fail in it. If there is a greater duty to perform and a smaller one to perform, and we see that there is some one who is able to perform the smaller duty in our place, we are justified in leaving it and taking up the greater. But if there is on one to perform the smaller duty and smaller was the first to appear, we must accomplish that one first; for after all it is nothing but a human concept of smallness or greatness. Everything is great in a way – and everything is small in a way. In a symphony one note is not more important than another note. They are all equally important. The most delicate note is just as important as the deepest sounding one, because each has its proper place. Therefore, we must not forget that Life is just as scientific as the music of an orchestra, and that if we want to live our lives harmoniously, we must play or part as conscientiously as we would in an orchestra. Life is one great orchestra. That is what is meant by living Life, TO DO ONE'S DUTY ALWAYS AT THE PROPER TIME AND NEVER TO WORRY ABOUT THE RESULT. THE RESULT WILL COME RIGHT INEVITABLY IF WE ACT RIGHTLY. There is a Law that will show the way. When we shall know the Law, we will move through our lives in serenity.

卐 Now what does it mean TO LIVE LIFE CONSCIOUSLY, INTELLIGENTLY – to demonstrate Mind in Life? Of course we are all thinking people; some of us are people of much knowledge, of great intellect; and yet to demonstrate Intelligence, Mind, in our lives means more than that. It means that WE SHOULD ALWAYS JUDGE RIGHTLY, ALWAYS KEEP TO THE MAIN ISSUES, ALWAYS TAKE THE ESSENTIAL AND GIVE TO THE NON-ESSENTIAL ITS PROPER PLACE. Above all, it means that WE SHOULD NOT LOSE OURSELVES IN DETAILS, that we should retain a proper mental perspective, because to lose oneself in details is one of the besetting sins of Humanity. If we wish to analyze a tree, and come so near to it that we can see only the leaves, we will find that we have no right impression of the tree as a whole. The study of a leaf will not reveal the character of the tree. We must stand at some distance in order to see the complete tree; then only is it possible to say, "There is the trunk, these are the branches, and these are the leaves." That is what we should do, and that is what so few of us do in life. We are usually losing ourselves in details, and giving to non-essentials a more import role than to essentials. TO LIVE INTELLIGENTLY MEANS TO GIVE TO EACH PERSON AND TO EACH THING THEIR PROPER PLACE, to keep one's judgment clear and to try to judge as impartially as possible. In other words, TO SIMPLIFY THINGS AND NOT COMPLICATE THEM. The complexity of life in every direction is one of the greatest failings of the world, especially of our modern civilization. The Great Principle is the One Point. There is nothing more simple than a point. At the same time the Great Principle is a Sphere. There is nothing more perfect, complete, and at the same time more simple than a sphere. It is perfection in absolute simplicity.

卐 Now what does it mean TO LIVE TRUTH? We are taught to be truthful, and we realize the offense of a deliberate lie. Yet to live Truth is more than that. It signifies that WE SHOULD MEAN ALWAYS WHAT WE SAY. Most of us human beings do not mean at all in our conversation what we say. We usually say one thing and mean another entirely different. We say, "I love you so much that I would die for you!" How many of us really mean this? With most it is only a manner of talking. We live in such an age of exaggeration, that when we come in contact with people who tell the truth, we do not always believe it. We have grown accustomed to discount the truth. People do not realize consciously the tremendous value of having the word correspond to the thought. In a certain passage of the Sacred Book called the Bible, a chapter begins: "In the beginning was the Word and the Word was with God and the Word was God." What does it mean? IN THE BEGINNING EXISTED THE VIRTUE OF OMNIPOTENCE, THE POWER TO MANIFEST, TO EXPRESS ITSELF, AND IT WAS WITH THE GREAT PRINCIPLE AND IT WAS THAT GREAT PRINCIPLE. Therefore is the word so tremendously powerful. A WORD SHOULD BE A CREATION, SHOULD BE LAW. How have we human beings used the word? As so many dead leaves, as so much worthless sound, as of no value. And this is a great loss for us because we are squandering one of the greatest powers in the Universe, the power of Truth. Therefore TO LIVE TRUTH IS ALWAYS TO MEAN WHAT WE SAY. When we say it is day, we must mean it is day, and when we say it is night, we must mean night; and if for some reason we feel that we cannot tell the truth, it is better not to say anything than to tell a lie, because of THE DISCONNECTION BETWEEN THE THOUGHT AND THE WORD. For thus both thought and word are rendered powerless. The law says that the effect must correspond to the cause. Therefore, in disconnecting the two, we are violating one of the fundamental Laws, the Law of the Great Principle, a Law so potent in our hands. THERE IS NO COMPROMISE WITH THE ABSOLUTE.

There is yet another point. We often tell untruths in jest. We do not mean it. We know it is an untruth and it is meant to be an untruth. We very often make fun of people and things without really meaning to be unkind or wishing to do harm. But there is a law which states that RIDICULE KILLS. IF WE MAKE FUN OF SOMETHING, WE KILL IN THE INDIVIDUAL THE SENSE OF THAT SOMETHING. If it is a good thing, something emanating from the Source of Perfection, it cannot be killed; but we can destroy in an individual his sense of that thing, which is the same as killing it in him. There is an orator who makes a speech full of intelligence and sincerity, and who impresses his audience with the power and beauty of his words. The opposing party can most easily destroy the effect of his speech by ridicule. A better or more noble speech would not as easily destroy it, but a few frivolous words of derision would make a burlesque of his speech, would make his audience laugh, and in that moment would destroy their sense of the value of the speech. Many know this power and use it. Many use the power and do not know it. It is important, therefore, to know that we can destroy whatever we want by ridicule, by laughing at it, but we must be careful that it is not something good, or sacred to us. Ridicule and laughter are like a two-edge sword-they destroy in both directions. If we have something which is sacred to us and which we would keep sacred for ourselves, we should never let anyone make fun of it, because in ourselves it will be destroyed. It is the operation of the law. Nature has given us the gift of laughter to neutralize negative impression, because there is so much disharmony around us, that if we did not have that gift we would be absolutely overwhelmed by disharmony. That is why, when we see something inharmonious, we laugh at it. If we were to take it seriously it would not be destroyed and would harm us; and as we do not want that, as we want only Harmony real to us, we laugh at disharmony and thus destroy our sense of it. And that is why we have theatres and other places where people can go and laugh and amuse themselves; because this life is so strenuous that it would require a great deal of mental effort to throw off the disharmony form the mind. There is the easier way – we go laugh it away. It seems that if we see something funny we relieve ourselves of the burden. This gift which Nature has given us let us remember to be very careful in using.

卐 Last comes LOVE—TO LIVE LOVE, TO MANIFEST LOVE IN OUR LIVES. What does that mean? To love is natural to us because it is a basic Law of Nature. There is no one on Earth who does not love somebody or at least something. There is the miser; he loves gold. He is supposed to be one of the most despicable of beings, yet he loves; only he loves a metal. It is a precious metal, a noble metal, and he therefore loves it. Some day he may love an animal, a still higher concept of Love; and finally he will love a human being; and again there are the various grades of human beings for him to love, always raising him higher and higher. Even the man who goes and steals something, who goes and kills somebody, why does he do it? Out of love for something. He wants to get that which is dear to him. That is a mis-application of Love, for the perversion of which he will some day pay the penalty, but still it has Love latent in it. Therefore, wherever we go we shall never fail to find people loving something or somebody. But to love completely, to demonstrate Love in our lives, is much more than that. It means that WE SHOULD ALWAYS TRY TO FEEL LOVING TO OUR FELLOW MEN, TO EXPRESS OUR LOVE-NATURE EVERY INSTANT AS MUCH AS WE CAN.

Lesson - One

"GIVE TO THE STRANGER THE RICHNESS OF THY SMILE," is the gentle appeal of Love. What does it mean? It means that we should give even to the stranger, whom we do not know, expressions of love. We all try to do our measure of good for our fellow beings, yet very often, in little things and things dear to the human heart, we omit gentleness, a smile. It is not the thing itself which counts, but the way the thing is done or the way it is given. One can give a little, simple gift with so much love in the way of giving that it will appear to be like the greatest treasure; and one can give away with the stroke of the pen a whole fortune, and people would take it because it is a fortune but would not feel the preciousness in it; for it is the motive which counts, the Love in the action. "NO MATTER WHAT YOU DO, IF THERE IS NO LOVE IN YOUR HEART TO SUPPORT IT, ALL YOUR SACRIFICE IS IN VAIN," is a wonderful and scientific statement found in the Bible. We may give to the needy the most valuable gifts, yet if there is no Love in what we do, all that is in vain. Love is that which, because of its constructive power, makes every service so precious; and that is why, especially in these days, we should always try to express the kindness we may feel to people. It is a very important thing that we should not keep Love unmanifested, but should at every opportunity disclose it, show it forth, manifest it, be it in a word, in a smile, in a look or in a handshake. "When he or she looks at you, you feel as if you have received a precious gift," is a very beautiful saying among the peasants in Russia. It means that one feels enriched by the simple look of an individual, regardless of whether it is a man or a woman, for whether it is a man or a woman, for sex does not make any difference; but the mere Love, the richness of the look, makes one feel as if one had received something worth a great deal. That shows how valuable Love is. All things can be bought; LOVE IS THE ONE THING WHICH CAN NEVER BE BOUGHT. That is why it is really precious and that is why we should never be ungenerous with it, because there is always enough for us to give. In fact, the more we give, the more there is to be given. Now that does not at all contradict what was said before in explaining the quadrangle, where Love faces Mind. ONE SHOULD NOT

31

SCIENCE·OF·BEING

SQUANDER LOVE AS A SPECIAL GIFT ON THOSE WHO ARE NOT
WORTHY BUT SHOULD RADIATE LOVE AS A GENERAL GIFT TO
ENEMIES AS TO FRIENDS, ALIKE TO ALL, JUST AS THE SUN SHINES
ON THE WICKED AS ON THE GOOD, ON THE FLOWER AS ON THE
WEED, ALL THINGS RECEIVING THE SUN'S RAYS EQUALLY, EVEN
IF THEY DO NOT MAKE EQUAL USE OF THEM.

LESSON - ONE

THE FIVE STATEMENTS OF BEING

~~~~~~~~~~~~~~~~~~~~~~

THE SUM OF ALL LIVES, THE ONE LIFE,
IS THE GREAT PRINCIPLE,
THE ABSOLUTE, CALLED GOD.

THE SUM OF ALL INTELLIGENCES, THE ONE INTELLIGENCE,
IS THE GREAT PRINCIPLE,
THE ABSOLUTE, CALLED GOD.

THE SUM OF ALL TRUTHS, THE ONE TRUTH,
IS THE GREAT PRINCIPLE,
THE ABSOLUTE, CALLED GOD.

THE SUM OF ALL LOVES, THE ONE LOVE,
IS THE GREAT PRINCIPLE,
THE ABSOLUTE, CALLED GOD.

THE SUM OF ALL BEINGS, THE ONE BEING,
IS THE GREAT PRINCIPLE,
THE ABSOLUTE, CALLED GOD.

These five scientific statements correspond to the five activities as expressed in the word "Principle." The first, to the activity of creating; the second, to the activity of constituting; the third, to the activity of governing; the fourth, to the activity of sustaining; and the fifth, to the activity of containing. They also correspond in the square to the four corners and the point,—Life, the Sum of all lives; Mind, the Sum of all intelligences; Truth, the Sum of all truths; Love, the Sum of all loves; and Spirit, the Sun of all beings.

• • •

What do they stand for? THE SUM OF ALL LIVES, THE ONE LIFE, IS THE GREAT PRINCIPLE, THE ABSOLUTE, CALLED GOD—means

SCIENCE-OF-BEING

that all individual lives (no matter if it is the life of a minute cell in the body, of a microbe, of an electron, or the life of a star, of a planet, of an individual, or any life in this Universe, lives small and great) all are bound together, are holding together as One Great Whole, like the drops of water holding together and forming the ocean. All these lives are One Great Life, as all the drops of water are one ocean, and that is the Absolute; and whenever we realize that we are a part of that One Life, we have then all the benefit of all the Forces and the Eternity of the One Life. But whenever we feel separate from that Life, then we lose our strength, and are at the mercy of circumstances, of fate; just as a little drop of water which is thrown out of the ocean and lies there alone on the sand, disappears because it is a separate unit, but which, when it is one with the ocean, has all the power of the ocean to sustain it. So it is with us. When we realize that we are one with the Great Life, one with the ABSOLUTE, the Great Principle, then we are strong, then we are what WE REALLY ARE; but if we think we are separate, we are weak, because we are left alone. That is so, not because we have been told that it is so, but because it is a Law; and when analyzed by Science, those lives taken together are found to be really ONE UNIVERSAL, ETERNAL LIFE.

• • •

卐 What does it mean, THE SUM OF ALL INTELLIGENCES, THE ONE INTELLIGENCE, IS THE GREAT PRINCIPLE, THE ABSOLUTE, CALLED GOD? It means that all intelligences throughout the whole Universe, all thoughts, the creative intellect of the genius, and the little mentality of a cell in the body, that has only enough sense to do its proper duty so as to work for us automatically, taking all of them as One Great Whole, make THAT ONE INTELLIGENCE WHICH WE CALL COSMIC MIND, THE SELF-CONSCIOUSNESS OF THE UNIVERSE. And whenever we feel one with that Cosmic Mind, we can draw all the knowledge there is from that Consciousness, and we Know; we can know all without studying, without the process even of reasoning. We do not need to go from one point to another, for we are then comprehensive and include all points. We have the

LESSON · ONE

Whole before us and we are a part of the Whole. Again like a drop, one with the ocean it is strong, outside it is weak. It is not because we like it or believe it to be so, but because IT IS THE LAW. ALL IS ONE INTELLIGENCE AND WE ARE PART OF IT.

· · ·

卐 THE SUM OF ALL TRUTHS, THE ONE TRUTH, IS THE GREAT PRINCIPLE. THE ABSOLUTE, CALLED GOD. That means that everything which REALLY IS from Eternity unto Eternity, every Law, no matter if it is a little law or if it is a Universal Law, every Truth ever thought or spoken, make ONE GREAT ALL, ONE UNIVERSAL TRUTH—AND WE ARE PART OF IT. Whenever then we realize that ONE-NESS with the Great Truth and stand for that Truth and live It, we have the whole of the Truth of the Universe back of us, because we are part of It, as a drop is part of the Ocean. The drop may be on the top of the wave; it is not the force of the drop which makes it rise, it is the force of the wave, and the wave is a part of the ocean. So are we. When we stand for the Truth we know that we are one with the Great Truth. We have then irresistible and invincible Power with us because the Great Principle—God—is that One Truth.

· · ·

卐 THE SUM OF ALL LOVES, THE ONE LOVE, IS THE GREAT PRINCIPLE, THE ABSOLUTE, CALLED GOD. What does it mean? It means every affection, every fervent emotion, every loving thought, word, look or deed—all these loves, be it the love which makes worlds vibrate, or the little unconscious love of two chemicals, put in the presence of one another and combining because they are mutually attracted—loves small and great, conscious or unconscious, sublime or low, taken together into One Great Whole, make THE ONE INFINITE UNIVERSAL LOVE FOR WHICH NOTHING IS TOO GREAT. Whenever we love unselfishly, not from our own personal little self, but from the Great Self, then that Ocean of Infinite Power and Harmony is immediately behind us in its GREATEST, MOST BEAUTIFUL MANIFESTATION OF LOVE—the manifestation which is last and yet is first

SCIENCE-OF-BEING

because it is the most important, and because it is THE GREAT PRINCIPLE, THE ABSOLUTE. Therefore, whenever we love unselfishly and manifest that Love, the whole of the Universe's Love stands behind us, and THERE IS NO GREATER POWER ON EARTH OR IN HEAVEN THAN THAT.

卐 And finally, THE SUM OF ALL BEINGS, THE ONE BEING, IS THE GREAT PRINCIPLE, THE ABSOLUTE, CALLED GOD. What does that mean? It means that all the individual beings, whether worlds, stars, planets, human beings, animals, plants, minerals, cells, atoms, electrons—the smallest things everywhere and the biggest things—make ONE, ARE ONE INFINITE, UNIVERSAL BEING, THE BODY OF WHICH IS THE UNIVERSE, THE MIND COSMIC INTELLIGENCE, AND THE SOUL INFINITE LOVE.

卐 Taken all together with their bodies, minds, and souls, holding together through the indissoluble Force of Attraction, yet retaining their eternal identities, moving freely in their own individual orbits, attracted one to another by the Law of Attraction, working throughout the Universe, THEY CONSTITUTE ONE GREAT BEING, just as each cell of our body, attracted to other cells, form this very body of ours. The body is made up of minute individual cells and yet it is a complete whole, which is strong and has its own powers. So it is with that One Great Being. It is made up of all of us; we are an eternal part of it; and THAT BEING IS CALLED THE GREAT PRINCIPLE, THE ABSOLUTE, OR GOD.

卐 Now the question may be asked, why are there five words which scientifically define the word "Principle," and not six or four or seven? Why does the Great Principle express itself in the four aspects of Life, Mind, Truth, and Love, culminating in the fifth aspect, Spirit? Why are there five Statements of Being, and not a lesser or greater number? Because we are living now in the Fifth Period of Humanity's evolution, represented allegorically in the Bible as the Fifth Day of Creation. The evolutionary number of this age being FIVE, that number is now continually expressed throughout the material and mental planes. That is why we have five senses, five extremities, five fingers, etc. The present human race (the Fifth Race) embraces five distinct types, the white, yellow, red, brown and black. This planet itself is geographically divided into five major parts. The Pentagram, or five pointed star, is the emblem of the Humanity of today. Instances of this sort can be cited indefinitely. Even human inventions express continually the number Five, or the Fifth Day of Creation. We read in the Bible that on the fifth day were created great whales, fish, birds, and all creeping things. What has the human mind brought forth today as mechanical inventions? Our gigantic steamers correspond to great whales, our submarines to fish, our airships and airplanes to birds, our trains, automobiles, etc., to creeping things. The inventive genius of Humanity bears the seal of the Fifth Period of our evolution. Most human beings of this age are, in mental or emotional development, creeping things, or at their best only birds. In our present state of consciousness we cannot even imagine the transcendent power, intelligence, and glory which will be ours when Humanity will reach the end of the Sixth Period of Evolution, that Sixth day of Creation, when, according to Biblical allegory, Divinity created Man in Its own Image and Likeness, and gave him dominion over all. When Man, through self knowledge and development of his inner latent qualities and powers, will be revealed to himself as he really is, the Son of God, the Witness of the Absolute, the Perfect Manifestation of the Great All, he will reach a greatness which passes all understanding. And this task of self development is the IMMEDIATE AND MOST IMPORTANT PROBLEM OF HUMANITY.

SCIENCE-OF-BEING

THE THREE ATTRIBUTES OF THE ABSOLUTE ARE:

OMNIPRESENCE, OMNISCIENCE, OMNIPOTENCE.

卐 Theological teachings state that Divinity has three distinct attributes, Omnipresence, Omniscience and Omnipotence. That is, the Great Principle, the Absolute, is omnipresent, omniscient and omnipotent.

卐 What is Omnipresence? The Great Principle has from Eternity, out of Itself, created everything there is. It is Its Own Center and Its Own Circumference. The Absolute, the Great All, is present everywhere, whether we are conscious of It or not. That means that whenever we wish to come in contact with the Great Principle, we do not need to think about something far distant, unattainable. All we need to do is TO KNOW THE IMMUTABLE FACT that Its first manifestation, Universal Energy, is always about us in its full power. It is closer to us than our own skin, which is in fact a part of it. Therefore, when anyone realizes that Presence consciously, THERE IT IS IN ITS FULL POWER. We again can make the comparison with the ocean. We cannot say that in any one place in the ocean there is more power than in another. There is power everywhere. Whenever one wishes to contact the qualities and powers of the ocean, one has simply to dip the hand into the water and one will feel all that the ocean is; and if one puts the hand in another part of the ocean, one will have the same result. Millions of people can do the same thing; at the same time, in millions of different places, and they all will contact the same fullness of the ocean. So it is with the Great Principle. Whenever we consciously contact the Absolute in Its manifestation as Universal Energy, THERE IT IS IN ALL ITS OMNIPOTENCE because It is all embracing. Therefore, it is not correct, as we very often find in literature, to imagine that there is somewhere in the Universe a Center of Powers and Forces from which all Forces radiate, acting most strongly upon those things which are nearest, and more feebly upon those farthest away. WE CAN ALWAYS RECEIVE EVERYTHING HERE AND NOW, ONLY WE MUST BECOME CONSCIOUS OF IT. It is our own unbelief, our fear, which prevents the Law from manifesting it. There are ways to overcome these unbeliefs, these fears, and they will be shown and explained in the following lessons.

卐 As the Great Principle is all-inclusive, It contains naturally all essentials of knowledge. Therefore, whenever we contact It in Its Aspect of Universal Energy we at the same time come in touch also with Its Aspect of Cosmic Mind, thus receiving all knowledge, all wisdom, because, as the Absolute embraces in Itself all there is, all knowledge which is in It must be there for us to contact, and thus to receive.

卐 The natural result of Omniscience is Omnipotence, because WHEN WE KNOW, WE CAN. We usually cannot do things only because we do not know how. Knowledge gives us the possibility to achieve; and since, therefore, Omnipotence is the direct result of Omniscience, whenever we contact Omniscience, logically, we inevitably achieve Omnipotence. That means, through THE REALIZATION OF THE ABSOLUTE HERE NEAR US, CLOSE AT HAND, WE IDENTIFY OURSELVES WITH ALL ITS POWERS. There is nothing closer to us than the Great Principle, because out of Its Own Self has It created us and IN IT WE LIVE, MOVE AND HAVE OUR BEING. It is within us and without us. Like a soap bubble, where there is air within and air without and a tiny film separating the two, so are we—THE ABSOLUTE WITHIN, THE ABSOLUTE WITHOUT, and nothing but a little film (our present state of consciousness) which separates the two for the time being; and some day even that tiny film will dissolve, and will be found no more.

TRINITY

卐 This subject must be also approached from the side of Religion or Philosophy, yet it is Science which will explain now this fundamental theological point.

卐 The idea of Trinity is a very ancient one. As far as we can go, through scientific investigation, we find in the most ancient religions this idea of Trinity. We shall analyze now three different kinds of Trinities in the most important religions, because they stand for three distinct conceptions.

卐 The first Trinity, the Egyptian Trinity,—OSIRIS THE FATHER, ISIS THE MOTHER, HORUS THE SON. Leaving aside the occult significance, there will be given here the direct and simple meaning of this Trinity. It means the Male principle, the Father; the Female principle, the Mother; and by the fusion of the Two, the Offspring, the Child. It is what we see in Nature everywhere. It is called the Natural Trinity or the Trinity of Nature. It is a Trinity, but it is in a way a primitive Trinity.

• • •

卐 Second comes the Brahmic Hindu Trinity, called "Trimurti"—BRAHMA THE FATHER, VISHNU ONE SON, SIVA THE OTHER SON. This Trinity means something entirely different. There is the Father, the One from whom all things have originated, the Eternally Unmanifest, and there are the two manifestations, the two Sons. There is no Mother. THE FATHER AND THE MOTHER ARE ONE. Out of the fusion of Two in One were brought forth Twins and these Twins are Vishnu and Siva. Vishnu the Law Giver, the Preserver; Siva the Destroyer and Regenerator. Translated into Christian terminology Vishnu, the preserver, the lover, would be Christ, LOVE; and Siva, the destroyer and regenerator, Lucifer, MIND. Mind, through his own mistakes, due to Pride, at first destroys his very life, but having REALIZED HIS MISDIRECTION starts to regenerate it, to rebuild it on a right basis. MIND, WHEN MISAPPLIED, DEBASES LIFE; PROPERLY USED, EXALTS IT. In the lesson on Mind Force will be explained in detail the destructive as well as constructive activities of Mind.

卐 What is the nature of Siva? In the Hindu mythology He stands for the destroyer and regenerator, and is therefore usually represented as destroying and at the same time creating life. There are the two Sons of God, who were both perfect once, but of whom one has fallen. Lucifer has fallen and become Satan, the Evil One, the one who claimed his power as separate from God; but in the Brahmic (Hindu) religion, he is still worshipped because he is of divine origin and a Son of God.

ᛉ Lesson - One

卐 There is a very deep idea hidden in this worship of Siva. His worshippers perceive within him the Divine Self, Perfect Intelligence; and even if he appears now to human consciousness as the Destroyer, the one to be feared (to be worshipped with fear) yet this present state is but a transitory condition, nothing but a dream, the veil of Matter, Maya, the Great Illusion. But some day the radiant Past will reappear in a still more glorious Future, when Siva and Vishnu will again be One in their Father-Mother, Brahma, MIND HAVING LEARNED THE LESSON OF LOVE AND BEING THUS REUNITED WITH HIS TWIN, HIS ETERNAL MATE, DIVINE LOVE. That is the Brahmic concept of the Trinity. It is an entirely different conception from the old Egyptian Trinity.

· · ·

卐 Last comes the Christian Trinity—GOD THE FATHER, THE SON, AND THE HOLY GHOST. This Trinity is the latest revelation to Humanity of the Absolute. In our present state of consciousness we cannot imagine anything more ideal than this Trinity, yet is has only one Father, one Son and one Holy Ghost, of Whom it is said the Three are One and yet are Three, God the Father, God the Son, and God the Holy Ghost. The ordinary explanation is that there is God, called the Father, the Son called Christ, and the Holy Ghost, the Spirit, emanating from the Father. The Roman Catholic Church says the Holy Ghost emanates also from the Son, and that affirmation of the Catholics "and from the Son" (Filioque), introduced into the Credo of the Western Church in 589 A.D. at the Council of Toledo (Spain) caused later on the separation of the Western and the Eastern Churches. Before that time the Churches were one; but when the words "AND FROM THE SON" (Filioque) were added to that passage in the Credo "The Holy Ghost proceeds from the Father," the Eastern Church, which claimed that it had received the Credo direct from the Apostles, whose teachings say only "from the Father," refused to accept that addition. From that time the two Churches separated and they have remained separate up to the present day. They are still divided and refuse to be reconciled. The reason why they seemingly cannot be reconciled is because they are seeing the same thing from two different angles. They feel intuitively that they are both right, yet appearances seem to show the reverse. All this seemingly disagreement can be explained away through Science. If we begin to reason from the point of view of Religion, what the Trinity is, and how it is that there are Three Persons in One, we can never come to any logical conclusion. Nor can we ever have a satisfactory explanation of why God Who is God, the Great All, has only one Son, the Only Begotten One. Why is it that human beings can have many sons, and the Infinite God has only one Son? Why is God, illimitable in other directions, so limited in that direction? He could have had more than the one Son we know of. In the Brahmic Hindu Trinity, there are two Sons, and yet in the Christian Trinity there is only One Son. There is a reason for it.

卐 Who is God? Who is the Father? The Father is that eternally Unmanifest Principle, the First Great Cause, the Absolute. That is the Father. Who is the Only Begotten Son? It is the Whole Universe, including Man. THE UNIVERSE AS A WHOLE IS THE ONLY SON OF GOD. God, the Unmanifest, the Great Principle, has never created another Universe, because from Eternity He has evolved it out of Himself and made it His exact counterpart. THE PROOF OF DIVINITY EXISTS. HIS ONLY CHILD, HIS WITNESS, IS THE UNIVERSE, INCLUDING MAN, and Christ is the ideal Man. The Universe is the Absolute made manifest; therefore IT IS OF DIVINE ORIGIN, COEXISTENT, COETERNAL, AND COEQUAL WITH THE FATHER.

卐 Who is the Holy Ghost? The Holy Ghost is that all pervading and sustaining Force expressed in the word "Principle," AS SUSTAINING POWER, which continually flows from the Father to the Son, from the Unmanifest, the Great Principle, to Its Manifestation, the Universe. That power, which conveys Life, Intelligence, Truth and Love to the Worlds, from Eternity to Eternity, is the Holy Ghost who proceeds from the Father and goes to the Son; and these Three are logically One. They cannot be separated. As the five activities of the word "Principle" cannot be separated, so the Three—the Unmanifest Great Principle, the Father, the Manifested Universe, the Son, and the Conscious, Loving Life Force, the Sustaining Power, the Holy Ghost—cannot be separated. THEY ARE ONE and yet they are distinctly THREE. Therefore the Eastern Church, which says the Holy Ghost proceeds from the Father to the Son, is right. Yet the Roman Catholics are also right, because after the Holy Ghost, the Intelligent Loving Life Force, has proceeded from the Unmanifest, the Absolute, the Father, to Its Manifestation, the Universe, the Son. It does not remain there. It has to go back to the Father, because the Father is the All-Inclusive Great All. If the Holy ghost were not to return from the Son to the Father, the cycle would be incomplete; yet the cycle must be completed because there is no other place for It to go (the Father being All) except to return to Its First Cause, the Father. There is a continual going forth, and returning to Its Own Origin, of that Eternal, Conscious, Loving Force called the Holy Ghost. Therefore THE HOLY GHOST PROCEEDS ALSO FROM THE SON, and the Roman Catholics are right as well as the Greek Catholics, The Greek Church seeing one side of the Eternal Fact and the Catholics seeing the other side also.

• • •

We are all looking for Divinity, the Great Principle, the Absolute; we are seeking It somewhere far away and yet we do not realize that WE LIVE ALL THE TIME IN THE CLOSEST CONTACT WITH THE GREAT ALL, AS WE ARE A PART OF IT. In the whole of Nature, in everything, in everyone, there is the Great Principle, Divinity, continually in Its three Aspects,—in the Unmanifest by what we feel, in the Manifested Aspect by what we perceive, and in its Third Aspect by what we know. Therefore the Absolute is always present in Its full force even though we are unconscious of Its presence. We cannot evade It; wherever we go, there is the Great All. When we contact nothing but air, there It is. Even the Ether is a manifestation of It. Whenever we are with human beings there we contact the Great Principle in Its highest Aspect on Earth, because EACH HUMAN BEING IS THE SON OF GOD, IS THE MOST TANGIBLE MANIFESTATION OF DIVINITY, IS A POINT IN WHICH ALL ITS FORCES AND POWERS ARE FOCUSED. Therefore whenever we are with human beings we must remember we are not away from the Absolute; we are in the midst of the Great Spirit manifested in body; we are in Divine company; and that is why, especially when we look into the eyes of people, we see something divine in their eyes, because THROUGH THE EYES OF MAN WE SEE GOD, Who looks at us through those windows of the Soul. Jesus said, "Whoever has seen me has seen the Father." And He told an absolute truth. He made a scientific statement, because in His clear eyes they could see His Father, God Himself. Through all our eyes, through the eyes of each individual, we can see God shining. When an individual smiles with the eyes, tenderly, sincerely, the look is so precious, is so wonderful, because IT IS DIVINITY SMILING. That is why people, when they love, look into each others eyes; they are never tired of doing it, for how can one be ever tired of looking at Divinity? The emotion of Love is for us the key which opens the gates of Heaven. In reality we do not love human beings; we think we do. We love Divinity through human beings. We have that longing and yearning within us to go back to the Father, to the Absolute, and whenever we find a channel through which we can achieve that return to Him, a channel opened by Love, we are only too glad to use it, because it is the inmost desire of our heart, it is the love of our Soul. The Great Principle is manifest everywhere and everywhere unmanifest; and therefore Heaven, Harmony, is not far away in unknown regions; it is always about us. IT IS OUR PRIVILEGE AND DUTY TO DISCOVER IT, NOW AND HERE. For this reason Jesus said that to "Love God with all one's strength, and to Love one's neighbor as one's self," are the two greatest commandments. He knew that IF WE LOVE IN THAT WAY, WE FULFILL AN ETERNAL LAW, WE BECOME ONE WITH THE GREAT PRINCIPLE: we have then reached absolute Unity with It, because we have united ourselves with Divinity in both Aspects, the Unmanifest and the Manifest.

LESSON - ONE

SCIENTIFIC DEFINITION OF MAN

MAN IS THE INDIVIDUALIZED PROJECTION OF THE GREAT PRINCIPLE INTO ITS OWN ETERNAL SUBSTANCE. PROCEEDING FROM THE GREAT PRINCIPLE AND INDISSOLUBLY CONNECTED WITH IT, MANIFESTING ALL ITS QUALITIES AND POWERS, MAN IS INDEED THE IMAGE AND LIKENESS OF THE ABSOLUTE. HE IS COEXISTENT AND COETERNAL WITH HIS FATHER, THE GREAT PRINCIPLE. TO KNOW MAN IN THE PRESENT STATE OF HUMAN CONSCIOUSNESS IS AS GREAT A PROBLEM AS TO KNOW THE ABSOLUTE ITSELF. MAN SEES MAN AS THROUGH A DARK CLOUD, VEILED. BUT WHEN MAN WILL BE REVEALED TO HIMSELF AS HE REALLY IS, THE WITNESS OF THE GREAT ALL, THAT DAY THE MYSTERY OF GOD WILL BE SOLVED, BECAUSE MAN FACING HIS OWN REAL SELF WILL THUS FACE GOD.

QUESTIONS & ANSWERS

LESSON ONE

1. QUES. What is the subject of the first lesson?
   ANS. A Scientific explanation of the Great All, and Man's relation to it.

2. QUES. What are the causes of the Great All?
   ANS. There is but one Causeless Cause, called the Eternally Unmanifest, the Absolute.

3. QUES. What is Primal Energy? Where did it originate?
   ANS. Primal Energy is the first manifestation of the Unmanifest, called God.

4. QUES. Is Primal Energy limited in Space, Time, or Power?
   ANS. No. It is filling all Space, is all-pervading, and therefore infinite. It endures through All Time, and is therefore eternal. It includes all Forces, and is therefore all-powerful.

5. QUES. What are the basic qualities of Primal Energy?
   ANS. Motion and Attraction.

6. QUES. How many kinds of movements are there in Motion?
   ANS. Two kinds, the rotary and the propulsory movements.

7. QUES. What word expresses most completely the nature and activity of the Absolute?
   ANS. The word "Principle."

8. QUES. What is the scientific definition of the word "Principle?"
   ANS. Principle is that which creates, constitutes, governs, sustains and contains all.

9. QUES. Who is the "Great Principle?"
   ANS. The Causeless Cause, the Unmanifest, the absolute called God.

10. QUES. What are the Aspects of the Great Principle in the present state of human consciousness?
    ANS. They are Life, Mind, Truth (Law) and Love which, taken all together, culminate in Spirit.

SCIENCE-OF-BEING

11. QUES. What is the relation of those Aspects of the Great Principle to the scientific definition of It?

    ANS. Life creates all. Mind constitutes all. Truth (Law) governs all. Love sustains all. Spirit contains all.

12. QUES. Are those Aspects simultaneous and instantaneous?

    ANS. Yes, they are, though kept in a certain logical order which cannot be changed.

13. QUES. What geometrical figures do they form?

    ANS. A Square and a Pyramid.

14. QUES. What do those two figures mean?

    ANS. Perfection, Harmony and Power.

15. QUES. What are the four corners of the Square?

    ANS. Life, Mind, Truth (Law) and Love.

16. QUES. What are the two greatest powers of today?

    ANS. Mind and Love.

17. QUES. What do they represent?

    ANS. Mind represents Lucifer fallen from his high estate, waiting for redemption. Love represents Christ.

18. QUES. Can Lucifer (Mind) be redeemed?

    ANS. Yes, through Christ (Love).

19. QUES. What are their relations to human beings?

    ANS. They are the two fundamental elements, the two poles in each human being.

20. QUES. How is the Pyramid formed?

    ANS. By simultaneously erecting the four corners of the Square (Life, Mind, Truth, and Love) to a convergent central point, which is Spirit.

21. QUES. What relations have the Square and the Pyramid of Life to human beings?

    ANS. The first is the foundation. The latter is the working out of the human character.

22. QUES.   How is that achieved?

      ANS.   By performing all actions energetically, intelligently, accurately and joyfully.

23. QUES.   What does it mean to live Life correctly?

      ANS.   It means to perform one's duties always at the right time.

24. QUES.   What does it mean, to live Life intelligently?

      ANS.   It means always to keep a proper sense of values, to take the essential, leaving the non-essential to its proper place. Above all, it means not to lose oneself in details.

25. QUES.   What does it mean, to live a life of Truth?

      ANS.   It means to be always truthful to one's own self, in feeling, in thought, in word, and in deed.

26. QUES.   What does it mean, to manifest Love in one's life, to live lovingly?

      ANS.   It means to give always, to everybody, under all circumstances, the radiance of one's Love.

27. QUES.   What practical result is obtained in living according to the four principles of the Square?

      ANS.   Spirit—that is, all freedom, all harmony, all power—is reached.

28. QUES.   How many Statements of Being are there in the present state of human consciousness?

      ANS.   There are five:

The sum of all lives	Is the
The sum of all intelligences	Great
The sum of all truths	Principle,
The sum of all loves	the Absolute,
The sum of all beings	called God.

29. QUES.   What do they mean?

      ANS.   They mean the Oneness of the Great Principle, the Great All.

30. QUES.   What is Man's relation to the Great Principle, according to those five Statements of Being?

ANS.   Man is an integral part of the Great Principle, of that Great All called God, described in those five Statements of Being. As long as Man realizes his actual Oneness with that Ocean of Force, Knowledge, Truth and Love, he has power; once apart from it, he is without power.

31. QUES.   Can Man's relation to the Great Principle ever be actually broken?

      ANS.   No, it can not, though Man may become unconscious of it, thus seemingly breaking away from the Great Principle.

32. QUES.   Why are there FIVE words which define "Principle," FIVE aspects of the Great Principle, FIVE Statements of Being, FIVE senses, FIVE fingers, etc. Why is the number FIVE everywhere so dominant?

      ANS.   Because Humanity is now living in the Fifth Period of its evolution, allegorically referred to in the Bible as the Fifth Day of Creation. For that reason also is the five-pointed star considered the emblem of the Humanity of today.

33. QUES.   What are the three attributes of the Great Principle?

      ANS.   They are Omnipresence, Omniscience, and Omnipotence.

34. QUES.   What is the practical value of those attributes to human beings?

      ANS.   In realizing Man's Oneness with the Great Principle, all Force, all Knowledge, all Power can be actually demonstrated in daily life.

35. QUES.   What does the word "Trinity" mean?

      ANS.   It means Tri-unity, or three in One.

36. QUES.   What are the three main concepts of the Trinity?

      ANS.
  1. The Egyptians: Osiris, the Father, Isis the Mother, and Horus the Son. (The Trinity of the Life Plane.)
  2. The Hindu: Brahma the Father-Mother, and two Sons, Vishnu and Siva. (The Trinity of the Mind Plane.)
  3. The Christian: God the Father, God the Son, and God the Holy Ghost. (The Trinity of the Soul Plane.)

37. QUES. Which of these concepts of the Trinity is most important?
    ANS. The Christian concept, because it is the latest revelation of Truth to Humanity.

38. QUES. What does the Christian Trinity mean?
    ANS. God the Father is the Eternally Unmanifest, the Great Principle, the Absolute. The Son is Its Eternal Manifestation, the Universe, the Only Child ever begotten of God, coexistent, coequal, and coeternal with the Father. The Universe is the actual proof of the existence of God. The Holy Ghost is the Force of Life, of Intelligence, of Truth (Law), and of Love, eternally proceeding from the Father, the Great Principle, to the Son, the Universe, and returning from the Son to the Father.

39. QUES. Where is the Great Principal?
    ANS. Everywhere.

40. QUES. Can one love God, the Great Principle, without first loving Man, animals, and Nature in general?
    ANS. No. Everything in Nature is an expression of the Great Principle, and no man can love that which he has not seen before loving that which he has seen.

41. QUES. What are animals, plants, minerals, etc., and what is their relation to Man?
    ANS. They are also perfect and eternal manifestations of the Great Principle, Man's younger brothers, who must obey Man and whom Man must govern and protect with love.

42. QUES. What is Man?
    ANS. Man is the highest known Manifestation of the Unmanifest, the Image and Likeness of God, the Witness of the Absolute. He is perfect, coexistent and coeternal with his Father, the Great Principle.

43. QUES. How can one know God?
    ANS. By knowing one's own True Self.

44. QUES.   Are the terms, "the Causeless Cause, the Unmanifest, the Absolute, the Great Principle, God," synonymous?

    ANS.   Yes, they are.

SCIENCE·OF·BEING

LESSON TWO

SCIENCE·OF·BEING
SECOND·DAY

LESSON·TWO
LIFE·ENERGY···1····
THEORY·

CREATION · FIRMAMENT·&·WATER
The·EARTH·AS·BOILING·MOLTEN·MATTER
ELEMENT · WATER·~·INVOLUTION
THROUGH·WATER
COLOR·~·RED·PURPLE

SCIENCE·OF·BEING
SECOND·DAY

I·AM·THE·FIRST·CAVSE·ALL·THINGS·GO·FORTH·FROM·ME·ALL·THINGS·RETVRN·TO·ME

LESSON·TWO
LIFE·ENERGY··1··

RIMAL Energy, as was explained in the first lesson, is the Fundamental Force of the Universe. It underlies, pervades, and sustains everything, fills all Space, endures throughout Eternity, and is the Source of all power. It is indeed the very Life of the Universe. As such, it is in perpetual motion, expressing itself through what are called vibrations.

SCIENCE·OF·BEING

IN THE ABSOLUTE THERE IS ONLY ONE KIND OF VIBRATIONS, THE SPIRITUAL. IN THE PRESENT STATE OF HUMAN CONSCIOUSNESS THOSE SPIRITUAL VIBRATIONS APPEAR AS A THREE FOLD RAY –

1). LIFE VIBRATIONS (MAGNETIC)
2). MIND VIBRATIONS (MENTAL)
3). SOUL VIBRATIONS (SPIRITUAL)

The present state of human consciousness, called THE TRIUNE STATE, acts like a prism through which we see those SPIRITUAL VIBRATIONS divided into three distinct rays, according to three planes, the physical, the mental, and the Spiritual. And each kind of vibration is expressing itself in a different way, which conforms to its own particular laws. Yet they all come from, and return to, the same Source, and have one UNIVERSAL LAW, called the Great Law, underlying all the other individual laws which govern them. Just as the prismatic lens splits into its component colors the white ray of the sun, so does the prism of our Triune State of consciousness resolve the Universal Spiritual Vibrations into their three primary aspects.

卐 Life, or Magnetic Vibrations, and Mind, or Mental Vibrations, can be readily demonstrated by us at any time. Life Vibrations, being the immediate object of our understanding, are naturally the easiest to deal with, as they belong to the physical plane on which we now live. Mind Vibrations are more difficult to handle, because we do not live completely on the mental plane. The proof that we do not yet live completely on the mental plane is that our thoughts must all be translated into material form in order to become tangible to our senses. As to what concerns the Spiritual Vibrations, only on rare occasions do we consciously contact them. Seldom do we perceive the Spirit now, though we are unconsciously in direct and constant relation with It. In the sixth lesson will be explained the science of Mental Vibrations, and in the seventh lesson how to reach the highest, the Spiritual ones.

LESSON-TWO

卐 Life Vibrations are also called Magnetic Vibrations, because they possess that fundamental quality of Attraction. In the first lesson, when describing Primal Energy, it was stated that it possesses two primary qualities, Motion and Attraction. In the practical application of Magnetic Vibrations, those qualities are continually used in order to obtain the desired constructive results. Magnetic Vibrations are essentially important because they not only permeate the whole Universe and underlie everything, but because they constitute the very element out of which our bodies and the whole visible Universe is made. The great practical value of those Life Vibrations is that we do not need concentration or strong mental effort to contact them. All we need to do is to become conscious of their continual flow into us, and thus establish the so-called contact. No matter what we do, be it a physical, mental, or emotional activity, we should never use our own very limited supply of life energy. This must be the cardinal point always to be remembered. We should always take the trouble to make the contact with the Universal Reservoir of that Force, and then the more we use it, the more we have, because it is the everlasting Fount of Life which always gives us more than we can receive. The question may arise, why is it necessary to make that contact with the Universal Life Energy? Are we not in direct and constant communication with it at all times? Yes, we are, but we are not conscious of it. On the contrary, we consciously believe that we are independent of it, that we have a life force of our own. We think we are separated from ALL POWER, and "as a man thinketh in his heart, so is he." Therefore we need to re-establish on the mental plane that which was lost there, though actually we have never lost that contact on the Spiritual plane. Spirit KNOWS that contact to be an eternal fact. On the physical plane one FEELS it. But mind, on the mental plane on which were produced all the mistakes and errors ever made, because of that original error of seeming separation from ALL POWER, believes in separation, and thus makes it real. As long as we are not conscious of that flow of Universal Life Energy through us, we do not derive much benefit from it, even though it is there.

卐 There are different methods of contacting Primal Energy. The easiest and the simplest way is through mental contact. In order to do it, we must relax

57

as completely as we can, physically, mentally, and emotionally. And when we feel harmony within us as a result of that relaxation, then we must say to ourselves the following words: "I AM ONE WITH UNIVERSAL LIFE ENERGY. IT IS FLOWING THROUGH ME NOW. I FEEL IT." Thus we open the mental door which separated the life force within us from the Life Energy without. And the force within, because of its inherent quality of Attraction, contacts the Force from without, which then begins to pour into us with an ever increasing power. Then the more we use that Force, the more it is supplied from the Infinite Source. In spite of the simplicity of the method, not everybody is at first able to use it successfully, because of the doubt which some people may entertain in their hearts of the efficiency of such a mental contact. We must also remember that on the mental plane we are a law unto ourselves. If we believe in a thing, and state our faith in it, it will be so. But if we doubt or fear, we ourselves thus prevent its realization. In order to overcome that difficulty and enable everybody, even the most skeptical and timid, to make successfully that conscious contact with the Universal Life Energy, there is another method which will be explained – a method of pure physical contact, based on the operation of physical laws. That second method has this advantage over the mental one, that it does not require any faith in it. It works for the reason that the physical laws are there put into operation, and the physical contact with the Universal Energy is made, not because we think it or want it, but because we cannot help it. Obviously, if we also think about the Universal Life Energy flowing through us at the moment of physical contact with it, it will work all the better. Yet if we do not think at all about it, it still will work, because of the aforesaid reasons. That second, the physical method, is based on a certain exercise, called the "STAR EXERCISE." The reason why this posture is called the Star Exercise is because the individual, when taking it, has to place his body in such a position that it will fit into the five points of a star. The Five Pointed Star, the emblem of the Humanity of today, the occult sign of the Fifth Period of Humanity's evolution, is also called the Pentagram. According to the alchemists of mediaeval times, the Pentagram was considered to be the key to all powers. The Philosopher's

LESSON·TWO

Stone, the Elixir of Life, and many other wonderful things, were supposed to be obtained whenever that sign was properly used. Yet the alchemists, though perceiving the truth back of that sign, saw only its geometrical form; that is, the dead letter of it, which had no actual power. The living force back of it, the spirit of it, remained veiled to them. In this Age, the veil is lifted, and the complete truth, spirit and letter, is revealed. And the mysterious sign, the Pentagram, becomes indeed a 'KEY TO ALL POWER', as it unlocks and brings forth in Man all his latent powers and forces. It is when the human body takes the position as shown in the diagrams following that the actual contact of the life energy within is made with the Universal Life Energy without. And a man's physical, mental, and emotional development will be thus stimulated by an ever increasing Force. Standing straight, but relaxed, with legs spread to a degree corresponding to the design, the arms stretched to either side on a level with the shoulders, and with head erect, the human body will fit into the five pointed star. Even the proportions of a normally built body will correspond to the figure of the star. The head fits into the upper point, the two arms into the two side points, the torso into the center, and the legs into the two lower points. The palm of the left hand should be turned up, and that of the right turned down. The whole body must remain erect, but not tense. The heart, situated on the left side of the human body, is not only the central pumping station which takes in and sends out the blood through the whole body, but is also the apparatus which sucks in and pours out Life Energy. The palm of the left hand, turned up, draws in through its complicated network of nerves the Universal Energy present in the surrounding atmosphere. That drawing action is due to the pumping activity of the heart, and the stream of Life Force pours into the body because of the attraction exercised on it by the inner life force of the body itself. Through the hand, arm, and heart the Life Energy flows to the solar plexus, whence it is distributed by way of the spinal nerve throughout the whole body. A certain amount of it is stored in the solar plexus, and the surplus sent out through the right hand, whose palm is turned down. It is especially through the finger tips of the right hand that the Force is flowing out the body toward the earth, which attracts it because of the same Law of Attraction. Thus is established a current of Universal Energy, penetrating from the Infinite Source into the human body, invigorating and purifying it, and flowing out of it only to return with ever increasing power. The left palm, turned up, takes the position of a receiving hand, and the right, with palm turned down, appears to bless. In fact, this is so. Our left hand receives all blessings from the Infinite, which our being, having assimilated, in its turn gives out as blessings through the right hand. Not only through the left hand does the Life Force penetrate into the body; it pours in also through every cell, and very strongly through the solar plexus. Yet during the exercise the main current is received as stated above. Shortly after having taken the position, one begins to feel a certain heaviness in the palm of the left hand. It is as if a heavy ball were pressing on the palm. And one is sensible of a kind of tingling in the finger tips of the right hand. These two different sensations are due to the influx and outpouring of Life Force. Thus the individual feels that the contact is established.

LESSON·TWO

·FIVE·POINTED·STAR·

·THE·PENTAGRAM·   ·STAR·EXERCISE·

There are a few more important points to be remembered in connection with that exercise. The best times to perform it are in the morning, immediately after getting up, before doing anything else, and at night before going to bed. When performed in the morning, this exercise will stimulate all one's physical, mental, and emotional activities, because of the ascending magnetic currents of the new day, which impregnate their local color in the exercise. In the evening, on the contrary, the same exercise produces an opposite effect. It soothes and disposes one to sleep, in harmony with all Nature, because of the downward curve of the local magnetic currents.

SCIENCE·OF·BEING

卐 Three to five minutes is all that is needed to perform the Star Exercise. For beginners, it would be inadvisable to do it longer, because of the very strong inpour of magnetic forces. But later on, when the body becomes accustomed to that inflow of magnetic currents, the duration of the Star Exercise can be prolonged to fifteen minutes, and the exercise taken more than twice a day. During that exercise, one ought to be dressed as lightly as possible, in order to leave the body free and without pressure on any part of it. A body without any covering is of course the most responsive. The exercise should be performed in front of an open window, and, if the temperature and circumstances permit, out of doors. The Star Exercise should never be taken immediately after a meal. At least an hour must elapse between the two; otherwise a most violent nausea, and sometimes indigestion, may result, as the magnetic current has the same effect on digestion as an electrical storm has on milk. It curdles the food in process of digestion, because of its strong chemical action. Deep, rhythmic breathing is very helpful in connection with the exercise, because of the stimulating effect of the oxygen. In the beginning, one's arms may feel tired in the performance of the exercise. No effort should be used to keep the arms in their proper position. Let them drop, and lift them again when rested. Otherwise the tension of the muscles and nerves resulting from a prolonged forced elevation of the arms will counteract, to a great extent, the flow of the Force through them.

卐 The exercise works so automatically that there is no imperative need to think about the Force flowing though the body. It will flow anyway, because of the Law of Attraction. There is no necessity of turning the face north, because the points of the compass are of no importance to those who use Universal Energy, which is limitless.

卐 The Star Exercise is exceedingly beneficial to children. It stimulates all of their bodies, especially their brain centers, and those glands which play such an important role in their growth and development. It also harmonizes their emotional side with the rest of their being, and establishes strength and poise where before was weakness and restlessness.

LESSON-TWO

✺ The Star Exercise ought to become a part of the daily routine for everyone, young and old, sick or healthy, weak or strong. It is to be carried on regularly though all one's life, to the very end, and the surprising positive results will exceed the most sanguine expectations. It is like watering a plant with Life Itself, so that it should grow with an ever-increasing vigor. It is indeed Life, in its strongest and purest form, that one is able to contact through the Star Exercise, and use for the greatest unfoldment of one's body, mind, and soul. For some time in the beginning that process of unfoldment may be rather slow. But one must persevere, and complete success will be the reward of that perseverance.

✺ When using Magnetic Vibrations, faith is not necessary. One can do without it. Nevertheless, faith is very helpful. The so called miraculous healings performed on large crowds who come to be cured by some of the Evangelist healers, is one of the easiest things to perform. It is much more difficult to heal patients singly. Each person in the crowd carries within him a certain light of faith, an open channel for the Life Force to flow through. Individually, these do not amount to much, but when counted by hundreds or maybe thousands, they become a great light, a tremendous power, a broad avenue of faith, over which the Magnetic Life Force is then conveyed as well to each individual singly as to the whole crowd collectively. There each person is benefited by the addition to his own little faith of all the other faiths present. Naturally the result thus obtained is usually a great success.

✺ Primal Energy, as was explained in the first lesson, has two fundamental qualities, Motion and Attraction. In its aspect of Life Energy, it has also two other qualities. First, it is SELF GOVERNING: second, it is BASICALLY HARMONIOUS. Like all elements, Life Energy is self-governing. Physical laws, expressing themselves through the elements, are back of that self government. For instance, water contained in any vessel, no matter what position that vessel may take, will always automatically maintain a level parallel to that of the sea. The air will rush into a vacuum through the most minute opening. Mercury, when broken into small particles, automatically takes the form of spheres, etc. Elements always choose the path of least resistance and seek equilibrium. The quality of self-government which Life Energy possesses is exceptionally practicable and valuable, and simplifies greatly the use of it. The following examples will explain how it works. Suppose there are two individuals, sitting one on the right side, the other on the left side, of the operator. The one on the right side, for some reason, feels very cold; the one on the left, hot. In order to re-establish normal conditions in the two, all the operator needs to do is to make the mental contact with Universal Life Energy, and then take in each of his hands a hand of either patient. The contact thus established, the Force flows through the operator to his patients. Being self-governed the Force automatically works to meet the requirements of the case. In the first instance it warms, in the second it cools, thus simultaneously establishing equilibrium in both. Especially in healing does this quality become invaluable. It does away almost entirely with the necessity of knowing the nature and location of the ailment. All one needs to do, in magnetic treatment, is to let the Force flow into the patient; and the Force, being self-governing, will always go to the spot where it is needed. For instance, a patient complains of heart trouble. The operator sends the Magnetic Force into the patient. The Force itself discovers in the patient some other unsuspected and possibly more serious ailments, perhaps in the lungs or kidneys. It will then automatically flow more to the lungs of kidneys than to the heart, because of the greater need. That is why everybody, even children who are too young to know the mental laws operating in mental healing, can so successfully use the magnetic current.

卐 Primal Energy, being the foundation of all there is, is by nature perfectly harmonious. Therefore, Life Energy, as its first aspect, must possess the same inherent quality. That is, it must be basically harmonious. It is mind alone which, when misdirected, covers that Life Energy with a negative film. But whenever that Force is taken direct from its Infinite Source there it flows, perfectly harmonious, healing, and constructive in every way. The magnetic current, when flowing from the Infinite, carries with it such a sense of harmony that it harmonizes even the very channel through which it flows – that is the operator – although he may have felt quite inharmonious when starting the treatment. The last quality gives to the Magnetic Vibrations a great superiority over the Mental ones, because no successful healing or other work can be achieved if the thoughts of the operator are not harmonious at the very start. The slightest disharmony on the plane of Mind is most destructive to the subject on which the thought is operating.

卐 Most of the physical discomfort is caused by either congestion or lack of magnetic forces in certain parts of the body, and needs the contact with an outside magnetic current to re-establish equilibrium. For instance, a sudden shock makes one's heart contract. Life force is thrown out of it. As a result, one feels a pain in the heart. Involuntarily one's hand is pressed to the heart. The magnetic current of the body, sent out from the solar plexus through the hand, fills the heart with its vivifying power. The heart resumes its normal condition, and the pain is gone. Or again, everyone has observed that when one thinks deeply, one unconsciously rests one's head upon the hands. The reason for it is that the brain, when very active, either accumulates too much energy, or not enough, in both cases having its functioning impaired. In either instance the magnetic current is required to correct the discrepancy. Nature sees that it should be done. Instinctively the hand is brought into contact with the head, and the magnetic current, flowing though the hand into the brain, or vice versa, re-establishes there the proper balance. The knowledge of how to contact and use the magnetic current is therefore so precious because it enables one consciously and scientifically to use that Force whenever there is need of it. What Nature makes us do instinctively, we can do with so much better results if we realize the Laws back of it and know how to apply them. All human emotions have the Magnetic Force back of them, and the way that Force works through them, being based on Laws, is so scientific, so accurate, that one can at once determine the kind of emotion, and how it should be met, by the way it expresses itself. Generally speaking, all emotions, positive and negative, produce, in certain parts of the body which exactly correspond to the rate of vibration of each emotion, and accumulation of the Magnetic Force. Such accumulation of Force makes the individual feel uncomfortable, and he unconsciously seeks de-magnetization by contacting that part of his body

SCIENCE-OF-BEING

with the part of another individual's body which will respond to the rate of vibration of his accumulated Magnetic Force. For instance when one loves, the emotion of love stimulates life currents throughout all the body. Starting from the heart, the magnetic current by and by permeates all the body, but concentrates especially in certain centers of it which, through their delicate and complex formation, are more apt to express it. According to a physical law, all vibrations naturally rise upwards. That being the case, they rise first from the heart into the head. There they concentrate, especially in the eyes and around the lips. The pupils are enlarged, and the eyes begin to sparkle, sending out magnetic waves which seek the eyes of another individual in order to be de-magnetized. The lips, in their turn, more and more filled with the Life Force, also unconsciously seek de-magnetization, which they achieve through what is commonly known as a "kiss." If the love of the two individuals is on the same plane, their lips will meet, because the magnetic currents are, in both instances, of the same rate, and seeking expression through the lips. But if the love of one individual is more of a mental type, his lips will seek de-magnetization, not on the lips of the other individual, but on the forehead, the seat of thinking powers. No other place on the face will do, because nowhere else could de-magnetization take place, on account of the different rate of vibration. Like attracts like. If one's love is of a more adoring kind, the lips, when charged with magnetic forces, will seek de-magnetization probably on the hands of the other individual, or maybe on the knees, or even at the feet, again on account of like seeking like. With all other emotions it is the same. In friendship, one's natural desire is to shake hands with the individual one loves, or to put the hand on the shoulder or around the waist. There the hand, the power to achieve, filled with the magnetic current, unconsciously seeks de-magnetization in another individual's hand. Or when the individual feels the emotion of protection, the impulse is to place his hand on the other individual's shoulder in a gesture of protection. Almost everyone has observed that when two individuals quarrel and a third one intervenes, they usually turn against him, and he gets from both of them the negative which he tried to destroy in them. Why? Because he unconsciously diverted their mutual negative passion of hatred and revenge in his direction. They were so full of negative vibrations that they needed mutual de-magnetization, which they sought in quarreling. A third party intervening at that moment directs the negative currents of both toward that new and open channel. Therefore, if one does not know how to approach a case like that, it is better to abstain from interference, and let people settle their own differences as best they can. All they need in such a case is de-magnetization, and after they obtain it they feel more at ease, no matter if the price they paid for it was some physical, mental, or moral bruises. The pressure which they could not bear is gone, and they feel at ease again. Those few main instances cited above explain clearly how the magnetic current works through our human emotions.

卐 All prominent and successful men and women of days gone by and of the present time have been consciously or unconsciously using the Magnetic Force in their lives. They possess an extraordinary vitality, which attracts everybody and everything to them. They have what is called a magnetic personality. Such a personality, such vitality and power, can be developed by everyone through the regular use of the Star Exercise, and the continual contact with Life Energy, through the mental method. By and by one becomes a living magnet, the power of which is ever increasing, because of its incessant use.

卐 The ancient sages and prophets knew a great deal about the Magnetic Force, and most of the so-called miracles performed by them were accomplished by the use of that Force. Its widest application it had in healing, where Life Energy was used most successfully to dispel all kinds of physical ailments. The methods sometimes employed were very extraordinary, and the following examples will give an idea of the results obtained. When crossing the Red Sea, Moses, who was well versed in all knowledge, prayed to God – that is, made the mental contact with Life Energy – and then extended his hand, holding his rod, toward the Red Sea. The magnetic current flowed through his hand and rod with irresistible force into the surrounding atmosphere, and there created a great disturbance. As a result, a strong wind arose and pushed back the waters of the sea, which was shallow at that particular place, and the Israelites walked on the bottom of the sea to the other side. Once safe across, Moses again made the contact, stretched forth his rod, and directing the Magnetic Force of the Universe through it, he reestablished normal atmospheric conditions. The wind subsided, and the waters, no longer pushed back by its pressure, resumed their proper position, and incidentally drowned the Egyptians, who were following them across the bottom of the sea.

卐 Elijah, when bringing back to life the son of the poor window in whose house he stayed, obviously used no other power than the Magnetic Force. Thrice after having prayed — that is, made the contact with the Universal Life Energy – did he throw himself on the body of the dead boy, so as to send from all his body the life current into the body which was bereft of it. And after the third time, the dead boy became alive.

卐 Through the use of the magnetic current did Jesus still the storm on the Galilean Sea. And when He was touched in the throng by a woman suffering from a blood issue, His words, "I felt a virtue coming out of Me," also showed that it was the magnetic current, the Universal Life Energy flowing through Him, which did the healing.

卐 The magnetic current can be easily concentrated also in inanimate objects. Those objects can be so charged with Magnetic Force that they become themselves dynamic centers from which the Force is flowing and carrying its healing vibrations to all those who happen to contact them. Thus are scientifically explained those healing properties which some of the so-called miraculous shrines throughout the whole world are supposed to possess. Either by itself or through conscious direction of it, the Magnetic Force was concentrated in those shrines, and they became real healing mediums. The healings performed by them were not what one would call faith cures. Of course faith was also an important agent, as it prepared the people to receive the healing. But the healings themselves were performed by the Magnetic Force which was actually emanating from them. It has been observed that water especially possesses to an extraordinary degree the faculty of storing

LESSON-TWO

in itself a great deal of Magnetic Force, and then giving it out when needed. Thousands of years ago that property was known to the Ancients, especially in Egypt, India, and other Southern countries where water, because of the great heat, is already a strong vivifying agent, and has been used for healing purposes. Most of their temples had sacred pools, the waters of which were blessed, or, in other words, were magnetized. Those seeking relief from their ailments plunged into those pools, and many of them emerged sound and wholesome. Even in our own day. Such pools are still in use in India, and the healing properties of their waters, sometimes even polluted with all kinds of germs of infectious diseases left by those who had sought relief there, are not thereby impaired. The Magnetic Force in the water is the stronger, and is able to heal in spite of the deadly germs. One can make some interesting experiments oneself in that direction. For instance, magnetize the water of the bath, or that to wash the face, or to drink. That magnetization is called by the Hindus "Pranization," from the Hindu word "Prana," or Life Force. All one needs to do is to make the mental contact with Universal Energy while standing in front of the water to be magnetized, with the hands extended toward it and the finger tips pointing directly to it, and remain in that position for a few minutes. The Life Energy will flow through the hands into the water and will charge it with Magnetic Force. That water can then be used, and the benefit derived from it is considerable. Those who suffer from insomnia can, by the same method, magnetize their pillows, sheets, and covers, and enjoy a sound, healthy sleep as the result of it. Infinite are the applications for that Force. In the fourth lesson will be given special detailed instructions concerning its use in daily life, in business, in general work, in healing, in achieving success and prosperity, and in overcoming old age through the regeneration of the cells of one's body.

QVESTIONS & ANSWERS

LESSON TWO

1. QUES.   What are Vibrations?
   ANS.   Certain oscillatory rhythmic movements of Primal Energy.

2. QUES.   How many kinds of vibrations are there in the Absolute?
   ANS.   One kind, the Spiritual Vibrations.

3. QUES.   How many kinds of vibrations are there in the present state of human consciousness?
   ANS.   Three kinds: Magnetic, Mental and Spiritual.

4. QUES.   Why are there three kinds of vibrations?
   ANS.   Because of the Triune State of the present human consciousness, through which everything is perceived as a three-fold ray.

5. QUES.   Which vibrations are the easiest to perceive and to handle?
   ANS.   The Magnetic, or Life Vibrations, because they are the immediate object of our understanding and are fundamental.

6. QUES.   From where do these Magnetic Vibrations emanate?
   ANS.   From their Eternal Source, called Universal Energy.

7. QUES.   Does that mean that Magnetic Vibrations are also a kind of Spiritual Vibrations?
   ANS.   Yes, they are, only of a slower rate.

8. QUES.   What are the methods by which Universal Life Energy can be contacted?
   ANS.   Mental and physical methods.

9. QUES.   What is the formula used for mental contact?
   ANS.   "I am One with Universal Life Energy. It is flowing through me now. I feel it."

10. QUES.   Why is it necessary to make the contact with Universal Life Energy on the mental plane?
    ANS.   Because the contact was once lost on the mental plane and must therefore be reestablished on that plane.

11. QUES.   Has that contact ever been lost on the Spiritual Plane?
    ANS.   No.

12. QUES.   What is the physical method of contacting Universal Life Energy?
    ANS.   The so-called Star Exercise.

13. QUES.   What is the Star Exercise?
    ANS.   It is a certain posture, the object of which is to fill the whole body and especially the solar plexus with Universal Life Energy.

14. QUES.   What is the solar plexus and where is it located?
    ANS.   It is a network of nerves, called solar because they radiate. It is located in the dorsal or anterior part of the abdomen. It is also called the abdominal brain."

15. QUES.   How is the Star Exercise performed?
    ANS.   Stand relaxed, feet spread apart, arms outstretched on a level with the shoulders, palm and finger tips of right hand turned downward, and palm and finger tips of left hand turned upward, slightly curved, as if to receive the current of Universal Life Energy that will flow quite noticeably through it into one and through the solar plexus to any weak part of the body, strengthening the same and flowing out through the right hand.

16. QUES.   Why is it called the Star Exercise?
    ANS.   Because it is a posture based on the geometrical figure of the Pent-Alpha, or Pentagram, the symbol of the present Fifth Race, the Fifth Day of Creation the Fifth Period of Humanity's Evolution.

17. QUES.   Should one observe any cardinal point such as turning to the East, or looking toward the North Star?
    ANS.   No. One must not limit oneself to the Earth's magnetic currents.

18. QUES.   Does one need to believe in the actual flow of Universal Life Energy during the Star Exercise?

SCIENCE-OF-BEING

ANS.   No. Universal Life Energy flows into the human body in obedience to physical laws.

19. QUES. Does this Exercise influence everyone alike?

      ANS.   No. It may cool one and warm another but it gives to each just what is needed, when it is needed and where it is needed.

20. QUES. What are the qualities of Universal Life Energy?

      ANS.   It is self-governed and basically harmonious.

21. QUES. Has Universal Life Energy some other qualities?

      ANS.   Yes. It has two fundamental qualities, referred to in the first lesson. They are Motion and Attraction.

22. QUES. What is the practical value of those qualities of Universal Life Energy in daily life?

      ANS.   Their practical value resides in the fact that because of those qualities, Universal Life Energy can be used automatically without any special mental concentration or application of will power. Magnetic Vibrations always produce constructive and harmonious results, because of their inherent qualities.

23. QUES. How often and for how long should one perform the Star Exercise?

      ANS.   For beginners, twice a day, in the morning and in the evening, from three to five minutes each time and whenever fatigued, but never too soon after a meal.

24. QUES. Why is the Magnetic Force without evil, constructive and harmonious?

      ANS.   Because it proceeds as a pure stream from its Infinite and Eternal Source, Primal Energy.

25. QUES. Can it become evil?

      ANS.   Yes, thought can make it in-harmonious by clothing it with a negative mental film.

`26. QUES. Does the magnetic current attract or repel?

      ANS.   It attracts, but by using will power and thought it can be made repellent.

LESSON-TWO

27. QUES. How do the Magnetic Vibrations affect the brain?
    ANS. They stimulate all the brain cells, thereby increasing the activities of the brain.

28. QUES. How often should one make the mental contact with Universal Life Energy?
    ANS. As often as there is any sort of work to be done, in any activity, physical, mental, or emotional.

29. QUES. What is the practical result of frequent mental contact with Universal Life Energy?
    ANS. All work will become easy, because of the increasing capacity for Manifesting Life Energy.

30. QUES. Can Universal Life Energy by used in business and how?
    ANS. Yes. By making the mental contact with Universal Life Energy every time one handles a business proposition or some articles, so as to make the Force flow through one during the transactions.

31. QUES. What result will this obtain?
    ANS. Success.

32. QUES. How can one develop a magnetic personality?
    ANS. By becoming a living magnet through continual contact with Universal Life Energy.

33. QUES. What causes most of the physical discomfort and pain?
    ANS. Excessive accumulation or congestion of magnetic currents in certain parts of the body.

34. QUES. How can such congestion by relieved?
    ANS. By demagnetizing the congested spot through laying on of hands.

35. QUES. What are emotions?
    ANS. They are manifestations of Magnetic Vibrations of different rates which, when accumulated in various parts of the body, create there congestions that can be relieved only by demagnetization of that part. Such demagnetization is achieved through a kiss, a   handshake, laying on of hands,

kind words, looks, thoughts, etc. Congestions of negative vibrations are ignorantly relieved by first blows, harsh words, looks, thoughts, etc.

36. QUES. What is magnetic chemicalization?
    ANS. It is a reaction following Magnetic Vibration. Somewhere in the body of the patient there may be negative thought-germs, discordant, but almost unnoticeable because possessed of little life force. When the magnetic current arouses them they become alive, inflate to the limit; then burst. After they burst they are utterly destroyed and the patient is healed.

37. QUES. What is the explanation of success in life?
    ANS. The use of Universal Life Energy.

38. QUES. Is it always used consciously?
    ANS. No. Sometimes consciously, most times unconsciously.

39. QUES. What power was used to accomplish more of the miracles in the past, and is now employed in the so-called "faith cures?"
    ANS. The Magnetic Force

40. QUES. Are the terms "Universal Life Energy, Life Force, Magnetic Force, Magnetic Current, Magnetic Vibrations, synonymous?
    ANS. Yes.

41. QUES. Why is there more than one term?
    ANS. To secure emphasis of one or the other of the qualities implied in the terms. "Energy" refers to power, "Life" to the quality of motion, and "Magnetic" to the quality of attraction, inherent in Universal Life Energy.

LESSON THREE

SCIENCE·OF·BEING
THIRD·DAY

LESSON·THREE
THE·RELATIVE·(MATTER)
THEORY·

CREATION · DRY·LAND·· THE·SURFACE·OF
·THE·EARTH·BECOMES·A·SOLID·MASS
ELEMENT · EARTH··THE·LOVEST
PLANE·OF·INVOLUTION
COLOR·· VIOLET·BLACK

SCIENCE-OF-BEING
THIRD-DAY

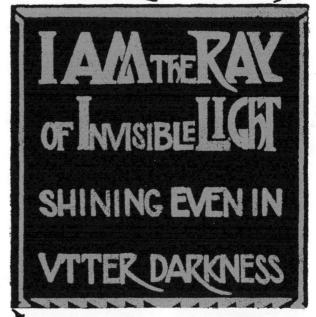

I AM THE RAY OF INVISIBLE LIGHT SHINING EVEN IN VTTER DARKNESS

LESSON-THREE
THE-RELATIVE-(MATTER)

ROM times immemorial, Matter has been a thing of greatest mystery, which Religion and Philosophy have tried more or less unsuccessfully to explain. Most religions of days gone by and those in use until now, qualify Matter as transitory, temporal, contra-distinct to the permanency of Spirit. They call it a

SCIENCE-OF-BEING

Veil, Dream, Illusion, Dust, etc. Some religious movements absolutely refuse to acknowledge the existence of Matter. Their teachings are based on its complete denial, they call Matter error, evil. Yet religions have never been able to explain Matter in a satisfactory way. After all it was not their province to do so. It is only Science – especially modern Material Science – which has been able to explain what Matter really is. Matter is called by the Hindus "Maya," the "Great Illusion," Why? Because seemingly we can never take hold of it. As soon as we think that we have hold of Matter, it eludes us. It is of all things the most elusive that we know. Matter appears to us usually in three distinct aspects – sold, liquid and gaseous form – due to different rates of vibrations. Certain manifestations of it commonly assume a solid aspect, such as stones, metals, wood, etc., some a liquid, such as water, mercury, etc., some a gaseous form, such as vapors, air, and different gases; but each of these material things may also be obtained in the two other aspects. If their rate of vibration is changed. For example, let us take ice. When a piece of ice is placed in a warm atmosphere, it melts. Thus we have the first transformation of Matter; from solid it becomes liquid. Ice becomes water. If the temperature is raised to a still further degree, the water evaporates, becomes steam, - another transformation, liquid taking a gaseous form. And steam is found to consist of molecules of water. Through disintegration of the molecule of water are discovered the atoms of the original gases, Hydrogen and Oxygen, the combination of which, in certain chemical proportion (H_2O) formed that molecule. Now an atom is such a small particle of Matter that it requires about 500 million of them placed side by side to cover a linear inch. In breaking up the atom are finally found electrons. The electron is the smallest division of Matter which Science has been able to obtain for the time being. The size of an electron compared to that of an atom is as our Earth in comparison with the whole Solar System. What is an electron? An electron is a tiny sphere which is rotating with extraordinary velocity on its own axis, and then revolving at a speed of about 10,000 miles per second around another microscopic sphere which acts as a central sun. They are kept in that relation by the Universal Law of Attraction, just like our planetary system in particular and like the

LESSON·THREE

Universe in general. It is, on a small scale, what we see there on a large scale. There are positive and negative electrons. The negative electrons are revolving around a central positive electron. It is the aggregation of these electrons in their revolutions around the central electron which constitutes the atom; and the relation of those electrons one to another, and their number in the atom of the analyzed element, determines its nature. The greater the number of electron in an atom of Matter the stronger and heavier is the material element. The Hydrogen atom, because it consists of one positive electron around which is revolving one negative electron, is accepted by the scientists of today as the standard atomic weight, this weight being taken as I. The analysis of the nature of the electron shows it to be radioactive, continually releasing Energy. Why? Because ENERGY IS THE BASIS OF THE ELECTRON. In other words the electron is made of condensed Energy. Energy is Force. Then what conclusion can be drawn? That the so-called material things are but condensed Forces, which are the most immaterial things that one can imagine. Material Science was therefore able, through investigation, to prove the absolute non-existence of Matter AS MATTER, in the generally accepted meaning of that word. It showed that everything is but Forces of different rates of vibration, in various combinations and relations one to another, and in different degrees of condensation. This evidence is so convincing, because it is scientific and it can be proven. It works invariably.

卐 For example, the diamond is supposed to be the hardest stone known on Earth. Its hardness is standard; it is ten. Next come the Corundum (Ruby, Sapphire); its harness is nine. They are both precious stones because they are made of a great deal of condensed Energy. Sandstone has only the hardness of about three. Now if the amount of Energy contained in the diamond were released, it would be found to exceed the amount of Energy contained the same volume of sandstone in exact proportion as the hardness of the diamond exceeds that of sandstone. According to calculations made by some modern Scientists, calculations based on scientific experiments, there is enough Energy condensed in one ounce of Matter, which, if suddenly released, would lift all the German ships sunk during the Great War from the bottom of the sea to the top of Mt. Everest, the highest mountain on Earth. Also, each human being has in his little finger enough condensed Force to run for several minutes all the trains in England, representing many thousands of horsepower. This shows what tremendous powers and forces are latent in us, waiting to be manifested and to be made proper use of.

卐 There are some metals which are called precious, and others which are called common. This is again the same thing. Precious metals are precious because they have so much condensed Energy within them that they can resist the disintegrating influence of the air. Gold is one of the metals which possesses this power. Common metals, because they have in themselves less condensed Energy, cannot resist those influences as easily as Gold, Platinum, Iridium, Palladium and other precious metals, and they oxidize – that is, disintegrate, die. The amount of condensed Energy in an element determines its preciousness, its real value. A diamond is precious not only because it is beautiful and rare, but especially because it has a real value from the point of view of its absolute superiority over other elements, on account of the greater presence of forces in it. And as it is with precious stones and metals, so it is with human beings. Those individuals who are called noble because of their noble character really express their life forces on a higher plane, in stronger, higher vibrations than others, and are therefore more powerful, and consequently more valuable to Humanity. The word "noble" in this instance is used in the sense of soul qualities and not as class distinction. It is evident that such investigations by Material Science explain Matter completely. Humanity owes that to the perseverance of the material scientist who were not afraid to use their own material means in order to disintegrate the very elements on which they were working. When one knows the laws which govern the so-called material phenomena, the present concept of Matter is done away with entirely. That is because of the Law and not because of one's affirmation that there is no Matter. The negation of Matter will not destroy Matter. That is why the success of mental healing does not depend on the negation of Matter, but on something entirely different. There are laws which are put in operation most of the time absolutely unconsciously by those who think that they bring

LESSON-THREE

forth result because they denied Matter. For example, let us take electric light. One can for a thousand years deny that it is shining, and still it will shine. But if one knows that there is a switch, that switch can be turned off and the light will not shine any more and it will be dark. There the Physical Law was made proper use of and it did work to obtain the desired result.

卐 The following scientific definition of Matter will clearly show what Matter really is: WHAT IS CALLED MATTER IS BUT THE CONSCIOUSNESS OF EFFECTS PRODUCED ON THE SENSES BY VARIOUS MANIFESTATIONS OF PRIMAL ENERGY. THEREFORE MATTER IS ONLY A STATE OF CONSCIOUSNESS, THE PRESENT MANNER IN WHICH THOSE EFFECTS ARE PERCEIVED.

卐 This proposition explains Matter completely. What then do we feel, what do we see, what do we perceive with our senses? Energy, forces, nothing but forces. Vibratory waves of Energy striking the senses produce certain impressions and those impressions we call sensations. When we have one kind of vibrations we feel it as touch, another kind we see, another we hear, another we smell, or another we taste. We say we perceive the thing materially, but in reality there is nothing material about it; it is all vibration.

卐 The question may be asked, how has the electron originated and why is it a sphere? Primal Universal Energy has two fundamental qualities, Motion and Attraction. Motion in its turn expresses itself in two distinct kinds of movement, one the rotary (centripetal) movement, the other, the propulsory (centrifugal) movement. That is seen throughout the whole Universe, therefore also in our own solar system. There is this planet, the Earth, rotating on its own axis and moving continually forward, but by the Sun's attraction kept circling around it. The rotary movement is expressed in the rotation of the Earth on its own axis. The forward movement is seen in the Earth's revolutions about the Sun. On a larger scale, our whole solar system turns around itself, and besides that moves forward at the speed of about 1,000,000 miles per 24 hours towards the constellation of Lyra. It moves in a seemingly straight line, but in reality not in a straight line; it revolves around a central sun which has

SCIENCE·OF·BEING

not yet been discovered by the astronomers, because it is so far away. There is no end to those ever increasing orbits, because the Universe is endless. And when we come down to the smallest things we find the same Law governing them. The electrons of which the atom is constituted, rotating on their own little axes, express the first movement of Primal Energy, and in revolving around their tiny sun they express the second movement. Now the first rotary movement is a condensary one. When individual units of vibrations of Primal Energy begin to rotate around their own little axes, their inherent quality of Attraction makes them condense into electrons. These electrons take the form of spheres, because a sphere is a perfectly balanced body, which can remain in that condition indefinitely, as all its constituent parts are in perfect relation one to another. For that reason physical bodies, in order to persevere in existence, take in Nature that simple and lasting form.

卐 On that principle is built the whole Universe. Out of a nebula which began to move and condense and revolve around its own axis, was formed this solar System. All other systems were formed in the same way; and the little atom and electron are formed according to the same law, because there is only One Universal Law, called the Great Law which pervades and governs everything in the same way, no matter if it is a star or if it is an electron. The electrons originated because of that first movement, the rotary condensary movement of Primal Energy. These Laws pervade everything and are continually operating also in our own bodies, and the knowledge of them enables us to work out problems in our life with mathematical accuracy.

卐 Our body is an aggregation of forces in different degrees of condensation; therefore it is a Dynamic Center, of which we are the rightful master.

LESSON-THREE

THE VISIBLE UNIVERSE IS MADE UP OF INVISIBLE, PRIMAL ENERGY. THAT WHICH IS SEEN IS MADE UP OF THINGS UNSEEN.

Almost everybody knows something about explosives. They are a very good illustration of how seemingly solid material things are in reality made of immaterial elements. Take a piece of dynamite. It is hard, has weight and density, etc. In striking that piece of dynamite, energy is used and produces certain vibrations which alter the relations of the atoms within so that the dynamite explodes – that is, some Energy is released and we have dynamite transformed into gases. It is a chemical reaction which takes place by shock. There is no need to pour any chemical on the dynamite in order produce an explosion. To strike – that is, to use energy – is sufficient. Energy makes the reaction. And what is obtained from that reaction? Perhaps thousands of times the volume of the original piece of dynamite. It is obtained in gases. It has entirely changed. Compared with the first thing which was handled, it is seemingly very immaterial. Of course the gases are also "material," as one can weigh gases, smell them, etc., yet there is already a tremendous change. That shows how Matter, when handled in a certain way, entirely changes its aspect and becomes a different thing, so that when it reaches its last hiding place in Energy, no one can call it "material" any more; it is the PURE FORCE.

卐 Everything in this seemingly material Universe is but a combination of Forces, in condensed and non-condensed conditions. In other words, the whole Universe is but an Infinite, Dynamic Center, which is, on a tremendous scale, the same as our bodies are on a small scale.

SCIENCE-OF-BEING

THE GREAT LAW OF ATTRACTION GOVERNS THE WHOLE UNIVERSE AND IS THE BASIS OF ETERNAL HARMONY.

When analyzing Primal Energy, it was explained that it has a basic quality, Attraction, and that this quality of Attraction makes possible the existence of the whole Universe, as everything in this Universe is kept in perfect relation through the Law of Attraction. Attraction and Love are synonymous; Love is the emotional name for Attraction. Because of the Law of Attraction, all the minute particles in everything are holding together and make up a whole. Why have we a body which we can touch and which has a form? Because of the Law of Attraction, which is keeping the cells together. The same is true of stone or of anything else. Why do we remain on the surface of the Earth and are not thrown into Space during its rotation around its axis? Because of the Law of Attraction. Why does the Earth revolve around the Sun? Because of the Law of Attraction. Without it, the Earth would be lost in Infinite Space. Why do all the celestial bodies move in such a harmonious way? Because of the Law of Attraction. This Law of Attraction is a Basic Law, a Fundamental Quality of Primal Energy; and here we have an explanation of the words in the Bible: "In Him we live and move and have our being." As it was previously stated, ATTRACTION AND LOVE ARE SYNONYMOUS. When we love we are attracted; when we hate we are repelled. It is the Law of Attraction which enables Universal Harmony to remain Harmony, because without Attraction, everything would become chaos, and the Universe would collapse. It is that Sustaining Power referred to in the explanation of the word "Principle" which makes it possible for the Universe to be eternally existing.

LESSON·THREE

SPACE WHICH SEPARATES THE WORLDS ONE FROM ANOTHER DOES NOT ISOLATE THEM. THEY ARE KEPT IN PERPETUAL COMMUNICATION ONE WITH ANOTHER THROUGH THE GREAT LAW OF ATTRACTION WHICH IS EXERCISED INSTANTANEOUSLY AND ETERNALLY THROUGHOUT ALL SPACE AND THUS FORMS INDISSOLUBLE LINKS BETWEEN WORLDS.

First must be explained the difference between the word "WORLD" and the word "UNIVERSE," for there is a great difference between these two words. THERE IS BUT ONE UNIVERSE; the word itself states it. This one UNIVERSE is made up of infinite numbers of Worlds.

What is called by astronomers a World is all that which can be seen through the telescope, and even much more than what can be actually perceived. All the seemingly infinite agglomeration of stars, suns, and planets extending in all directions – some of these stars being so far away from the Earth that their light takes millions of years to reach us, although light speeds through Space at a rate of about 186,000 miles per second – constitutes this World. Many stars do not exist any more, yet we see them because their light is reaching us only now. It is impossible, in our present mental development, to realize the stupendous size of this World. Yet what we see around us, seemingly infinite as it appears to be, IS FINITE AND HAS AN END; and when we come to what we call the limit of this World, we would see the following picture. On one side myriads and myriads of stars, the Milky Way, beautiful combinations of lights, etc., which, all taken together, would appear as an infinitely large Sphere; and on the other side, utter darkness, darkness so complete, so terrible, that here on Earth we could have no idea of it. It seems to be void of everything, dead; and if we would travel through that darkness, where not a star is shinning, even no vibration of the Ether perceptible, for a seemingly endless time and through immeasurable space, we would again come to another World, to a different agglomeration of what would appear to another infinite number of stars and suns and planets.

SCIENCE-OF-BEING

⌘ That would be another World; and that World, taken as a whole, is again a Sphere, a gigantic Sphere floating in that Endless Ocean of seeming Voidness, seeming Darkness; and that Endless Ocean, which has NO LIMIT, with those floating Spheres in it, which are the Worlds, THAT IS THE UNIVERSE; and that UNIVERSE, BOUNDLESS, INFINITE, IS THE ONLY CHILD, THE ONLY SON EVER BORN OF THE ONE GOD, OF THE ONE GREAT PRINCIPLE, THE ABSOLUTE. When we visualize Divinity from the point of view even of Astronomy we have such a gigantic, overwhelming concept of what the Great Principle is that all religious ideas of It are nothing but pale, limited thoughts, because they can never give us, as Science does, that wonderful proof of the greatness of God, that Great One, call the Absolute, who is our Father.

⌘ Our Earth is a beautiful star floating in that Infinite Ocean, the Universe. The Law of Attraction, a BASIC LAW OF UNIVERSAL ENERGY, PERVADES THE WHOLE UNIVERSE. Even in that Void Space, where there is seemingly nothing, where even the visible light vibrations cannot penetrate because they are too dense and are therefore circumscribed to their respective Worlds, there the Law of Attraction, of Love, is still operating. That Law cannot be avoided; there is nowhere in the Universe a place where Attraction, or Love, does not exist; and Love is an Aspect of Divinity, the highest we know of now. These scientific statements correspond exactly to the words of the Psalmist: "IF I ASCEND UP INTO HEAVEN, THOU ART THERE; IF I MAKE MY BED IN HELL, BEHOLD THOU ART THERE; IF I TAKE THE WINGS OF THE MORNING, AND DWELL IN THE UTTERMOST PARTS OF THE SEA, EVEN THERE SHALL THY HAND LEAD ME, AND THY RIGHT HAND SHALL HOLD ME."

⌘ The Law of Love, the Law of Attraction, pervades the seeming voidness of interstellar space and is exercised instantaneously and eternally, because Time and Space do not exist for that Law. It is just as infinite as Infinity and Eternity. And the Law of Attraction is the great bond of Love uniting the Worlds, the bond which Humanity has always consciously or unconsciously recognized, because it is a Universal Law. Why do human beings congregate and form communities, cities, countries and nations? Why is it that we like to league ourselves together, to have brotherhoods, societies, unions? Because of that Law. All the Worlds and all the Stars are brothers; so are we all brothers; and if the Worlds are placed in that relation one to another, and the Law of Attraction is functioning so perfectly there, why should it not be also consciously exercised among us human beings? That would be THE FULFILLING OF THE LAW OF LOVE, OUR ETERNAL PRIVILEGE AND DUTY. Scientist now realize the infinite possibilities opened by that Law of Attraction, and they try to communicate, through vibrations, with the different planets, because they know that vibrations will reach anywhere. These are the indissoluble links between the Worlds, formed by the Vibrations of Attraction, the Basis of Universal Harmony. Therefore, these Worlds, these Stars and Planets, which seem to be isolated are in reality not isolated, and form One Great, Perfect, Eternal Whole. They are no more isolated one from another than are the cells in our bodies. ALL IS COMPLETE UNITY, AND WE OURSELVES ARE ALSO NOT SEPARATE BODIES AS WE APPEAR TO BE; WE ARE PARTS OF THE ONE GREAT UNIVERSAL BODY, UNITED AND HELD TOGETHER BY THE LAW OF ATTRACTION.

ENERGY IS INDESTRUCTIBLE, THEREFORE ETERNAL.
SUBSTANCE IS INDESTRUCTIBLE, THEREFORE ETERNAL.
THE UNIVERSE IS INDESTRUCTIBLE, THEREFORE ETERNAL.
THE SOUL IS INDESTRUCTIBLE, THEREFORE ETERNAL.

• • •

ENERGY IS INDESTRUCTIBLE, THEREFORE ETERNAL. Primal Energy, being the basis of everything, is indestructible. That was explained in the First Lesson. It cannot disperse itself anywhere because it pervades Infinite Space, is One with it. There is nothing which can destroy it because it is all there is, and once it is indestructible, it must be eternal because it must remain in that condition forever. It has always existed and always will be existing.

• • •

SUBSTANCE IS INDESTRUCTIBLE, THEREFORE ETERNAL. What is Substance? What is the difference between Substance and Matter? Substance and Matter are two very different things. Matter is a phenomenon, a condition of continual changes, elusive, mutable. Substance is, on the contrary, a noumenon, something stable, permanent. The word Substance itself expresses it. It means something which underlies, stands under as a foundation, from the Latin word "Substare" – to stand under, support. Substance is the first condensation of Primal Energy, due to its rotary movement. There is the free Energy and the so-called condensed Energy, and from the combination of these two is formed everything which exists. Substance being made of an indestructible, eternal element, Primal Energy is just as indestructible and eternal as the latter.

卐 First there is the Unmanifest, the Causeless Cause, the Great Principle, the Absolute called God. Its first manifestation is Primal Energy. Primal Energy becomes in turn a cause by itself. Its direct manifestation is Substance, which is the underlying basic element from which the whole Universe is made. Substance is therefore universal. Being a noumenon, it is immutable, but expresses itself in infinitely varied and continually changing phenomena.

• • •

THE UNIVERSE IS INDESTRUCTIBLE, THEREFORE ETERNAL. The Universe is an infinite and eternal structure, conceived in the creative imagination of its great Architect, Cosmic Intelligence, reared out of Substance through the agency of Free Energy, and indissolubly cemented by the immutable Law of Attraction. All these elements which contribute to its existence being indestructible, the Universe itself is indestructible therefore eternal.

• • •

THE SOUL IS INDESTRUCTIBLE, THEREFORE ETERNAL. Finally we have the Soul, indestructible, therefore eternal. At first the question may arise, "What is a Soul? Is there a Soul and can it be proven that there is a Soul?" It can – by logical deductions. WHAT IS A SOUL? THE *SOULS OF EVERYTHING, BE IT MAN, ANIMAL, PLANT, MINERAL, OR GAS, ARE THOSE SELF-PROJECTIONS INTO SUBSTANCE OF THE UNMANIFEST, ETERNALLY PROCEEDING FROM THE GREAT PRINCIPLE, THE ABSOLUTE, RANGING FROM THE MOST SIMPLE TO THE MOST COMPLEX, AND CULMINATING IN THOSE INDIVIDUALIZED, CONSCIOUS, COMPOUND PROJECTIONS CALLED MEN.*

卐 The Soul creates channels through which to express its activities. These channels have certain definite forms, and an aggregation of them is called a body. The plane on which the Soul is functioning, be it the physical, the mental or the Spiritual, determines the appearance of the body and the elements of which it is formed. In other words, the body is the direct result, the proof, of the Soul's existence. But the body dies. What then happens to the Soul? Does the Soul also disintegrate, die? No! The body is nothing but an effect, the Soul being the cause; therefore the destruction of the effect can in no way impair the cause. One body destroyed, the Soul builds up another body, always of a stronger, better material, until it reaches a stage where its body is made of indestructible elements. Such a body becomes then eternal, because it is indestructible.

Therefore the death of the body does not mean the annihilation of the Soul, for the Soul cannot die, nor can it ever be lost. But the sense of the Soul can be lost, and when that sense of the Soul is lost, then happens what is called in the Apocalypse, THE SECOND DEATH, which means that the unit called a Soul is thrown back into the very deepest plane of Involution, from where it has to start all over again the millions of years of experience until it reaches once more the stage in which it lost the sense of its own existence. Each one of us, in our present state of Evolution, is the product of millions and millions of years of hard, very hard work. We have been through such experiences that if most of us could consciously remember our past, it would become one of the greatest curses Humanity could have, because we would be so weighed down by the remembrance of these experiences. Fortunately we have it now behind us. Divine Wisdom has covered that sad past with a veil of forgetfulness. Otherwise, life on Earth with all its efforts, aims and endeavors, would become almost impossible, on account of remorse for that past. In each successive incarnation, it is given to men to start their lives anew.

THE SOUL IS INDIVIDUAL. WE HAVE A GREAT NUMBER OF PERSONALITIES WITHIN OURSELVES AS REMNANTS OF PAST INCARNATIONS, BUT WE HAVE ONLY ONE INDIVIDUALITY, the individual being compared to the note in music or the number in mathematics. That is our individuality, OUR ETERNAL IDENTITY. MAN IS INDIVIDUAL. Personality is but the human concept which we have for the time being of our own self, and our present personality is made up of many personalities.

THE BASIS OF MAN'S EXISTENCE AND IDENTITY IS THE SOUL. THE BODY IS BUT A TRANSITORY CONDITION OR EXPRESSION OF THE SOUL'S PRESENT ACTIVITIES. THEREFORE, AS THE ACTIVITIES OF THE SOUL CHANGE, SO DOES THE BODY CHANGE ALSO.

In this proposition we have something basic, fundamental – the Soul;

that is, the direct emanation of the Great Principle, the Absolute, of Divinity, conscious and perfect in every way, Its image and likeness. The question may be asked, "Is there an infinite number of souls,?" Yes, there is. Because, even if each soul manifests the completeness of the Absolute, the perfect image and likeness of which is represented in it, the Infinity of the Great All can only be represented by infinite number of souls that make up that Great All, as in their infinite number, they stand for the Infinity of the Absolute. Each soul is identical with Divinity in quality, not in quantity; but taken all together, they are identical with the Great Principle also in quantity, and thus constitute the Great Compound Soul of the Universe. It is a Law which is continually expressing itself in Nature. For instance, take a solution of salt, or any other crystallized chemical, and when that solution is saturated and crystallization begins, it crystallizes in thousands and thousands of small crystals. What is the Law back of it? The solution is full of energy, manifested in vibrations going in different directions. There are a great many of those vibrations, each unit of which individually expresses itself through the chemical elements in the form of a small crystal, all the crystals together representing the quantity of the solution, and each crystal having also all the qualities of that solution. Nature works in this way, and Nature always expresses itself exactly according to Universal Laws, manifested in that ordinary experiment with the solution of any salt. The same Laws also governs the relation of souls to their Primary Cause, the Great Principle.

卐 The Soul, therefore, is THAT WHICH STANDS AS THE BASIS OF OUR EXISTENCE, of our life, of our identity and individuality. Individuality is in the soul. Each soul has from Eternity its own fixed identity which no other soul can have. Never two souls alike, never two lives alike. Each has its own place in the Universe. When the Soul has found that place, it will keep it for Eternity. That is why the basis of man's existence and identity is the Soul.

卐 What is the body? The Soul acts. Its qualities, its forces, are expressing themselves through its activities, and the aggregate manifestations of those activities, outwardly outlined, from a body. Body does not mean only a material form; it may be a mental, a Spiritual body. It depends on the plane on which the Soul expresses its activities. What do the eyes stand for? They stand for perception. We perceive, we see through the eyes. What do the ears express? They express discrimination. Each part of our body expresses a certain activity of the Soul – the heart, emotion; the brain, capacity to think, to coordinate, or the governing power; the shoulders, power to bear responsibilities; the feet, the foundations on which we stand; the legs, the power to move forward, to advance; the hands, the power to act, etc. The body is but a transitory condition or expression of the Soul's present activities. When the activities of the Soul change, the body also will be modified according to the changed activities of the Soul. Human beings of today are said to belong to the Fifth Race. Its emblem is the Pentagram – the five pointed star. That is why we are now expressing, manifesting, the number Five. We have five fingers, five senses, etc. The previous Race, in whom the activities of the Soul were less developed, were supposed to have only four senses, perhaps only four fingers. Four was their dominant number. The next Race, the Sixth Race, will have six senses; it will manifest, express the number Six. Their bodies will be modified according to their Soul's activities. Its emblem will be the six pointed star, - the Star of Wisdom where the two principles, the male and female, combine in one.

卐 It is a scientific fact that the body is renewed periodically. Every seven years (some authorities say three, others every year) each part is made new – tissues, bones, etc. Why is there this divergence of opinions? Because some individuals whose vibrations are slow renew their bodies slowly. Those whose vibrations are rapid renew them quickly. Their vibrations are higher and therefore their change is much quicker. They can renew in three, perhaps in two years, or even in one year. That renewal is all due to the activities of the Soul. In that first proposition the material body, our present body, does not enter yet, as a separate concept. It refers in general to "a body." WE SHALL ALWAYS HAVE SOME KIND OF BODY. THE SOUL MUST HAVE A BODY, because that is the outward manifestation of its inner qualities. What form the body will take we do not know now, but it certainly will have a form and always a more and more beautiful, a more advanced form. Everything has a form; form is a quality of the Soul; therefore bodies will always have some form. On the higher planes, where the activities of the Soul have finer elements through which to express themselves, the bodies continually change in their appearance. Those whose eyes are trained to perceive the life vibrations of the body, called the Aura, know that the color and the force of the Aura change all the time. When we have one kind of thought or emotion the Aura is one color; with another kind another color; all due to the activities of the Soul.

THE SOUL OF MAN, OR THE REAL SELF, WHICH IS MAN, IS A COMPOUND, INDIVIDUALIZED, SELF-CONSCIOUS PROJECTION OF HARMONIOUS VIBRATIONS, PROCEEDING FROM THE INFINITE SOURCE OF ALL ENERGY AND BEING THEREFORE ETERNAL. IN PENETRATING INTO THE MATERIAL WORLD THE SOUL ATTRACTS FROM ITS SURROUNDINGS (AIR, WATER, EARTH, ETC.) ALL THE NECESSARY ELEMENTS TO CONSTRUCT A VEHICLE OR BODY FOR ITS EXPRESSION ON THIS EARTH PLANE. AFTER IT HAS EXPRESSED ITSELF ON THIS EARTH PLANE FOR A SUFFICIENT LENGTH OF TIME, THE GREAT LAW CALLS IT TO PROCEED FURTHER TO DO SOME OTHER WORK. THE SOUL LEAVES THE BODY, WHICH BEREFT OF ITS COHESIVE POWER, DISINTEGRATES AND GIVES BACK TO ITS NATIVE ELEMENTS THE MATERIALS OF WHICH IT HAS BEEN CONSTITUTED.

Here we have again the Soul of man, which means the inner self, the Real Self, the manifestations, the ray, of the Absolute, called also the son God, and which is an individualized compound projection of harmonious, self-conscious vibrations. When there was given, the First

SCIENCE-OF-BEING

Lesson, a definition of what man is, a different wording was used because it was approached from the point of view of the Absolute, where even vibrations were not mentioned as being a too material concept. But now the same subject is taken up from the point of view of the science of vibrations, and in a way vibrations are very tangible things – tangible as far as their perceptibility is concerned. The Soul is a compound unit of these vibrations; that is, all the infinite varieties of vibrations of the Absolute, focused in an infinite number of individual points, are souls – conscious, harmonious, individual projections of Self-Consciousness, proceeding from the Infinite Source of All Vibrations and being therefore eternal, because they have eternally the nature of their Father, the Great Principle. When these souls, these aggregated self-conscious vibrations, focused in individual points, penetrate into this material world, in order to have a body, a material vehicle, through which to express themselves on this plane, they attract (the force of Attraction being their inherent quality) around themselves all the different minute electrons, atom, and so forth, and build with those elements a body. That is done, as we all know, through the mother by means of gestation. The Soul which is to be incarnated sends its vibrations into the mother's womb; there it touches, in the female egg, a unit of the male seed which had penetrated there; from there the life begins to unfold and the Soul to express itself more and more through that little seed, combining its own activities with those of the mother, and thus forming little by little the body which it will call its own. The mother provides the building material through breathing, eating, and so forth, and feeds the body of the future child; and the Soul continually attracts around its own activities the material elements provided by the mother, thus forming its future body. During that physical union between men and women, the main object of which is the conception of another being, some of the strongest physical, mental, and emotional vibrations are brought forth. In that moment is determined what kind of a soul shall be incarnated in the mother's womb. Like attracts like. If the vibrations of the two parents are harmonious and of a high rate, a highly evolved soul will be attracted. If, on the contrary, both parties, or even one, will manifest vibrations of disharmony, vibrations of a low rate, a soul whose vibrations correspond to that rate will be thus attracted.

LESSON-THREE

THEREFORE IT IS MOST ESSENTIAL THAT THE PROSPECTIVE PARENTS CONSIDER THAT BODILY UNION AS SOMETHING VERY SACRED AND PURE, AND THAT THEY PERFORM IT WITH A HIGHER OBJECT IN MIND THAN THE MERE GRATIFICATION OF A CARNAL APPETITE. IT MUST BE A GLORIOUS HYMN OF LOVE, IN WHICH EVERY FIBER OF THEIR TRIUNE BEING, BODY, MIND, AND SOUL, SENDS OUT ITS MOST PERFECT VIBRATIONS. No physical union should ever be tolerated when the two parties are not in complete harmony with each other at that moment, else most disastrous effects will descend upon the child born of such a disharmonious union.

The Soul which incarnates is not within the seed; it only overshadows it, combines its individual life force with that of the seed, thus making the seed grow and become the channel for its expression on this Earth plane. When the nine months of gestation are over, the body is completely formed and the child is born and becomes a separate entity. The Soul then acts through the child as through a separate, individual channel, not needing the mother any more. The Soul expresses through the body of the child all its functions only when the child reaches the age of puberty, and is ready for procreation. When the Soul has expressed through the body all its functions, even the function of procreation (which is a Divine quality, and one of the greatest the Soul possess), then only is it fully equipped to fulfill properly its mission on this Earth. The Soul then continually expresses itself through that body, the vehicle built by it for its own use. The material body is the instrument, the channel, through which the Soul contacts the outer world and manifests itself and is perceptible on this material plane. When the time comes for the Soul to go to another plane to work there, it happens so that through circumstances (the individual having become sick or old) the Soul leaves the body; and as soon as it abandons the body, the latter, being no longer held together by the cohesive power, the force of Attraction inherent in the Soul, begins to disintegrate, to give back to the elements the materials of which it has been formed. There are the words of the Bible: "Dust thou art, and to dust thou shalt return." Out of dust was the body created, and to dust does it return. Out of invisible little particles is formed the material body – sometimes a very beautiful body – but when the Soul goes away, that body reverts back to dust.

SCIENCE·OF·BEING

Thus we see that the body really returns to its primitive condition of simple elements. Therefore, when we lose somebody on this plane, we should never morn over the body, which was dear to us as the visible manifestation of the Soul we loved. That body is just as outworn as an old suit of clothes. It may be a remembrance to us, but it is a worn-out garment, which the Soul has replaced with another garment much more beautiful.

We see continually in Nature this changing of bodies. Let us take the caterpillar as an example. The caterpillar dies as a caterpillar, becomes a chrysalis. The soul of the caterpillar is on longer satisfied to crawl on the ground; it wants to fly. By and by that consciousness unfolds in it, and when it has unfolded itself perfectly, and has created all the necessary apparatus to be able to fly, the chrysalis bursts and the butterfly comes out. That is why the butterfly is considered the symbol of the Soul which frees itself from the old body. The Soul, by the successive putting on and leaving off of its different bodies, creates more and more perfect vehicles for its expression, until it finally reaches a stage where its body becomes as perfect and indestructible as is the Soul itself.

卐 When we are born again, we start life anew. We have within us all our past experiences, although most of us are not conscious of it. Even those who are the most advanced have to work hard for a number of years in order to become fully conscious of their own knowledge. It took Jesus over thirty years before He was able to unfold within Himself all that was needed for His divine mission, and yet He knew, from the very day when He entered this material plane, that He was to save the World. Tradition says that He went into the Ephesian schools to study the Science of Being. That Scientific study, that period of inner development, was necessary in order to bring back to Him in His material embodiment that which He already knew from Eternity. If we consciously express the Laws of Harmony now, we shall be able to prolong our lives, and especially we shall be able to keep to the very limit of our days a strong body – a body strong not only in its activities, but also young and harmonious in form. If people would live as Jesus did, they would not need to die. They would raise their vibrations higher and higher until finally they would be translated into another plane, as were Jesus, Elijah, Enoch and others,

LESSON-THREE

thus overcoming the last enemy, Death. It is not the changing of one body for another that makes people fear death; it is the pain connected with it, because most people suffer terribly when those ties between Soul and body are served. It is also an acute mental agony, especially for those who love life and yet do not believe in a life hereafter; and that is why, after all, the process of dying is such a sad thing. When our mental attitude towards it will have changed, then our physical experience of that transition will also be greatly modified, and we will not fear it any longer. On the contrary, the ABSOLUTE CERTAINTY THAT WE ARE GROWING INTO A BETTER, FINER BODY, raising us into a higher condition, will make us almost desire that change.

THE HUMAN BODY IS A CURRENT CONTINUALLY RENEWED BY THE ASSIMILATION OF GASES THROUGH BREATHING, AND THE FEEDING OF THE MOLECULES, DIRECTED, ORGANIZED, GOVERNED, BY THE IMMATERIAL FORCE WHICH ANIMATES IT AND WHICH IS CALLED THE SOUL.

The previous proposition simply gave us man born, the Soul incarnated, manifesting itself through a material body. It gave us the process of that incarnation, the process of building the body, but it did not say how it will keep the body, how it will live in that body. This proposition explains that. It says the body is a current, which is scientifically correct. It is a current of vibrations, a current of Life continually flowing through us. That vital current which flows through the nerves, through the bones and through every cell in the body – that current, aggregated, outlined, is the body itself; and that current is kept alive first of all through breathing, or the assimilation of gases. The gases feed that current. We usually think that the feeding of our body by means of the mouth and through the stomach is the most important. But this is not so at all. In the year 1920, the Mayor of Cork, MacSwiney, showed that he could live a very long period, approximately seventy-six days, without eating, yet he could not have lived five minutes without breathing. That proves how much more important breathing is than the actual material food. People of today realize that more and more, and that is why there are so many different systems of scientific breathing. Some of them are exceedingly good. TO BREATHE PROPERLY, THAT IS, TO BREATHE SCIENTIFICALLY, IS ONE OF THE VERY IMPORTANT THINGS FOR US TO KNOW IN ORDER TO KEEP STRONG AND HEALTHY; yet, unfortunately, our knowledge of that is very limited. Most human beings do not know at all how to breathe properly. They live such an artificial life that even that most essential function of the body is undeveloped. There are different kinds of systems of breathing; the best are those which are evolved in the very country where they are to be used. That is why the Oriental systems do not suit so well the Western people, and vice versa.

卐 There are, throughout the world, a great number of systems of diet. One of the best, up to the present, is considered that of Horace Fletcher, an American. If people would follow Fletcher's or any similar system, they would never know what stomach trouble is, and also there would be no shortage of food, because he proved scientifically that people could eat half of what they eat now and yet be stronger and healthier. It is only necessary to masticate the food properly.

卐 The digesting of the food is done first by the mouth, then by the stomach. When the food is broken to pieces through mastication, a certain amount of energy is thus liberated, absorbed by the mucuses of the mouth and conveyed directly to the brain, which is therefore the first to receive Life Force in that liberated condition. The masticated food is then sent through the alimentary canal to the stomach, which starts its digestion. In order to digest the food properly, the stomach produces gastric juices, whose chemical qualities are so powerful that they can dissolve almost anything they come in contact with. The gastric juices produced by the stomach are of a different kind for each food. Therefore, in dietetics, a simple food is always advisable in larger quantities – more of one kind and not so many different kinds combined. For each kind of food we absorb, the stomach must produce the corresponding

gastric juice. Suppose there is a dish composed of six or seven ingredients. Then the stomach has to produce at the same time six or seven different gastric juices, which naturally it cannot do, because it can produce only one kind of juice at a time. Not being able to solve the problem in a satisfactory way, it loses its head, and losing of the stomach's head means indigestion; therefore, people who eat very complicated food, usually discover that in their older days they can hardly eat any food at all. Those who live on simple food, on the contrary, even if they become very old, still keep their stomachs in a fine condition to the very end, because they never gave to their stomachs work which that organ could not do properly. Fresh, well prepared but simple food, in a sufficient quantity, especially vegetables and fruits, well masticated, is all anyone needs to insure proper digestion. The current of Life Force is therefore also fed by the chemical reaction, called the burning process, which is produced by the digestion of the food. That is what is meant by the feeding of the molecules, a work which is all done – the current directed, properly organized, and governed – by that invisible, immaterial, individualized, conscious force, which we call the Soul. Even there, in that material body, the dominant power is not the visible body, but that invisible entity which is underlying, governing and sustaining it – the Soul. It is all so systematically arranged that it seems to work automatically. THERE IS NOTHING MORE WONDERFUL AND BEAUTIFUL ON THIS EARTH PLANE THAN A PERFECT HUMAN BODY, THE "TEMPLE OF THE LIVING GOD," as an Apostle calls it.

THE HUMAN BODY, AS MATERIAL AS IT MAY APPEAR TO US, IS BUT A HARMONIOUS GROUP FORMED BY THE IMMATERIAL FORCES OF THE SOUL.

The last proposition, which closes the cycle of the body, seems very much like the first, in which it was stated that the basis of man's existence and identity is the Soul, and the body is but a transitory condition or expression of the Soul's present activities. Those two propositions appear to be alike, yet they are not. The first one refers to "a body." It does not state a material body; it mentions only a body. It could just as well be a mental body, an astral body, or a Spiritual body. This last proposition applies specifically to a material body, which material as it may appear to us, is after all but a harmonious group of cells, of molecules, of atoms, of electrons, of vibrations, formed by the immaterial forces of the Soul, and held together by the Law of Attraction. The invisible forces of the Soul have moulded that visible form, that living statue, called a human body; and these forces are also permeating it, sustaining it, and are the very substance of that body. After the very deepest point of involution has been reached, where one seems to be at the bottom of Matter in its densest aspect, the scientific fact is discovered, that even there it is NOT THE SO-CALLED MATERIAL BODY WHICH IS THE GOVERNING POWER, BUT THE SOUL which has formed that body through its own activities. And as the Soul has formed it, so can the Soul also modify and change, even now and here, on this material plane, this body of ours. In other words, reaching the bottom of matter, we find there SPIRIT; THAT IS, SPIRIT IS EVERYWHERE.

What applies to the human body also applies to any other body, to the bodies of animals, plants, minerals and gases. They are all formed in the same way, according to the same principle, the same law, as human bodies. The reason why only the human Soul and body are mentioned is because they are the highest in Nature; therefore, naturally, when one speaks of the highest, the lesser is also included in it. Jesus, in His Sermon on the Mount, did not mention that we should love animals, plants, and so forth. As far as we know, He very seldom even referred to them, because He understood that if we loved Man, the highest, naturally we would love everything below. Why then did Buddha teach such wonderful respect to all Nature? He lived in a country where animal and plant life reached an extraordinary development; it expressed itself in most cases in very beautiful forms and became a very important part in the daily life of the people. Buddha taught His fellow beings to love as their younger brothers all those entities belonging to the different kingdoms of Nature, to respect their lives. Thus He prepared His followers to love better their own fellow men, the highest manifestation in Nature. Great teachings always make the best practical use of their immediate surrounds, be it of place or of time. They are always attuned to the period in which they are given, so as to make the process of Evolution as easy as possible. Jesus, when He was giving His teachings, said to His disciples: "Many things have I to tell you, but you cannot bear them now." In spite of being continually with Him, His disciples could not understand all of His teachings, because they were not ready. When Krishna, who lived long before Buddha, came to proclaim the gospel of Truth, He did not speak about Nature in the way Buddha spoke; His teachings remind one much more of those of Jesus. Why? Because it was again a different period in which He lived. That period of Humanity's Evolution required teachings which appear to be more similar to the teachings of Jesus than those of Buddha. The same was with Vishnu. Yet Jesus, Buddha, Krishna and Vishnu are One, because there is only one Savior of the World, who comes to this Earth at different periods, under different names, as a different personality. The Eternal Individuality back of all those personalities was, is, and ever will be the same One. Vishnu, Krishna and Buddha were just as much Saviors of the World as was Jesus, and as there cannot be several Saviors, they must all be One Eternal Savior – Love Divine.

"FOR THE PROTECTION OF THE GOOD, FOR THE DESTRUCTION OF EVIL DOERS, I AM BORN FROM AGE TO AGE," IS THE MESSAGE OF LOVE TO SUFFERING HUMANITY.

QVESTIONS & ANSWERS

LESSON THREE

1. QUES.   What is Matter?
   ANS.   Matter is certain vibratory phenomena perceptible through the senses. It is by Nature changeable.

2. QUES.   What is the origin of Matter?
   ANS.   Primal Energy is the noumenon, or basis, from which the phenomenon called Matter originated.

3. QUES.   What is the nature of Matter?
   ANS.   It is essentially elusive. It is called the Great Illusion.

4. QUES.   What are its aspects?
   ANS.   Solid, liquid, and gaseous form.

5. QUES.   What are its qualities?
   ANS.   Weight, density, volume.

6. QUES.   What is the smallest known particle of Matter?
   ANS.   The electron.

7. QUES.   How many kinds of electrons are there?
   ANS.   Two, the positive (male) and the negative (female) electrons.

8. QUES.   What is an electron?
   ANS.   An electron is a tiny sphere, rotating on its own axis, and made of pure, condensed Primal Energy.

9. QUES.   How is an electron formed?
   ANS.   Individual units of vibrations of Primal Energy, in rotating around their own axes, become condensed and form a microscopic sphere called an electron.

10. QUES.   What is an Atom?
    ANS.   An aggregation of electrons, a planetary system in miniature.

11. QUES.   What is taken as the unit of atomic weight?
    ANS.   An atom of Hydrogen, which has only two electrons, a positive one around which revolves a negative.

102

SCIENCE-OF-BEING

12. QUES.   What is a molecule?
    ANS.   It is an aggregation of atoms. Molecules constitute all material elements.

13. QUES.   What determines the weight and the hardness of a material element.
    ANS.   The number of electrons in an atom of it. In other words, the amount of condensed Energy determines the qualities of the element.

14. QUES.   What other quality does Matter possess?
    ANS.   It is radio-active. It emanates Primal Energy.

15. QUES.   What is the cause of radio-activity?
    ANS.   The disintegration of Matter, the release of Primal Energy contained in it.

16. QUES.   Are all material elements radio-active?
    ANS.   Yes.

17. QUES.   Which is the most radio-active so far as is known now?
    ANS.   Radium.

18. QUES.   What determines the preciousness of an element?
    ANS.   The amount of condensed Energy contained in it.

19. QUES.   What is the difference between a noble individual and a common one?
    ANS.   An individual of noble character expresses his energies on a higher plane, in stronger, higher vibrations than others, and is consequently of more value to Humanity.

20. QUES.   What is the scientific definition of Matter?
    ANS.   Matter is but the consciousness of effects produced on the senses by various manifestations of Primal Energy. Therefore Matter is only a state of consciousness, the present manner in which those effects are perceived.

21. QUES.   What is the human body?
    ANS.   It is an aggregation of vibrations in different degrees of condensation. It is a dynamic center.

SCIENCE-OF-BEING

22. QUES. On what principle is the Universe built?
     ANS.   On the same principle as is formed the electron – through condensation of Primal Energy.

23. QUES. What is the basis of the visible Universe?
     ANS.   Invisible, Primal Energy.

24. QUES. What is the Fundamental Law of the Universe?
     ANS.   The Great Law of Attraction which governs the whole Universe and is the basis of Eternal Harmony.

25. QUES. Are the words "Attraction" and "Love" synonymous?
     ANS.   They are. Attraction is the scientific name for Love.

26. QUES. What is the connecting link between the component parts of the Universe (worlds, planets, etc.)?
     ANS.   The Great Law of Attraction, which is exercised instantaneously and eternally throughout all Space.

27. QUES. What is the difference between the word "World" and the word "Universe"?
     ANS.   There is but one limitless and eternal Universe, which is made up on an infinite number of Worlds.

28. QUES. What is our Earth?
     ANS.   A beautiful star, floating in that infinite Universe.

29. QUES. What is Man's eternal privilege and duty?
     ANS.   The fulfilling of the Law of Love.

30. QUES. Why is Primal Energy indestructible?
     ANS.   Because it is the effect of an indestructible Cause, the Great Principle Itself.

31. QUES. What is Substance, and why is it indestructible?
     ANS.   Substance is the first condensation of Primal Energy. Being made of an indestructible element, Primal Energy, it is also indestructible.

32. QUES. Why is the Universe indestructible?
     ANS.   Because its basic elements, Primal Energy, Substance, Cosmic

LESSON-THREE

Intelligence and the Law of Attraction are indestructible.

33. QUES. What is the Soul, and why is it indestructible?
    ANS. Souls are individualized self-projections of the Unmanifest into Substance. They are eternal because they are the manifestations of the Great Principle Itself.

34. QUES. Is the Soul individual?
    ANS. Yes.

35. QUES. What is the difference between "Individuality" and "Personality"?
    ANS. Individuality is man's eternal identity. Personality is but a transitory human concept of that Individuality.

36. QUES. What is the basis of man's existence and identity?
    ANS. The Soul.

37. QUES. What is the body?
    ANS. The body is the aggregated manifestations of the Soul's activities, outwardly outlined.

38. QUES. Does the body change?
    ANS. Yes. The body is modified to conform to the changing activities of the Soul.

39. QUES. How often is the body renewed?
    ANS. Every one to seven years, according to the individual.

40. QUES. Shall we always have some kind of a body?
    ANS. Yes, because the body is the proof of the existence of the Soul.

41. QUES. Has the Soul only a material body?
    ANS. No. It evolves bodies correspond to its different stages of evolution.

42. QUES. What is the difference between the Soul of Man (his real self), and Man himself?
    ANS. None.

43. QUES. How does the Soul incarnate itself on the material plane?

SCIENCE-OF-BEING

ANS.   It attracts from its surroundings (air, water, earth, etc.), all the elements necessary to construct a vehicle, or body, for its expression on this earth plane.

44. QUES.   Through what medium does that incarnation take place?
      ANS.   Through the human mother, by the process of gestation.

45. QUES.   What attracts the Soul which is to be incarnated?
      ANS.   The extraordinarily strong vibrations projected by the parents during their physical union.

46. QUES.   Why is it important that such physical union should be something sacred, inspired by the highest emotions?
      ANS.   Because of it immediate effect on the Soul to be incarnated.

47. QUES.   Is the Soul which incarnates contained in the seed?
      ANS.   No. It only overshadows it.

48. QUES.   When does the Soul express all its functions through the body of the child?
      ANS.   When the child reaches the age of puberty, and ready for procreation.

49. QUES.   Is procreation a quality of Matter or of Spirit?
      ANS.   Of Spirit.

50. QUES.   Why does the body die?
      ANS.   Because the Soul withdraws from it, being attracted to a different plane, where it will have to do some other work.

51. QUES.   What becomes of the body?
      ANS.   It disintegrates, being bereft of its cohesive power which resides in the Soul and returns to its native elements, out of which it has been formed.

52. QUES.   Explain the statement, "Dust thou art, and to dust thou shalt return."
      ANS.   According to material science, it is the history of Matter itself.

53. QUES.   Is the Soul re-incarnated again?
      ANS.   Yes, in order to learn its lessons.

LESSON-THREE

54. QUES. Will Reincarnation ever stop?
    ANS. Yes, when the Soul has learned all its lessons, and will have realized its eternal Spiritual Status and its oneness with the Great Principle. There is no Reincarnation on the Spiritual Plane.

55. QUES. What is the human body?
    ANS. It is a current continually renewed by the assimilation of gases through breathing, and the feeding of the molecules.

56. QUES. Which is first in importance, breathing or eating?
    ANS. Breathing.

57. QUES. What are the advantages of scientific, rhythmic breathing?
    ANS. It invigorates and purifies the body, and stimulates all its activities.

58. QUES. Why should food be properly masticated?
    ANS. In order, first, to release the Primal Energy by breaking up the atoms of the food, and second to transform the food being masticated into a homogenous mass which will simplify the work of digestion for the stomach.

59. QUES. Why is the simple food preferable to the complicated?
    ANS. Because the simple food, even if of coarse quality, and taken in large quantities, is more easily digested by the stomach than a complicated food.

60. QUES. What is the invisible power which is directing, organizing and governing all activities of the human body?
    ANS. The Soul.

61. QUES. Is the human body material?
    ANS. No. It is only a harmonious group of condensed vibrations, formed by the immaterial forces of the Soul, and held together by the Law of Attraction.

62. QUES. When one has reached the densest aspect of Matter, the bottom of Involution, what does one discover?
    ANS. That Spirit, the most immaterial thing that we know of is at the bottom of it. As Spirit is also at the top of Matter, the logical

conclusion to be drawn is that Spirit is EVERYWHERE.

63. QUES. Do those propositions concerning the human Soul and body apply also to the souls and bodies of animals, plants, minerals, etc.?

ANS. Yes.

64. QUES. Why did Buddha teach such great love for Nature?

ANS. Because he knew that everything in Nature is a manifestation of the Great Principle, and is therefore closely related to Man.

65. QUES. Why did Jesus, in His teachings, scarcely ever refer to Nature?

ANS. Because if human beings will love their fellow men, they cannot help but love Nature also. Who can do more can do less.

66. QUES. What is the message of Love to suffering Humanity?

ANS. "For the protection of the good, for the destruction of the evil-doers, I am born from Age to Age."

LESSON FOUR

SCIENCE·OF·BEING
FOVRTH·DAY

LESSON·FOVR
LIFE·ENERGY ··2··
PRACTICAL·APPLICATION
AND·DEMONSTRATION ·

CREATION · SVN·MOON·STARS
THE·DISPERSING·VAPORS··
DISCLOSE·THE·HEAVENLY·BODIES
ELEMENT · EARTH··THE·BEGIN
NING·OF·EVOLVTION
COLOR·· VIOLET·BLVE

SCIENCE·OF·BEING
FOVRTH·DAY

I AM · THE LIFE OF·THE VNIVERSE ITS·ONLY REALITY

LESSON·FOVR
LIFE·ENERGY ··2··

IFE Energy, when expressing itself through the human body as individualized life, vibrates, or radiates, from that body in what is called a Human Atmosphere or Aura. That radio-activity does not only belong to human beings. Animals, plants, minerals, and even gases, possess also their own radio-activity. In other words, everything there is, has an Aura, a luminous atmosphere, surrounding it, and there are infinite varieties of Auras, due to the different kinds of Magnetic Vibrations. Auras of all bodies are formed in the same way, yet the Aura of the human body is the most interesting for investigation, because it presents the greatest number of varieties. The human Auras vary according to the sex, state of health, and age of the individuals, and also according to their physical, mental, and emotional development. There are no two Auras alike. As a general rule, women have a more pronounced and larger Aura than men. The human Aura consists of three distinct strata. The first, the invisible stratum, which surrounds the body like a band about half an inch thick, is called the Etheric Double. Out of that Etheric Double emanates the second stratum of the Aura, called the Inner Aura. It is of a misty appearance, like a delicate vapor surrounding the body. It is usually about two inches thick. Both strata, the Inner Aura and the Etheric Double, preserve a uniform thickness all over the body, following its contours. Surrounding the Inner Aura, and emanating from it, is the third stratum of the Human Atmosphere, called the Outer Aura. That Outer Aura has the appearance of rays which contact the outside atmosphere. Through those rays Life Energy both pours out of the body into Space, and pours into the body form Space. There is a continual coming in and going out of Life Force through those Auric Rays. When the contact is established between the life force within the human body, and the Universal Life Energy outside it, it is through those Auric Rays that the Life Energy pours into the body. The Outer Aura is colored. The six colors of the spectrum are perceptible in it. Usually one definite color is so dominant that the other colors become almost imperceptible. That dominant color in the Human Atmosphere is the so-called Individual Color of the person whose Aura is being investigated. Individuals in the lower stages of evolution have often their Auric Colors rather clouded with an unpleasant grayish-brown tint. But the higher the individual is evolved, the purer and more luminous those Auric Colors become. If the Auric Colors of two individuals blend, they will feel in harmony with each other. In the opposite case, they on the contrary will have an unpleasant sensation and will become restless, or even antagonistic. That accounts largely for the fact that we instinctively like to be with some individuals and resent the society of others. The thickness of the Outer Aura varies with different parts of the body, and displays marked difference between the Auras of different individuals. In some it has a thickness of from three to five inches, but its size may be varied by changes in the physical, mental, and emotional qualities and conditions of the individual. The Outer Aura is exceptionally strong around the head. When flowing through the finger tips, the Life Force is perceptible as a sort of misty waves of different lengths. The strongest current proceeds from the thumb. There, its visible length is about two and a half inches. Next comes the index finger, whose current appears to be about two inches long. The fourth finger's current is visible only for about an inch and a half. The small finger's current appears for about an inch. The middle finger, the biggest of all, has a visible current of only about a quarter of an inch. The visible length of these waves is increased in proportion to the strength of the magnetic current flowing through the hand. The Outer Aura reaches sometimes a thickness of several feet in certain individuals with a very strong mental or spiritual development. In the latter case, the whole nature of the human Aura is changed. Such individuals seem to be surrounded by rays of light, of very beautiful and changing colors. Their Auras are not only very beautiful to look at, but are also very soothing and healing to an appreciable degree. It is often sufficient merely to be in the presence of such people in order to be benefited in every way, physically, mentally, and morally. With a healthy person, the human Aura is of a pleasant, pure appearance, and quite regular in its stratification. Abnormal or unhealthy people, on the contrary, have a very irregular Aura, full of protuberances and cavities. The human Aura, when expressing Life Energy alone, is not self luminous, and can be perceived only by its reflection of light. Yet the same Aura is shining with its own luminosity whenever expressing thought or emotion. A great many diseases are nowadays diagnosed by the appearance of the human Aura. For that purpose are used certain chemical screens impregnated with very sensitive chemicals, on which is seen, as luminosity, the human Aura, as soon as the individual places himself behind the screen. Another method of detecting the human Atmosphere is to place the individual in front of a dark background, in a comparatively dim artificial light. In this instance, little glass screens filled with certain chemical solutions which, when one is looking through them, increase the sensitiveness of the eye, are used in order to enable the untrained eye to perceive the Aura. Yet one can train one's eyes to perceive radio-activity without artificial aids. Those methods are used a great deal now in hospitals, by up-to-date physicians.

卐 Life Energy, being the Fundamental Power of the Universe, ought to be used in an ever increasing degree in everything we do. No matter what kind of work we undertake, we should first make the contact with Universal Life Energy, by the mental method indicated in the second lesson. Especially in business and in human relations in general, Life Energy becomes invaluable. The salesman can magnetize the products which he is selling; the business man can embody Life Energy in his advertisements, and make them attractive; the politician can employ it to strengthen his speech, the minister to vitalize his sermon, the artist to find inspiration, and the scientist to solve his problems and make discoveries. It is not only the privilege, but also the duty, of human beings TO USE THAT LIFE FORCE IN EVERY DEPARTMENT OF THEIR LIVES, TO USE IT ALL THE TIME, AND FOR EVERYTHING. In doing so, an extraordinary change will come to those who have been faithful and have persevered to the end. They will notice by and by that they can endure more work and strain without feeling the same sense of fatigue as before. They become mentally more efficient, because Life Energy flowing to their brain cells with an ever increasing force stimulates them, and makes them work more quickly and better. Reasoning becomes clearer and more logical. And because of the excess of Life Forces radiating from every center of the body, work becomes what it ought to be, a pleasure instead of an onerous duty. The individual grows always stronger through the continual use of that Life Energy. The Magnetic Force can be used for realization of almost all human wishes. In order to obtain that which we want, all we need to do, when thinking of or working for the fulfillment of our heart's desire, is to make the mental contact with the Universal Life Energy, and to feel it flowing through us. And the Life Force, pouring into us, will eventually make us living magnets, which will attract, because of the Law of Attraction continually operating through Life Energy, the very thing we wish. It will come to us, not because of the

exercise of an exceptional will power, but because of the operation of natural law, the Law of Attraction. We can attract everybody and everything to us if we develop within ourselves a magnetic personality, as we can do very readily by continually contacting, physically and mentally, the Life Energy of the Universe. It is one of the first duties which we owe as well to our selves as to others, if we want to succeed in life and become useful members in the great Human Family. Forces are universal. Nature expresses those Forces through every available channel. We human beings are some of the most important channels for their expression. Therefore we must be strong, and desire and develop that strength all the time, thus rapidly advancing along the path of Evolution. Weakness is not only an impediment, but is unnatural, because it is in direct contradiction to All Power.

卐 Whenever one wants to use Life Energy for healing purposes, the best method of procedure is the following. Have the patient comfortably seated, in a chair with body erect, yet not tense, relaxed physically, mentally, and emotionally. Then make the mental contact with Universal Life Energy. After that contact is made, and the operator feels that Force flowing through him, he must place his hands on the shoulders of the patient in such a way that the two thumbs are joined on the seventh vertebra of the patient's spinal column. The seventh vertebra is that prominence generally thought of as the joint of the neck. It is one of the most sensitive spots on the spinal column, and the spot where the spinal nerve can be most readily and most easily influenced. The other four fingers must be placed on the shoulders, pointing down the body. As the magnetic current always flows through the hand in the direction in which the finger tips are pointing, it is advisable, as a general rule, whenever treating the upper portion of a patient's body, to have the finger tips turned down. That process must be reversed – that is, the finger tips must be pointed upward – when the lower portion of the body, from the waist down is being treated. The reason for this is that in every instance the magnetic current must be directed toward the solar plexus, which is the great reservoir of that Force in the human body. After his hands have been placed in the proper position, all the operator needs to do is consciously to remain an open channel for the Life

SCIENCE-OF-BEING

Energy, that it may flow through him. There is no special need to know which part of the patient's body is in a disharmonious condition. Life Energy, being self-governed, will do its work automatically, and will flow to those parts of the body which are in the greatest need of its healing powers. The operator must keep his hands on the shoulders of the patient until he ceases to feel the life current flowing through him. At that moment the patient's body has reached the point of saturation, and can no longer absorb the Magnetic Force. To continue the treatment would be a waste of time and energy. As a general rule such treatments ought to last from five to fifteen minutes. No more precise indications can be given concerning the duration of the treatments, because each case must be handled individually, as there are no two people alike, and as even the same person may react differently at different times. It is left to the inner sense and intuition of the operator to determine when he is to stop. In practicing magnetic healing, one very soon is able to develop that inner sense. A fairly good indication that the treatment is finished, is a peculiar desire to take one's hands away from the shoulders of the patient. In case one wishes to treat a particular local trouble, one can, in addition to that first treatment, give another, placing the hands on the ailing part, and keeping them there until one ceases to feel the Force flow. If the diseased portion of the body is very small, as in the case of eye, ear, brain, heart, or other localized trouble, one can bunch the fingers, bringing the tips together against the tip of the thumb, and thus concentrate the five individual rays of the Force upon one point. Such a concentration of the Force acts very strongly, and must therefore be handled carefully, especially when treating delicate organisms such as the eye.

卐 As soon as the patient begins to feel a certain burning sensation, due to that concentration of the Magnetic Force into one ray, the operator must remove his fingers immediately. Otherwise he may burn the patient, as if with fire or scalding water, and burn him badly enough to produce a blister. In the event of such a magnetic burn, all that is necessary in order to cure it is to pass one's hand lightly over the injured spot, as if softly brushing it away, and all traces of the magnetic burn will vanish like magic. It is important to remember that whenever a new treatment is started, even if on the same patient, it is advisable to make a fresh contact with Universal Life Energy. This applies especially to beginners, who do not know how to keep themselves consciously open to the continual flow of the Force they use. Later on, that renewal of contact for each treatment becomes unnecessary, as the conscious contact with the Universal Life Energy, once established, remains for quite a considerable length of time.

卐 The method of treatment described above is the classical method, which can be modified and varied in infinite ways. For instance, if the patient is lying in bed, or is otherwise so situated that the operator cannot put both hands on his shoulders, one hand, the left one, can be placed so that the index finger touches the seventh vertebra, and the thumb rests on the shoulder, pointed downward. The right hand of the operator grips the left hand of the patient in such a manner that the index, middle and fourth fingers rest on the inner side of the wrist, point up along the arm. If, for some reason, only the patient's hands are available, or even one alone, it is quite sufficient for the operator to make the aforesaid contact with that. In exceptional cases, where no physical contact of any sort is possible, the operator can send the current into the body of the patient by merely directing his finger tips toward it, using one or both hands. The position of his arms is of little consequence, as it is the position of the finger tips which determines the direction of the magnetic currents. These act like light rays emanating from a reflector, and are directed upward if the finger tips are pointing upward, or downward if the finger tips are pointing down.

卐 The magnetic current is naturally attracting, but it can be made repelling by a simple effort of will power.

卐 In cases of self treatment, the way to proceed is as follows. Since one cannot conveniently place one's hands on one's own seventh vertebra, so as to convey the magnetic current into the body, the mental contact with the Universal Life Energy is sufficient. As soon as one feels that the Life Force has sufficiently saturated the body, one can then use one's hand as described above to heal any local trouble, by placing it over the diseased spot. The general way of procedure is thenceforth identical with that employed in treating someone else. The only difference is in the beginning, when the contact with the seventh vertebra and shoulders is omitted.

卐 It is sometimes noticeable, in treating one's self and others, especially in cases of chronic organic troubles, that after a few successive treatments, when the general condition of the patient seems to have been greatly improved, suddenly there occurs a relapse, and the patient may feel even worse than before the treatment. That relapse is due to the fact that the diseased part of the body was, before the treatment, lacking in vitality.

卐 The disease was like a crust of carbon impeding the normal functions of the affected tissues, and cutting them off from the nutrition essential to their health, When the vivifying current of Life Energy is directed against the diseased spot, it acts like a blast of pure oxygen brought into contact with carbon. Just as carbon, upon its chemical union with oxygen, glows to a sudden fierce incandescence, and then vanishes, so disease when exposed to the purging current of Life Energy, must burst into an intense flame that consumes it utterly, thus burning away the barrier between the sick tissues and the flow of vital forces. That is called magnetic chemicalization. It is an unpleasant, but favorable symptom. Therefore all one has to do in such cases is to continue the magnetic treatment with increased energy. The ailment will be eventually completely destroyed, and the diseased part of the body thus restored to its normal condition.

卐 When treating, the operator must take toward the patient an attitude of love because one of the qualities of love is expansion. Expansion of the inner gateways through which the Life Energy is flowing into the operator enables the Force to enter in greater volume, thus insuring a more successful treatment.

卐 One of the many applications of the magnetic current for healing purposes is the inducing of the so-called magnetic sleep – that is, a sleep induced by the use of the magnetic current. Individuals who suffer form insomnia, or who, for some other reason, are unable to sleep, are greatly benefited by this magnetic sleep which, no matter how short it may be, rests and invigorates the body beyond anything one could ever expect. When induced in the daytime, about fifteen minutes of magnetic sleep is all that a patient can ever need. After that, the patient must be awakened, because to let him sleep longer would mean to go against the natural ascending movement of the Earth magnetic currents of the day. This would result in a feeling of heaviness, or often in a headache. A quarter of an hour of magnetic sleep during the day is equivalent to six or seven hours of ordinary night's sleep. When the magnetic sleep is induced at night, there no necessity to awaken the subject, as the magnetic sleep will presently lapse into normal sleep of its own accord. In order to induce magnetic sleep the following method is recommended. To start with, make the mental contact with the Universal Life Energy. Then place the hands, in the manner previously indicated, on the seventh vertebra of the subject, who should be comfortably seated in an easy chair, with head reclining. When the body of the patient is saturated with the Magnetic Force, take the hands from his shoulders and stand in front of him in such a way that his knees are facing the knees of the operator. The hands of the latter, thumbs joined and finger tips pointing toward the forehead of the subject and lightly touching it, must remain in that position for several minutes. Thus the magnetic current will flow into the brain, will fill it to capacity, and will then begin to condense because of the law of Attraction, which continually operates with the current and cements together all the successive magnetic waves proceeding from the hands of the operator. The operator must move his hands slowly down across the face of the subject, but without touching it, as low as the solar plexus. From there the hands are returned to their original position each slowly describing a half circle outward on its own side, and meeting the other before the forehead. From five to fifteen minutes, according to the individual, is sufficient to put the average subject into a magnetic sleep. In some exceptional cases, the magnetic sleep is induced almost instantaneously, while in other cases it may require several successive trials. Those movements of the hands which induce magnetic sleep are called magnetic passes. Slow passes condense the magnetic current, that is, put the individual into a magnetic sleep. Quick passes awaken, dispelling the condensed forces. To awaken a subject plunged into a magnetic sleep, all one needs to do is to repeat the same passes, only very quickly instead of slowly. The subject will awaken for the reason explained above. If the subject does not feel completely awakened, a quick brushing movement by both hands from the center of the forehead outward to the temples, and similar operation from the back of the head, will entirely dispel every lingering sensation of drowsiness. When properly treated, the subject must awaken from the magnetic sleep refreshed and invigorated, and with a pleasant feeling of buoyancy. An opposite effect would indicate that the operator consciously or unconsciously used his will power, and not the natural law, to put the individual to sleep. In other words, he willed, or hypnotized, his patient into slumber. Such a method is very objectionable because of its disharmonious effect on both operator and subject. Therefore the operator must guard carefully against employing his will power during the magnetic passes, and must let the law of Attraction operate unimpeded. Thus he will obtain the most favorable results.

卐 In case of self-inducement of the magnetic sleep, the method of procedure is quite different. There the individual, who is both operator and subject, must clasp his hands behind his head, and then make the mental contact with the Universal Life Energy. The Force will flow through his hands, and will do its condensatory work, as a result of which will come the magnetic sleep. In order to awaken in due time, if that sleep is induced during the day, one must impress upon one's Sub-consciousness, before going to sleep, the order to awaken at the prescribed time. And the Sub-consciousness, in obedience to the command, will do it with a surprising readiness and a mathematical precision. No hesitation or doubt should be in one's mind when commanding the Sub-consciousness, as otherwise failure will be the result.

卐 There is another problem which is bothering Humanity today, as it has done throughout all times. That problem is, how to attain Success and Prosperity. All kinds of devices and means are used by human beings in order to reach this goal. Needless to say, illegitimate Prosperity attained through wrong means, by taking unfair advantage of other people, is not and cannot be lasting, because it is unnatural, transgressing Universal Laws, and is ultimately most destructive to its possessor. True Success and legitimate prosperity are always based on the Laws of the Absolute. They are the result of our harmonization with Infinite Harmony, which is Power. That Power then flows through every channel which we open to it. Yet why is it that some people, who seemingly follow and live in accord with the Laws of Universal Harmony, are apparently unable to demonstrate in their lives Success and Prosperity? In such cases, the cause must be sought in the individual himself. For some reason the channels through which affluence and harmony normally flow are either undeveloped, paralyzed, or dried up. In each of those instances the Universal Life Energy must be used in order to give those channels their natural functions. This once achieved, Success and Prosperity will be obtained. In the Absolute, - that is, in the realm of the Real and the Eternally Harmonious – everything, every action, every cause culminates in a perfect effect, which is complete Success. Affluence in everything good, in all supply of all forces and powers, is another eternal reality. The only reason human beings do not always achieve it is because they are not always in accord with it, or are closed to it. There again the Magnetic Force, being the Universal Panacea for all ills and troubles, sets matters aright. All one needs to do, after having made the mental contact with the Universal Life Energy so that one feels it flowing through all one's being, is then to FEEL SUCCESSFUL, TO FEEL PROSPEROUS AND RICH IN EVERYTHING. Thus Life Energy will vivify those channels within the inner self of the individual, and open them to the inflow of Universal Life Energy which, with its magnetic power, will establish the connections with all the things we may desire. Naturally, after that contact with Universal Energy has been made, one should not remain idle, and simply wait for the blessings to pour in upon one. On the contrary, CONSTRUCTIVE ACTIVITY IS REQUIRED IN ORDER TO ACHIEVE THE DESIRED AIM. And as a final result, Success and Prosperity in an ever increasing degree will come through the use of the Magnetic Force. Mere mental affirmations of Success and Prosperity will not bring them into one's life. The attractive power of the magnetic current, combined with constructive activity, is needed to do this.

SCIENCE-OF-BEING

That explains why, with so many people, affirmation of positive things does not achieve them when that affirmation is not sustained by Life Energy, the Fundamental Power of the Universe.

卐 One of the sad experiences which Humanity, especially, has to go through, together with the rest of this material world, is old age and death. In this world of material phenomena, in this present state of consciousness, where everything has a beginning and end, because of the limited concept of Time and Space, the privilege of Youth, of Strength or Power, of Beauty, is but a fleeting moment in human lives.

Strange to say, man supposed to be the highest manifestation of the Absolute, has the shortest space of time allowed him for the enjoyment of those privileges. Animals, plants, minerals, all seem to be much more favored in that directions. About one third of the human life is spent in developing that organism which the Soul needs for its expression on this earth plane. The second third permits the enjoyment of that life. The last third is marked by a rapidly declining curve. It is a continual disintegration and loss of that which has been so painfully built up during the first period of one's life. Whenever one thinks about it, one must inevitably conclude that there is something fundamentally wrong and destructive, either in the Universal Laws and Forces of Nature, or in man. Universal Laws ARE fundamentally constructive and harmonious. So are the Basic Forces underlying all Creation. Therefore it is obvious that they cannot be wrong or destructive. Then, the only logical conclusion is that the wrong and destructiveness abide in man himself. There – and there alone – must be sought the cause for all human ills and troubles, sorrow and suffering. The cause once discovered, proper means can be used in order to remove that cause. One of the greatest privileges and powers man has is FREE WILL. That Free Will he can use constructively or destructively. Man creates his own heaven and his own hell. They are man-made, not created by God. They are states of consciousness, not localities, and they last as long as one remains a willing host to them.

卐 Scientifically speaking, the average human beings do not die a normal death. They commit suicide, consciously or unconsciously. If they would only leave their bodies alone, to be developed and sustained according to the laws of Nature, their bodies would live almost indefinitely. It has been proven nowadays that individual cells of the body, even when separated from that body, if kept in proper surroundings, can not only sustain their life, but can even develop and increase. And as the body is composed of about fifty billions of those cells, one must come to the logical conclusion that the whole of the body could live and prosper for long periods of time, if permitted to do so. Ignorance is the cause of all the trouble. We do not know the vital importance of attuning ourselves to the Laws of Universal Harmony, which means Life Eternal. We are relying all the time on the limited reserves of life forces within us, and are spending them faster than our bodies supply them to us, instead of being in constant conscious communication with Universal Life Energy. We continually transgress natural laws, by eating improper food, as well in quality as in quantity, and by wearing inappropriate clothes which interfere with the normal functions of the body, either through pressure or through preventing the body from getting all the benefit of the invigorating action of the surrounding atmosphere, and the purifying and stimulating influence of the sun rays. Such clothes are against common sense and the Laws of Harmony and Beauty. We do not sufficiently exercise that body of ours, and we undermine its resisting qualities by resorting to medicines and all sorts of drugs in case of illness, and by the immoderate use of alcoholic drinks and more harmful drugs when we are well. We think inharmoniously, and those thoughts of ours – unaware in most cases as we are that they will some day be visited upon us – act most destructively on us. The same is true of our negative emotions, such as hatred, jealousy, revenge, etc. Even if we feel these emotions toward other individuals, ultimately we are the ones who will be most harmed by indulging them, because of the law of Retribution. In addition to all this, that body of ours also has to fight continually all kinds of outside disintegrating influences, such as sudden changes of temperature and atmospheric conditions, and the incessant assault of innumerable armies of microbes and deadly germs of all sorts of diseases. And finally we prey upon our own body, like vampires in drawing upon each cell for life force, which we usually then consume within our own self, wasting it in countless ways. Instead of supplying and stimulating each cell of our body with Life Force from within and from without, we tax each of those cells to the limit of its endurance. No wonder that after a certain time they become depleted of life force, their activities are lessened, and they exhibit the symptoms of old age and decrepitude. Under those conditions it is really surprising that our material body can live at all. The only reason why it can is because of its extraordinary power of resistance. In order to do justice to our own selves, and to do at least as well as animals and plants, which increase in size, strength and beauty until almost the very end of their earthly existence, we have to start to live a normal and constructive life, physically, mentally and emotionally. We have to take into consideration the Laws of the Universe, and Forces of Nature, and do our best to attune ourselves to them. And above all, we must make continual conscious contact with the Universal Life Energy, which by and by will fill to its utmost capacity every cell of our body, thus making it grow and prosper in every direction. Each one of us ought to devote from a quarter to half hour daily to the general invigorating and rejuvenation of all our body. In order to obtain that, proceed in the following way. Seated in an easy chair, make the mental contact with the Universal Life Energy, and when the Force is felt flowing, consciously direct it into the brain, into every organ of the body, into the tissues, the skin, the cells. Think it that way, wish it that way, feel it that way. The guiding thought, backed up by constructive will power, will make the best use of the inherent qualities of the Life Energy, namely, self-government and harmonization. Think Harmony, Youth, and Beauty; wish them, feel them, knowing that they are the result of the Eternal Law of Life and Love, CONTINUALLY EXPRESSING ITSELF THROUGH EACH INDIVIDUAL. It is like bathing the whole human organism in a living stream of Life Force and, if faithfully performed, the result of it will exceed all expectations. Each cell of the body will exhibit a greater constructive activity, each organ of the body will perform its duties with an every increasing power and precision, thus giving all members of the body the possibility of manifesting in a most perfect way the activities of the soul. The whole body will be gradually regenerated according to a new and better standard. We must always bear in mind that our body is a statue moulded by our soul with the chisel of our thoughts, the Life Force of the Universe supplying both the material and the Energy which the soul needs to perform that work. The harmonious co-operation of all three is necessary, yet in a way the Life Force is most important, because with it thought and even the Soul itself are powerless. The more one feels the Life Force flowing through one's self during that conscious stimulation of the body, the better the process of reconstruction and rejuvenation will proceed; and a new, vigorous, harmonious, and beautiful body, a proper channel for the expression of the Soul, will ultimately be the result. Thus the limits between death and birth of human beings will be removed further and further apart from each other, health and longevity increased, and especially one greatest advantage obtained, namely, the preservation of our physical, mental, and emotional powers in a state of strength and activity, giving us the sensation and appearance of youth and beauty to the very end of our earthly days. And that will finally bring another result which will come as the logical sequence of that work of rejuvenation. Death, the last enemy of the human race, will be destroyed, and man will then be translated into higher spheres of action by merely raising the vibrations of his body to the plane of his next activities. That transition will take place without involving for a single moment the loss of consciousness, without any apparent interruption in the course of life, and will be as natural as to step form one room to another. We will become invisible to those whom we have left, because their lower rate of vibration will render it impossible for them to see us any longer. And with that obliteration of death, the whole process of generation will also be modified. There will no longer be any need for human parents to act as channels through which the Soul must make its physical appearance on this earth plane. The Soul will be able to draw directly and almost instantaneously from its immediate surroundings, air, water, earth, and all the necessary elements to form a body for its expression on the material plane. In other words, the Soul will suddenly appear visible

SCIENCE-OF-BEING

through its human body in the full development of a glorious youth, thus starting its actual material existence as a useful member of the Great Human Family from the very beginning of is earthly days, to continue so throughout its life until the last moment when, hearing the Call of the Great Law, and consciously obeying that Call, it will leave this material world painlessly and joyfully, simply disappearing without any trace. The sting of death will be thus removed, and UNINTERRUPTED, ETERNAL LIFE, NOW ONLY A WONDERFUL HOPE, WILL THEN BECOME A RADIANT REALTY.

QVESTIONS & ANSWERS

LESSON FOUR

1. QUES. What is the human atmosphere, or Aura?
   ANS. It is the radio-activity of the human body, due to the emanation of Life Energy from it.

2. QUES. Does that radio-activity belong only human beings?
   ANS. No. Animals, plants, minerals, and even gases possess also their own radio-activity.

3. QUES. Is the Aura self-luminous?
   ANS. No. It is rendered luminous only by light striking it.

4. QUES. Are all human Auras alike?
   ANS. No. They vary according to the sex, state of health, and age of the individual, and also to the physical, mental and emotional development.

5. QUES. How many strata has the human Aura?
   ANS. Three. The Etheric Double, the Inner Aura, and the Outer Aura.

6. QUES. Which stratum is colored?
   ANS. The Outer Aura which expresses the personal color of the individual.

7. QUES. If the auric colors of two individuals blend, what is the effect?
   ANS. They will feel harmony with each other. In the opposite case, they will feel indifferent or even antagonistic.

8. QUES. How thick is the ordinary human Aura?
   ANS. From five inches upwards.

9. QUES. How can the Aura be perceived?
   ANS. By mechanical means, or by training one's eyes.

10. QUES. What is the practical use of investigating Auras?
    ANS. To find out the general condition of health, etc., of the individual.

11. QUES. How often, and where, should Universal Life Energy be used?

ANS.   It should be used in every department of human life, all the time, and for everything.

12. QUES.   What practical result is obtained through the continual use of Universal Life Energy?

ANS.   The individual grows stronger in every way, physically, mentally, and spiritually.

13. QUES.   How should Universal Life Energy be used in order to obtain one's heart's desires?

ANS.   Contact it, and let it attract all the elements necessary for the realization of one's desires.

14. QUES.   How is Universal Life Energy used for healing purposes?

ANS.   First contact it, then send it through the hands into the body of the patient.

15. QUES.   At which point is the Magnetic Force most readily conducted into the body of the patient?

ANS.   The seventh vertebra of the spinal column.

16. QUES.   Does the magnetic current flow equally through all fingers?

ANS.   No. It flows strongest through the thumb, and the weakest through the middle finger.

17. QUES.   What direction does the magnetic current take when flowing through the hands?

ANS.   The direction in which the finger tips are pointing.

18. QUES.   Does the magnetic treatment work automatically?

ANS.   Yes, because Universal Life Energy is self governing.

19. QUES.   How do magnetic forces work?

ANS.   Always to re-establish equilibrium.

20. QUES.   How long should a magnetic treatment last?

ANS.   As a general rule, from five to fifteen minutes.

21. QUES.   How does one know when to stop it?

ANS.   By an inner sense that the patient can absorb no more, because his body has reached a point of saturation.

22. **QUES.** How should one treat a local trouble?

   ANS. By placing one's hand on the diseased part, and letting the current flow.

23. **QUES.** How is the magnetic current most strongly concentrated on a small area.

   ANS. By bunching the finger tips.

24. **QUES.** How is a magnetic burn cured?

   ANS. By passing the hand lightly over the injured spot.

25. **QUES.** Does one need to make a new contact with Universal Life Energy for each successive treatment?

   ANS. For beginners, yes.

26. **QUES.** What would be the result if a treatment were started without first making the contact with Universal Life Energy?

   ANS. The patient would immediately absorb all the available amount of Life Energy stored in the operator, and would leave him completely depleted.

27. **QUES.** Is it necessary, when treating a patient, to contact him physically?

   ANS. No. The magnetic current, if properly directed can be sent at a distance.

28. **QUES.** Is the magnetic current attractive or repellent?

   ANS. It is naturally attractive, but it can be made repellent through an effort of will power.

29. **QUES.** How shall one proceed in treating oneself magnetically?

   ANS. First make the mental contact with Universal Life Energy and let it flow through the body. When the body is properly saturated with it, use the hands as indicated above.

30. **QUES.** What is magnetic chemicalization, and what are its causes?

   ANS. It is the seeming increase of the negative condition of the patient, due to the vivifying power of the magnetic current.

31. **QUES.** Should the treatment be stopped because of the chemicalization?

ANS.   No. It should be continued with increased energy, and the ailment will eventually be completely destroyed.

32. QUES.   What should be the attitude of the operator toward the patient during the treatment?

      ANS.   One of compassion and love.

33. QUES.   Is it necessary to treat the patient mentally at the same time?

      ANS.   No, though a scientific mental treatment, combined with the magnetic one, produces better results.

`34. QUES.   What is the magnetic sleep?

      ANS.   It is a sleep induced by the use of the magnetic current.

35. QUES.   What is the difference between magnetic and hypnotic sleep?

      ANS.   The first, based on Life Power, is beneficial; the second, based on will power, is detrimental.

36. QUES.   When is the magnetic sleep needed?

      ANS.   In case of insomnia or weariness.

37. QUES.   How long should it last?

      ANS.   About fifteen minutes when induced in the daytime; throughout the whole night when induced at night.

38. QUES.   What is the method of procedure?

      ANS.   Make the mental contact with Universal Life Energy, and let the current flow through the hands into the brain of the patient. Then move the hands slowly down, without touching the face of the patient, as low as the solar plexus. From there the hands are returned to their original position, slowly describing a half circle outward, and meeting before the forehead of the patient. Repeat.

39. QUES.   How long does it take to induce a magnetic sleep?

      ANS.   From a few minutes upward varying according to the individual.

40. QUES.   What is the correct method for awakening one from a magnetic sleep?

      ANS.   Use the same movements, only quickly instead of slowly.

LESSON-FOUR

41. QUES. What are those magnetic movements called?
    ANS. Magnetic passes.

42. QUES. Why should a magnetic sleep induced in daytime last only fifteen minutes?
    ANS. Because it is against the ascending movement of Primal Energy.

43. QUES. How is the magnetic sleep induced on oneself?
    ANS. By clasping the hands behind the head, and making the contact with Universal Life Energy.

44. QUES. How does one awaken oneself from a self-induced magnetic sleep?
    ANS. By commanding the subconscious self, before going to sleep, to awaken one at the desired time.

45. QUES. What are the usual causes of poverty and material limitations?
    ANS. Undeveloped, paralyzed, or dried-up channels through which affluence and harmony should normally flow.

46. QUES. How are such conditions overcome?
    ANS. Contact mentally Universal Life Energy, and when it flows feel successful, think successful, and gradually success will come into one's life, attracted by the irresistible power of Universal Life Force.

47. QUES. Is it sufficient to be satisfied with that contact only?
    ANS. No. After that inner work has been completed, one must strive to work it out in actual life, and success and prosperity will be the result.

48. QUES. Is it necessary for human beings to grow old?
    ANS. No. Human beings can live as long as they choose if they know how.

49. QUES. Why does one grow old?
    ANS. Because one spends more life energy that one produces.

50. QUES. How can that be obviated?
    ANS. By the continual contact with Universal Life Energy.

SCIENCE-OF-BEING

51. QUES. What is the method of procedure to rejuvenate an old body?
     ANS.   Make the mental contact with Universal Life Energy, and consciously send it to every part of the body, to every organ, to every cell.

52. QUES. How often should this be done, and how long each time?
     ANS.   Every day for about a quarter of an hour each time.

53. QUES. What will be the result?
     ANS.   The body will be completely renewed and made stronger, younger, and more harmonious.

54. QUES. Is it necessary to die?
     ANS.   No. When human beings will know sufficiently how to control their own selves, they will be able, by raising their vibrations, to translate themselves from this material plane to a higher one.

55. QUES. Has it been done before?
     ANS.   Yes, so far as is known, by Enoch, Elijah, Jesus, and others.

56. QUES. What promise given to Humanity about two thousand years ago will thus be realized?
     ANS.   The Sting of Death will be removed, the Last Enemy overcome, and Uninterrupted Eternal Life, now only a wonderful dream, will then become a Radiant Reality.

LESSON FIVE

SCIENCE·OF·BEING
FIFTH·DAY

LESSON·FIVE
LAWS·
ABSOLUTE & RELATIVE

ιΧθύς

CREATION - FISH·AND·BIRDS

ELEMENT - WATER - - - REGENER
ATION·BY·WATER

COLOR - - BLUE·GREEN

SCIENCE·OF·BEING
FIFTH·DAY

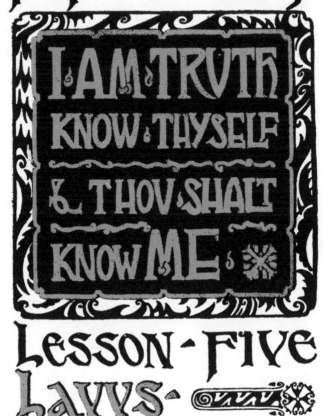

I·AM·TRUTH
KNOW·THYSELF
&·THOU·SHALT
KNOW ME·

LESSON·FIVE

 LAWS·

EVEN LAWS IN THE PRESENT STATE OF HUMAN CONSCIOUSNESS GOVERN THIS WORLD. OF THOSE SEVEN LAWS, THREE ARE ETERNAL, IMMUTABLE, LAWS OF THE ABSOLUTE, AND FOUR ARE TRANSITORY, MUTABLE, LAWS OF THE RELATIVE.

SCIENCE-OF-BEING

THE THREE LAWS OF THE ABSOLUTE

1. LIFE, MIND, TRUTH, LOVE, SPIRIT, IS ALL IN ALL.
2. THE SAME LAW GOVERNS ALWAYS EVERYTHING, EVERYWHERE, IN THE SAME WAY, FROM THE GREATEST STAR DOWN TO THE SMALLEST ELECTRON.
3. EVERYTHING IS VIBRATION.

In the Absolute, those three Laws are One Law, called the GREAT LAW. To our present state of consciousness that One Great Universal Law; manifests itself as a triune ray; we perceive it in its threefold aspect, our consciousness acting as a prism; therefore, as we are studying these Laws now, we must consider them as they appear to us at present.

LIFE, MIND, TRUTH, LOVE, SPIRIT, IS ALL IN ALL. These Five which were explained in the first lesson are the Alpha and the Omega, the beginning and the end of everything; they are a Law by themselves, the Law of Life, of Mind, of Truth, of Love which is the Law of Spirit. They include everything, and that is why Jesus, who knew these Laws, said, "Love thy God (The Great Principle) with all thy heart, and all thy soul, and with all thy mind, and with all thy strength, and love thy neighbor as thyself," and when He was asked further, "what about the other commandments?" He answered, "All the laws and all the prophets are in those two commandments." The Great Principle, the Absolute, is all Life, all Mind, all Truth, all Love, all Spirit; all there is, is in the Great All, and if we apply that Law, the Law of Life, of Mind, of Truth and of Love, to all problems of our daily life, we work out, without noticing it, all the perfection we can ever aspire to, we buildup the Pyramid of our own life and reach the Point of Spirit, and we do not notice how it

136

# LESSON-FIVE

happens, because it is the Great Principle Itself Who is working to that end through us. It is Its work as much as ours. All we have to do is to be conscious, open channels for that.

THE SAME LAW GOVERNS ALWAYS EVERYTHING, EVERYWHERE, IN THE SAME WAY, FROM THE GREATEST STAR DOWN TO THE SMALLEST ELECTRON. The wonderful simplicity of that Universal Law is that there is but ONE LAW which underlies all other laws, operates on all planes, and expresses itself through everything, always in the same way. The formation of the electron, of the atom, of the body, of our planet, of this World, of the Universe are ALL BASED ON THAT ONE LAW. Everywhere is seen the operation of that Law, which is also called the Law of Analogy, "AS IT IS ON THE HIGHEST PLANE SO IT IS ON THE LOWEST." That is, that One Pattern is expressed through millions of aspects and yet is always One. For instance, let us take the sphere. An electron is a microscopical sphere. Vapors are made up of tiny spheres of water. A dewdrop is a sphere, and so are the particles of mercury or the little red and white corpuscles in our blood. A soap bubble is a sphere, our Earth also, and all other planets, the sun, the stars, and the worlds. Why? Because the Great Law says that everything which wants to persevere in existence must take the form of a sphere, which is a body in which all parts are in perfect relation one to another and also to its center, and which therefore is so perfectly balanced that it can offer the maximum resistance to all kinds of outside disintegrating influences.

卐 Another example: All vibrations emanate from a given point in all directions in waves, forming continually increasing spheres. A stone thrown in water starts spherical vibratory waves, which, where they touch the surface of the water, appear as circles, enlarging till they reach the shore of that body of water. It is the same with all other vibrations, sound, light, Hertzian waves, magnetic waves, also thoughts and Spiritual Vibrations, all this again because of the Great Law, which decrees that all vibrations must normally proceed in waves, forming continually increasing spheres which are kept in that condition by the Law of Attraction perpetually operating through those vibrations. That Law is so infinite, so universal, that in our present mental development we can only begin to perceive its numberless manifestations. That Law is often also called the Great Law. The knowledge of that Law enables one to calculate with mathematical precision even things the nature of which is as yet unknown to us.

卐 Geometry, mathematics, all exact sciences, have the Great Law as foundation of their individual laws. For instance, three times three makes nine, and three million times three million makes also nine plus as many zeros as there are zeros in the two numbers. Why is it so? Because of the Great Law expressing itself through the mathematical laws. Those who study zoology also discover very soon the various manifestations of the Great Law. There are so-called wild animals, lions, tigers, panthers and so forth. Their coats are of certain colors, arranged in certain designs, which are expressing their qualities. The same characteristics are found among birds of prey, eagles, hawks, owls, etc., as these occupy amongst the birds the corresponding place to that occupied by wild animals among the beasts. It is the same among fishes, insects, mushrooms, trees, plants and minerals. The same distinguishing color schemes, the same combinations, throughout the whole round of Nature. Take the rainbow, that wonderful bridge, shining with the six colors of the spectrum and connecting Heaven with Earth. Its iridescence, produced by the refraction of light, is found on the soap bubble, on oil-coated water, in the diamond, also in the opal, that stone both precious and mysterious; it is displayed on the wings of certain butterflies, on different insects, on birds, and even in the hair of human beings, where there is a certain iridescence. Why? Again because of the Great Law. Throughout the whole cycle of Creation are everywhere seen these wonderful expressions of the Great Law. Infinite are the aspects through which it continually manifests itself. There is the glorious sunset, wonderful colors in the sky. But the sun's rays have no color, they are white; the clouds have no color, they are also white; the air has no color, it is transparent; yet taken together in a certain combination, they all make a wonderful sunset. It is the relation of the different lights, one to another, shades and light, white rays

LESSON·FIVE

broken up in different rays, interpenetrating and combining one with another – colorless elements, yet producing the most wonderful colors. All this is the result of the One Great Law.

ALL IS VIBRATION. This is the third and last of these Absolute, Immutable Laws. Is it possible that Vibrations will be eternal? They will be, as they always have been. Even Spirit Itself communicates through vibrations. Maybe some day they will be called by another name, but it is not the name which is so important, it is the nature of the thing itself. THE WHOLE UNIVERSE IS BUT VIBRATION. When we speak the sound is conveyed through vibrations; through vibrations do we also see, smell, taste and touch. Everything is done through vibration. Sound is vibration, light is vibration; so are the emanations of radium, wireless telegraphy, telephony; all use vibrations as agents. Thoughts also are vibrations; so is love; everything is vibrating; vibrations are penetrating all planes, and therefore even in the Absolute everything is vibration. There are different rates of vibrations, infinite varieties of them, some so high, so subtle, that of them we cannot have any concept just now. ALL IS ETERNAL VIBRATION BECAUSE VIBRATION IS LIFE ITSELF, AND LIFE IS ONE OF THE FUNDAMENTAL ASPECTS OF THE ABSOLUTE, THE GREAT PRINCIPLE. The operation of this Law is explained in detail in the second, fourth, sixth, and seventh lessons.

SCIENCE-OF-BEING

THE FOUR LAWS OF THE RELATIVE

1, THE LAW OF POLARITY.

2. THE LAW OF RHYTHM.

3. THE LAW OF GENDER.

4. THE LAW OF CAUSE AND EFFECT.

THE LAW OF POLARITY: EVERYTHING IN THIS WORLD IN THE PRESENT STATE OF HUMAN CONSCIOUSNESS APPEARS TO HAVE TWO POLES, THE POSITIVE AND THE NEGATIVE POLES – GOOD AND EVIL, HEAVEN AND HELL, LIFE AND DEATH, LIGHT AND DARKNESS, DAY AND NIGHT, WHITE AND BLACK, SOUTH AND NORTH, PEACE AND WAR, YES AND NO, POSITIVE AND NEGATIVE, ETC.

Everywhere, no matter where we turn, there is the law of Polarity or Duality. It is the law of the Pairs of Opposites. Any opposites, even men and women, come under that law. It is a very important law, which pervades the whole World. It is a law which we think we cannot master, to which we must submit, as it has taken possession not only of the physical but also of the mental plane. In the most ancient religions, the law of Duality or Polarity is manifested, prevalent. There are the Days and Nights of Brahma, the Absolute, - Manavantaras and Pralayas, periods of activities and periods of rest, periods of manifestation and periods of non-manifestation, periods of being and periods of non-being. It is believed to be an immutable Law, a Law of the Absolute, but that is not correct. In one of the sacred books of the Hindus, in the Bhagavad-Gita, Krishna, the One Who Knew, when speaking about the Absolute, about Divinity, said that GOD IS ABOVE THE PAIRS OF OPPOSITES; that means, ABOVE THE LAW OF DUALITY OR POLARITY. The law of Duality therefore cannot be a Divine Law if God is above it because God and Divine Laws must be one. UNITY IS THE LAW OF THE ABSOLUTE. Yet religious, philosophical and sometimes scientific teachings are based on the law of Duality. As long as the law of Duality, or Polarity, will be accepted as an immutable law, it will keep this World

LESSON-FIVE

enslaved. Peace and Harmony will remain but a beautiful dream, because that law means a continual warfare between the two principles, the positive and the negative – and there is the question, which one of them will win? One will for a time, and under those conditions, Harmony can never be attained. When opposites are coming together they emphasize each other's opposition. It is only like which attracts like, and thus becomes one whole; but there is no possible unity between two opposites.

It is one of the most subtle and powerful laws on Earth, that law of Polarity or Duality, but it is not an eternal law, despite the assertions of some of the oldest Religions and greatest Philosophies. Humanity is hypnotized by it, and as long as human beings will submit themselves to that law, it will operate and they will always be swinging between life and death, good and evil, peace and war, and so forth. If we analyze that law from the point of view of Science, we find that it is not a true law. We say there is light and there is darkness, yet this is not a correct statement. THERE IS ONLY LIGHT. Darkness is but a suppositional absence of light. There is no such thing as real darkness, because light vibrations penetrate everywhere. We think that light is only what we see. Yet we perceive only the range of rays from red to violet – that is, the six colors of the Spectrum. There are also rays below the Red and beyond the Violet which we do not see, and those invisible rays are the most powerful. Light visible and invisible is everywhere, therefore there cannot be, THERE, IS NO DARKNESS. There are only degrees and different kinds of light. ALL IS LIGHT. Even that seemingly utter darkness and void of the inter-steller space is penetrated by vibrations, invisible to the human eye, of the Absolute Light, which is Attraction or Love. The same with good and evil. There is no absolute evil. There are only conditions of relativity, of good. There is the ultimate good, and there is the very first starting point of good, and naturally there is all the scale to develop from the point to the infinite. It is obvious that if the point and the infinite are placed together, the contrast is so great that they appear to be opposites. Yet such a comparison is not right, as there is all the infinite number of links between them, each successive link being a part of that endless chain or circle which has no beginning nor end.

SCIENCE-OF-BEING

This scientific fact cannot be ignored. GOOD, taken from the scientific point of view, IS EVERYWHERE, OMNIPRESENT. There are degrees of good, that is all, but no evil. Evil is but a suppositional absence of good, therefore non-existing, as good is all-pervading. The same is found to be true with every other pair of opposites which one begins to analyze. Soon the fact is discovered that it is only the positive which has a real existence. The Earth has two poles. One is called the North and the other the South pole. The South pole is a high mountain, the North pole is a cavity; but we call them North and South poles because we imagine that there is a top and there is a bottom. If we change our position, then really the North pole would be below and the South pole above. One must try to visualize those things also from the point of view of the Absolute and not only from that of the Relative. Scientifically speaking, there is no East or West, as a definite location; it is but a direction, pointed out by the magnetic needle, relative to the point from which one is taking it. When we are in China, the East will be in America, but when we are in Europe, America becomes West to us and China would then be East. These are only human concepts, created and used by us to distinguish the Unlimited with our limited perception; to find, to direct ourselves in the Infinite, which has no direction.

卐 There is the YES and NO. How few people know that as soon as we make a positive statement and, "Yes, I am going to do that," immediately from somewhere out of the unknown arises the silent opposition "No." And it works so strongly against us, that we usually then have all kinds of difficulties in performing that which we intended to do. Why does it happen? Because of the law of Polarity. The law of Polarity continually interferes with all our human affairs. That is why we are all the time swinging between good and evil, between hope and fear, between success and failure. There is another law still worse which usually works together with the law of polarity, and is the so-called law of Rhythm. Both are there, ready to stop all human endeavors, to destroy our works, and thus prevent us from progress. A great many people have had experience in that direction, and they have grown wise; they never will say "I am going to do that;" they say "I am going TO TRY," because they have noticed that as soon as they make a positive statement, something seems to be continually interfering with it. Yet nothing of that kind happens if a neutral form of speech is used. What is the reason? Why does the negative seem to be so strong when the positive should be the stronger? When we make an individual statement, a positive one, we simply state the positive from our human point of view; we back it up only by our own limited forces. It is just as circumscribed as we humanly are circumscribed; yet it is not a little part of the negative, but the whole of it, which the law of Polarity causes to rise automatically each time as a negation, in opposition to our positive statement. That is why it is so overwhelming. Just as the whole of the ocean striking a little piece of wood carries it away, so the whole of the negative, in which Humanity believes, and utterly fears, sweeps away and destroys our individual positive statements. YET, POSITIVE STATEMENTS CAN BE MADE IN SUCH A WAY THAT NOTHING CAN DESTROY THEM. If we say "WITH GOD'S HELP," or 'WITH THE HELP OF THE GREAT LAW I am going to do that," such a statement covers the whole ground, because NEITHER GOD NOR THE GREAT LAW HAVE OPPOSITES. Satan once attempted to oppose Divinity, but that opposition proved itself a complete failure. The world is not divided between good and evil. The Great Principle is the ONLY ONE, and IT IS ALL. Therefore, when we place the Absolute or the Great Law behind our statements, we can make any statement we want, because there is no possible opposition to those two.

Another way to neutralize that law of Polarity is continually to refuse to see the negative, always place the weight in the positive scale, to try to see, even in things most unpleasant, something good. Thus we cast the weight in the right scale, in the positive, and the result is, that by and by the law of Polarity will be neutralized, and finally will cease to operate in our lives at all. Then, ONLY the positive will come to us. Usually there is always the negative coming together with the positive because of that very law of Polarity; but when we will have overcome that law, we will realize that there are no opposites any more, no days and nights, but, metaphorically speaking, only an Eternal Day. In the Revelation, the Inspired Writer, when describing the Holy City, which lies foursquare - that is, the Realm of Perfection – says "There is no night there." There is NO NEGATIVE, NO LAW OF POLARITY IN THE ABSOLUTE. THERE ALL IS UNITY.

卐 We must not only affirm good, but SEE GOOD, KNOW GOOD; not try to excuse evil, but to explain it. We must, through our own reasoning process, see the real motive behind everything, and then we will always find something positive. There is never a complete absence of good. When we make statements in our daily life, WE MUST BE POSITIVE, but positive with the Great Law behind us to back up our words. We should recognize the law of Polarity only to the extent of endeavoring to overcome it, and we should always know it to be a TEMPORARY MUTABLE LAW above which we must some day rise. When we overcome that law, we rise to a power unknown to us now, because we become One with the Great Law. The best way to get rid of something negative, is first to detect it; second, not to fear it, and finally, to DESTROY IT BY REALIZING ITS NONEXISTENCE IN THE REALM OF ETERNAL HARMONY. Simply to close one's eyes and say there is no such thing as evil is not practical at all, as that very thing will then usually happen, precisely because of the operation of the law of Polarity. If we want to do something, LET US DO IT, AND KNOW THAT THERE IS THE GREAT LAW BEHIND US, WHICH WILL GIVE US AID AND ASSISTANCE IN ALL THAT IS RIGHT.

卐 Everybody knows how difficult it is to keep a secret. It seems to be burning on one's lips; one is almost compelled to give it away. Why? Because of the law of Polarity. When we are told NOT TO TELL, the Silent Opposition, due to the continual operation of the law, says, "DO TELL," and we usually yield to that silent command. People call it temptation, the voice of evil; in reality, it is but the working of the law of Polarity.

卐 Very often we find ourselves undecided as to what we have to do. Why is it? Again because of the law of Polarity. We take a decision and as soon as we take one, we almost regret that we did it. With some people that law of Polarity is working so strongly that they are always undecided as to what they shall do. It is not because they cannot decide, for THEY CAN DECIDE, but because they are so subject to that law of Polarity, so one with it, that whenever they make a decision, immediately there arises the silent opposition which makes them change their decision, and take another one. As soon as they have taken that new decision, the old one comes up again, and so on, until by an effort of will power, they keep to one.

卐 Take people who have what is called the spirit of contradiction. Whenever we begin a conversation with them, they must always contradict what we say. They like to argue, because of the law of Polarity. They argue sometimes against their own convictions. They cannot help it.

卐 We can try them with a little experiment, which shows how the law of Polarity is working. When they start to argue, concentrate for a few moments and silently deny the law, deny its power, and affirm Unity, Harmony, so as to cast the weight into the scale of the positive. Then probably the individual, instead of continuing to argue, will say, "What is the use of arguing?" There we have not only a good example of how to get the best of somebody's spirit of contradiction, but also, and what is more important, of how to overcome the law back of it. And when we do that, we must not say, even mentally, to the individual that he is not going to argue; that mental process must be done within ourselves impersonally, entirely forgetting about the person who does the arguing.

卐 Action and re-action is another manifestation of the same law. When people have been going for some time in one direction and have reached a certain limit, they turn suddenly back and go in the opposite direction, to return again to the first one, and so on indefinitely.

卐 That is especially noticeable in all kinds of religions, scientific or political movements. After a great spiritual uplift, the people get very realistic; after a very materialistic age, the people again are seeking something spiritual. The reason why it is so difficult sometimes to work in certain directions, is because with each step one takes forward, there is that tendency to go backward, due to the law of Polarity, in connection with which usually operates also the so-called law of Rhythm.

卐 Students of psychology know well that peculiarity of the human character. Yet that characteristic of most human beings is not an integral part of them; it is but the law of Polarity expressing itself through human channels, who, in most cases, not knowing how to rise above that law, become helpless tools in its hands. Therefore, it is very important for us to study, to analyze that law and to learn how to master it.

卐 The law of Polarity was first brought down into Involution by Mind itself; it is its creation, its own child. Later on, however, that law grew so strong that it subdued its own creator, and became one of the most relentless of masters. It has taken possession of the two planes, the physical and the mental; from there it governs the world with a rod of iron; but we can, and with the help of the Great Law, WE WILL, some day, overcome that law of Polarity and be free again.

THE LAW OF RHYTHM: EVERYTHING IN THE WORLD, IN THE PRESENT STATE OF HUMAN CONSCIOUSNESS, INHALES AND EXHALES, GOES UP AND DOWN BY COMPENSATED OSCILLATIONS.

This law is also called the law of the Pendulum, because its operations are in a way similar to the swinging of the pendulum. The pendulum goes up one side, down again, up again, and so on. That law operates in our life on two planes, the physical and the mental, in many different ways. To start with, its functioning on the physical, material plane will be explained. This is especially noticeable in waves during a storm on the sea or on any other body of water where waves are brought forth by a storm. The following design show how the energy of the wave is directed by that law.

LESSON-FIVE

⌘ The upward and forward movement of energy carries the wave higher and higher, until it reaches a culminant point. Then comes a moment when, through its own weight, the wave breaks down and falls, seemingly to continue again its forward and upward movement. That is only an appearance, however. In reality, the energy which has raised that wave, after it has reached its highest point, does not proceed at all the way it seems to. The law of Rhythm entirely reverses its movement. After it has reached the culminant point it suddenly turns within and goes all the way down and backward until it reaches the farthest point back, the point where it stated its forward movement. And when it has reached the farthest and lowest point, then it starts to go up again, first under the water as an invisible, propulsory force, then appearing on the surface again as a wave, to reach its climax and then start back again under the water. A certain part of its forward movement is done on the surface as wave, but all its backward movement, and a part of its forward movement, are done under the water unseen but still most strongly operating. That is how the waves of the ocean are moving. Every swimmer knows that undercurrent; it is called the undertow, which is so dangerous because it sucks in. But how few realize that it is all due to the operation on the physical plane, of the law of Rhythm.

⌘ As on the physical plane, so also does the law of Rhythm operate on the mental plane, because in both instances it is governed by the one immutable Great Law. We, who consciously live on these two planes, are under that law of Rhythm as long as we have not learned how to rise above it.

⌘ As are the waves on the ocean, so is Humanity's Evolution. It goes forward and upwards until it reaches the highest point, then begins the decline into its backward movement. It goes down with ever increasing speed until it reaches its lowest and farthest point, from which it starts its climb again.

卐 As we see the energy of the ocean moving partly on the surface of the water as a wave, partly under the water as the undertow, so it is also with Humanity's Evolution. The progress of Humanity begins to be noticeable only when the law of Rhythm becomes apparent in social life, just like the visible waves on the ocean, the beginning of whose ascending movement remains unseen under the water, until it bursts forth as a visible wave. But all the important work was really done, so to say, in the secrecy of the ocean itself. The silent, unseen progress is due to the hidden forward movement.

卐 When the backward movement starts, at first it is almost unnoticeable, but its speed increases all the time until it has reached the lowest point. There again, as in the ocean the backward movement is not so much seen as felt. On the surface things seem to be still moving forward, but there is the undertow, which sucks in and down all those who are not strong enough to resist that backward and downward movement. The backward movement is so strong as to bring Humanity almost to the same point from which it started, and the little gain still made is due exclusively to the operation of another law called the Law of Evolution, which in some measure counteracts the operation of the law of Rhythm.

卐 If we would express in mathematical figures the advancing movement of the Human Race, and then its receding movement, due to that law, they would read as follows: In the forward movement, Humanity has in its progress advanced, metaphorically speaking, twelve feet, but when the backward movement starts, the law of Rhythm throws Humanity back eleven feet, eleven and three-quarter inches, and the whole progress is thus reduced to one-quarter of an inch. That is the reason why Humanity's Evolution is so very slow. We have lived countless ages and yet we have progressed comparatively very little, all because of that law of Rhythm. If it were not for that law, which keeps it back, Humanity would long ago have solved its problems of Evolution. That law would have kept Humanity for eternity in its clutches, if there were not the Law of Evolution, which states that "ALL VIBRATIONS TEND NATURALLY

LESSON·FIVE

TO RISE UPWARDS IN THE SCALE OF ETERNAL HARMONY."
That Law is a ray of Hope, sent by Love to suffering Humanity to uplift it, to
counteract to some extent the operation of the law of Rhythm. Because of that
Law of Evolution we see all vibrations always striving upwards in spite of the
law of Rhythm working continually against it.

卐 It will be explained now how that law of Rhythm works in our daily lives.
Most of us have had the experience that there are certain days when everything
is successful and other days when anything we start is a failure. It is the
upward and downward movement of the law of Rhythm which produces these
differences. It must be remembered that as there are big waves on the ocean,
there are also smaller waves. Each big wave is made up of smaller ones, and
each little wave is governed by the same law and manifests the same kind of
movement forward and backward, as does the big wave, the law of Rhythm
working in identically the same way on the all waves.

卐 Men of business also know that law, sometimes consciously, most of the
time unconsciously. There are certain periods in their business when things go
well, and periods when things do not go well. Those periods are sometimes
long, sometimes short, just like waves on the ocean, and repeat themselves.
In History certain facts also continually repeat themselves and we then say:
"History repeats itself." It is the law of Rhythm which is the underlying cause
of those forward and backward movements. People who have been successful
in their life are those who have mastered that law; that is, they acted like good
swimmers on a stormy sea. When the law started to draw them back, they did
not lose courage or begin to fear; on the contrary, again like good swimmers,
they courageously did their best not only to remain afloat on the top of the
wave, but swim so vigorously as to advance even in spite of the opposing
current, until by and by, at each attempt, they won some point. The result was
that finally those waves, instead of drawing them backward, really began to
carry them onwards. Sometimes it may be a slower, other times a quicker
movement, but it will always be a forward movement. There is no longer any
backward movement possible. Under those conditions, when it happens on

the water of the sea, we say the storm is over. When it happens in our life, we say we have mastered unsuccess – we are successful. If one analyzes the lives of most successful people, no matter to what department of life they may belong, be it Religion, Science, Business, Statesmanship, Arts or Politics, one will find that any man or woman who has ever been successful has had the same experience. In the beginning, great hardship, handicaps and failures, yet they persevered, failing maybe hundreds of times, but advancing still, full of energy, and still hoping that some day they would meet with success. One day they did meet with success, and that day they neutralized that law to the extent that we humanly can in our present state of consciousness. Even then the law can bring them a little down but still it always remains a forward movement.

卐 Now there is the question, how to neutralize that law and take advantage of its forward and upward movements. The first thing to do when we see that the law of Rhythm is carrying us backwards is not to fear, not to be discouraged, and to try to swim as vigorously as we can against the opposing current. Even if, in spite of our efforts, we are carried far back and deep down, after all it does not matter how much backwards we are carried by the law; the important point which we must always keep in mind is that some day, because it is the law of Rhythm, it must start again its forward and ascending movement. Being a law, it must be true to itself. Therefore, even at its worst, there is always a hope for us that we will leave the bottom some day, if we will persevere, and if we do not let ourselves be discouraged and remain on the bottom like a stone which cannot be carried forward by the ascending movement of the law. That is why we say that "a man may be down but not out." When the bottom is reached, then the ascending movement starts, and finally the highest point is reached. Wise people know that then is the time to be careful. We can master the law, yet we must watch it till we have really overcome it. That does not mean to fear the law, but to be cautious, and when we see the backward movement starting again, to polarize ourselves on the positive and simply refuse to be carried back, like a good swimmer fighting the undertow.

LESSON-FIVE

When the law of Rhythm begins its backward movement, we must persevere in what we already have on hand, because it is our duty to hold on to that; but must never start anything new once the backward movement has set in. It usually turns out to be a failure. Naturally, if one can stand through the backward movement till it has reached its very lowest point, then some day one may become successful; but why waste all that energy in order to fight the backward movement, when it is much easier and more rational to wait for the ascending movement of the law. Success will come then by simply waiting for the positive operation of the law. Thus we will have saved all the energy which otherwise would have been wasted in fighting, and then we can use it to better advantage in combining it with the forward movement of the law of Rhythm.

In our lives we all have periods of success and periods of unsuccess, due to the operation of that law. Therefore, whenever we see that we are on the way to success, we must DO ALL WE CAN during that time in order to take in every direction every possible advantage of the positive side of the law of Rhythm. That law is an automatic, unconscious law, but WE ARE CONSCIOUS. We can, therefore, outwit the law, and we have for that the divine authority and help because it is a transitory law which we must some day overcome. Like the law of Polarity, it originated when our involution into material consciousness started, and it will disappear when we will have evolved out of that state of consciousness. Take, for instance, that story in the Bible, the dream of Pharaoh about the seven fat cows and the seven lean cows which ate up the seven fat cows and still remained lean. It was the law of Rhythm which the Pharaoh perceived in a dream and which Joseph was able to interpret correctly. Joseph was wise. He knew the operation of the law of Rhythm and how to overcome it and so he said: "During the seven prosperous years gather and bring together all you can." That is, use the upward movement of the law of Rhythm to the very limit in every direction; and then when you will have received all which can be obtained during those seven prosperous years, when the years of famine, or the backward movement, will start, you will have everything ready to meet that backward movement, and being prepared, you will thus overcome the law. We should and can do just the

SCIENCE·OF·BEING

same and follow the example of the Pharaoh. When the forward movement of the law of Rhythm starts, let us use its power in every possible direction. No matter what we will endeavor to do during that time, it is bound to be a success, but when the backward movement starts again, then we must be careful, watch, and refuse to be carried away by that movement. The more we act that way, the more and more do we neutralize that law, and by and by we will notice that those backwards movements will become weaker and weaker till they will disappear entirely, leaving only the forward movements. When we have reached that condition, the storm on the sea of our lives will come to an end and we can say we have mastered that law of Rhythm; the negative operation of it will cease, leaving only the positive force, which then will help us all the time. The following design shows how the law of Rhythm operates when consciously mastered.

It is very necessary for us to know those laws and their operation because we are seemingly so helpless when confronted with them. People become so frightened by their manifestations that they grow superstitious. Somebody says: "How well you look," or, "How successful you are in your business?" Immediately most people would tap wood. Why? To counteract so called negative influences. The superstition that we must tap wood was really brought on because people noticed that whenever a compliment about their good health or success was made, soon some misfortune happened to the one who was complimented. Back of all that trouble are those two transitory laws, the law of Polarity and the law of Rhythm. Many superstitions were brought forth to meet those laws, but in reality they were never able to do so. It is only our mental attitude, the knowledge of the operation of the laws, and faith in our God-given power to overcome them, which enable us to master those laws.

LESSON·FIVE

LAW OF GENDER: EVERYTHING IN THIS WORLD IN THE PRESENT STATE OF HUMAN CONSCIOUSNESS HAS TWO GENDERS, THE MALE AND THE FEMALE GENDER.

The law of Gender expresses itself most forcibly throughout the whole round of Creation in the so-called opposite sexes, the male and the female. It is manifested not only through human beings, but also through animals, plants, minerals, electrons, electrical and magnetic currents, etc. Not only on the physical plane does that law of Gender function; it is also manifested in the mind of each human being, be it man or woman. They have the two genders expressed also in their mental selves. The mind of each individual has a Self-consciousness which belongs to the male gender, and a Sub-consciousness which belongs to the female gender. These two are definitely expressing two sides of our individual minds. As the most important part of the process of thought operation is based on the law of Gender in the human mind, details about it will be given in the sixth lesson, which deals with Mind Force.

卐 There is also a third constituent part in our mental selves, called the Super-consciousness, which will be taken up in the seventh lesson.

卐 In this lesson the law of Gender will be explained in its operation through the fundamental characteristics of what we call, in our present state of consciousness, the two opposite sexes. We have now in Humanity, on one side Man, and on the other side Woman, and these two are like two halves of a sphere, which, when they come together, combine to form a whole sphere. The generally accepted belief of today is that they unite for the purpose of procreation, to continue the human species on this Earth. No matter how important procreation may appear, a still greater and higher purpose is there for them to achieve. That ultimate purpose is that by learning their lessons through association, and by mutually developing their latent complementary qualities, they may work out completeness within each, after which they are automatically separated. Yet after their separation they are no longer the same as they were before. A great change has taken place within them. Before their meeting, they appeared as halves, but after the object of their association has been attained, they separate because each one of them has become a COMPLETE SPHERE. In Man, who is the outward expression of the male qualities, which are energy, self reliance, intellect, etc., are also latent and ready for expression all the female qualities. On the other hand love, patience, intuition, gentleness, etc., latent in men, whenever expressed as dominate qualities, manifest themselves in what we call Woman. Yet women have also latent within them all male qualities. This is so not only in character of the individuals, but also in their physical bodies. For instance, the embryo of a child, until about the fifth month of gestation, has the two sexes within itself physically expressed. Yet afterwards it develops one sex or the other, and thus determines the sex to which it is born, boy or girl. Yet within the body of human beings are still discernible traces of the opposite sex. As it is with our physical bodies, so it is with our characters, and from each individual can be drawn out and developed the latent complementary parts of their characters. The main purpose of marriage and in general of the association of men and women is therefore to work out that development, to make them complete individual spheres, the image and likeness of the Infinite Sphere, called the Great Principle, the Absolute. In the first chapter of Genesis we read, "And God created Man in His image and likeness: male and female created He them." Only a being possessing both qualities referred to can be the perfect image and likeness of the Perfect One. That is the goal toward which each step in Humanity's Evolution is bringing us daily nearer and nearer.

The following diagrams show three pairs of halves, each half representing a man and a woman placed in a certain juxtaposition one to another, and forming three distinct groups. The whole of human relations can be classed under those three main headings. Yet each case is an individual one, and there are no two alike. The first pair shows the two halves, man and woman, directly facing each other, thus establishing between them as many connecting lines of Attraction, or Love, as their open surfaces allow. When in that relation, there is an irresistible drawing from one to another which unites them

LESSON·FIVE

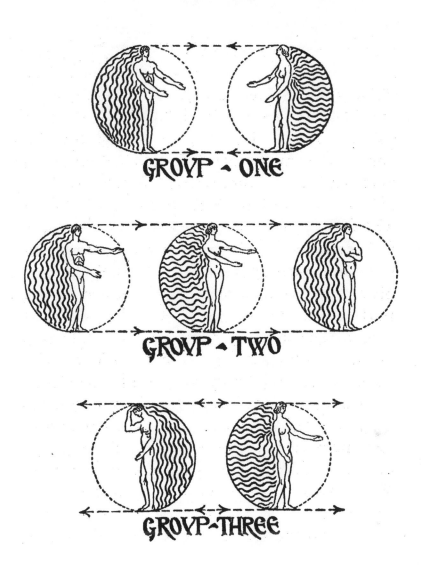

GROVP · ONE

GROVP · TWO

GROVP · THREE

into a complete sphere. It may happen sometimes instantaneously, when two individuals chance to be in that relation one to another. It is then called "love at first sight." When the two seemingly become one, everything seems to be in common between them – common interests, a common axis about which their lives rotate. And when individuals are in that condition, they feel such an overwhelming sense of completeness and harmony that they call it perfect bliss, and because of it would never like to part even for a moment. The slightest separation causes them intense suffering, because of the lack of the complementary part. It is like an open wound when they are put apart, and

155

SCIENCE-OF-BEING

they are only happy when they are again together. And they expect to remain in that condition not only throughout this life but even throughout Eternity. When two individuals are in that relation to one another they are harmless, but also useless, to the rest of the world. They cannot help it. All their interests are centered within themselves. Most of their energies are used to keep those two halves together, the man to meet the demands of the woman, the woman to meet the demands of the man. They live in a world of their own and are happy. The world around them does not exist for them. Naturally in such a case they cannot express anything outside of themselves, and therefore one of the fundamental Laws of the Universe, the Law of Attraction, cannot operate outside of them as it should, for the Law of Attraction must be operating outside as well as inside in order to keep everything in perfect equilibrium and harmony. If the whole Universe would be filled with compound spheres of the above kind, nothing would be flowing from one sphere to another, each being centered in itself; and the Universe deprived of the cohesive power of Attraction, would fall to pieces. But the Great Law takes good care that such a condition shall be only transitory, and nothing but a stepping stone to work out higher problems. When the two halves, man and woman, combine into a sphere, those halves apparently fit each other completely, but that is not the case. There is always some little space between them where they are not completely adjusted. Compared with the great harmonization of the other qualities, that little maladjustment is almost unnoticed by them; yet in that little space where they seemingly do not accord, and which forms a sort of a vacuum, the latent complementary parts of each are growing in, because Nature does not permit a vacuum. The manifested male qualities of the man draw out of the woman her latent male qualities, because the law says that "like attracts like." And the manifested female qualities of the woman, in their turn, draw out of the man his latent female qualities. Thus two incipient halves are gradually growing out in the open space between the two. The more they grow, the more independent of each other the two individuals become. This process of development is unfolding so gradually that neither of them notices the change in their relations one to another until they have become two complete spheres rotating around their respective axes, independent and free, yet still most intimately related one to another. Then only do they realize that some fundamental change has taken place within them, and their opened eyes perceive with amazement that they have grown into a new and higher condition. Their association has achieved its purpose; the law has been fulfilled. Two complete beings have been evolved from a half-developed condition, and brought to the Universe TO COOPERATE CONSCIOUSLY IN THE GREAT ETERNAL SCHEME.

But a question may arise, Is all that love, that tender relation between them, gone once and forever? No! By no means. On the contrary, never before did they feel a greater sense of love, a more intense feeling of completeness and harmony, than since they became complete individual spheres. When they were halves, they could express one to another only the love of a half, but the moment they became complete spheres they expressed complete love to each other in all its infinite manifestations. Being complete spheres, and rotating around their own individual axes, they continually see one another in all their different aspects. It is like incessantly discovering in each other some new and precious qualities. Naturally, under those conditions, their love becomes infinitely greater and more perfect than it had ever been before. On account of their completeness they must also radiate love to everyone and everything about them in every direction, thus fulfilling the Law of Love, of Universal Brotherhood. Then they become useful members of the Great Human Family, because they love everybody, only they will love their mate more, because their relations are at the time the closest, one to another. That is why they are called mates, or affinities, or twin souls. But their mutual love by no means excludes love to other beings also. Through incarnation after incarnation we have all been working out that problem of ours, by gradually developing our inner qualities. Usually, when two individuals are in that position facing each other, as described above, it is due to previous incarnations which prepared them for that relation. That is why, when they meet, they cannot help but love each other. When two such individuals have worked out their completeness, and reached a state of individual spheres, they do not think any more of their own happiness. All their life, all their thought, all their love, is for their mate's or their friend's happiness. They are never expecting anything in return, but, being complete spheres, it is inevitable that they should receive in return as much as they give. It is the highest love we can imagine now in our present state of consciousness, because it is a love which loves, not for what it can get, but for what it can give. It is the nearest to the Love of Divinity, for Divinity also gives first, then receives. God first loved us; that is why we, in our turn, are to love Him. Even bodily separation or death cannot break such ties once they are established.

卐 Diagram number two shows another group, much less harmonious, but much more common. There the man loves the woman, who does not reciprocate his love because her affections are fixed upon another man, who, in his turn, is indifferent to her. Under these circumstances it is much more difficult to work out the completion, because there is no help whatsoever from the side of the corresponding party. Still, the problem of completion is solved, but in a different way. First the man, not having the woman's manifested qualities directed toward him to awaken within him the latent qualities of love and gentleness, has to draw out of himself, through his own efforts, stimulated by his love, the complementary female qualities. Love does it. More and more, because of the woman he loves, all the latent female qualities, as love, patience, gentleness, intuition, etc., are brought out of that man by his love. It is a slow and painful process, because he has to do it alone, without the help of the woman he loves. Yet he does it, because he loves. When he has worked out his completion, his whole attitude toward that woman changes. In the beginning it was selfish; but the more he loves, the less selfish he becomes. At first he suffered because his love was not answered, and was jealous of the other man to whom that woman was giving her love. The completeness once attained, all these negative feelings disappear entirely, because he has found harmony within himself. Then he no longer thinks of his own happiness; he finds his happiness in the happiness of the woman he loves. No sacrifice is too great for him, for he is a changed being.

卐 There is the woman, in love with another man, who is indifferent to her. She has also to work out the problem of her completion without the help and assistance of the man she loves. Through love again is that problem solved. Her own love makes her more self-reliant and energetic, compels her to make greater use of her reasoning qualities, etc. And thus, through much hard work, sorrow, and trouble, she becomes eventually a complete sphere. Then her whole attitude changes. She begins to feel toward the unresponsive object of her love a mother's affection, caring for him without ever expecting to get anything in return, entirely forgetting her own self for his sake. She also is then ready for any sacrifice, because she has worked out her completion.

卐 And when the two, the first man and woman, have become complete spheres, their mutual relations are then also modified. To their surprise they discover that bonds of love exist from both sides. They become friends, and the woman who spurned, perhaps for many years, the love which the man lavished upon her in such measure, begins in her turn to love him also. Why that sudden change? Because, as a complete sphere, she cannot help but love everybody; and that first man, perhaps her husband, being so close to her, naturally must get the radiations of love emanating from her in every direction.

卐 The third group represents two individuals, a man and a woman, who are married, yet turn their backs upon each other. Worldly considerations were probably the cause of their loveless marriage; or maybe it was a match arranged by their parents, who did not consult the personal feelings of the two chiefly concerned. Such a marriage must be an unhappy one, and an utter failure in regard to the problem of working out their own individual completeness. It is one of the most inharmonious of human relations, because it is unnatural, the Law of Attraction, the Basic Law of the Universe not finding expression in their mutual relations. They are of no use one to another, as they are turning their backs to each other, Yet, as the problem of completion must be worked out also in that case, they are seeking an affinity, a love, outside of their matrimonial ties. And when they have found somebody to love they separate, because they realize that otherwise happiness would remain for them a mere dream. Because of worldly considerations, it may take them many years before they make that final decision, yet it is inevitable. Soon or late it must come, and the sooner the better.

卐 That last group teaches human beings a great lesson, that marriage is there to build the character, to develop Love to its highest manifestation, and not to attain material ease and comfort.

SCIENCE-OF-BEING

卐 The problem of Completion is continually worked out in life through association of individuals one with another. Women constantly contribute to men some of their qualities, and men do the same toward women. That is why co-education has so many strong points in its favor. Even the association of individuals of the same sex has also its own beneficial results. Especially large educational, social, and military bodies play a very important role in that respect. There, individuals belonging to different classes in social life come together, each one contributing some characteristic, some quality, to their fellow beings. Angles are rounded off, rough surfaces made smooth, and individuals promoted a few degrees further toward completion.

卐 COMPLETION IS PERFECTION, and as such is a very wonderful thing to seek and to strive for. But we must also realize that a problem of that magnitude cannot be worked out by individuals in the span on one life. Many returns to Earth, many reincarnations, are needed for each one of us before we become perfect beings, the image and likeness of that Supreme Being, the Source of all Perfection, Whom we call God.

 # LESSON-FIVE

THE LAW OF CAUSE AND EFFECT: EVERY EFFECT HAS ITS CAUSE AND EVERY CAUSE HAS ITS EFFECT.

. . .

This law pervades the three planes, the physical, mental, and Spiritual. It is a law which has its root in the Spiritual plane because there is the First Great Cause, the Principle, the Basis of everything. But there also is the effect, the Universe. On the Spiritual plane, cause and effect are simultaneous and instantaneous; there they are so blended together that they cannot be separated; but on the other planes there is always a certain time, a period of space between cause and effect, due to the human concept, in our present state of consciousness, of Time and Space. That law is operating in this way; every time we start something, be it thought, word or action, we create a certain cause which will some day materialize in a corresponding effect. If we start a positive cause, a right cause, there will be in due time a positive effect, and vice versa. Just when that effect will take place, no one can tell; it depends upon many circumstances; but it is unavoidably due, like a logical result in a mathematical problem. Whenever we have started a cause, we are powerless over its effect, can never change the effect. Yet human beings do not realize that at all, as is indicated in the common belief that if people will regret their sins, they will be forgiven and ushered into Heaven. That is an utter impossibility because it is against the Law. If a person regrets a mistake, a sin, it is forgiven in the sense that there is always the possibility to make it right, to start a new positive cause. But the penalty for the wrong is also always there, and that penalty it is impossible to avoid because it is our own creation, the effect for the cause we started coming back to us. And there we have the explanation of those words of Jesus in the Bible, when He said: "WHOSOEVER SOWETH THE WIND SHALL REAP THE WHIRLWIND." He knew the law of Cause and Effect and He stated it, but naturally He could not explain that law to the people who were living at that period as scientifically as it can be explained now. He presented it in another way. He used the allegorical form, yet it was the same law. When we know that law and apply that knowledge to our daily life, we can shape

SCIENCE-OF-BEING

our own destiny exactly as we wish it. Naturally we CANNOT straighten out past mistake, but we CAN TAKE THEM AS LESSONS.

卐 When those mistakes, those negative causes, materialize into our lives as negative effects, those who are wise profit by the experience of their mistakes, which then become for them good lessons not to repeat those mistakes. In order to use that law successfully in our lives, we must learn to handle it properly. The first and most important thing to do is TO LIVE IN THE EVER PRESENT NOW. What does that mean? Are we not living right now? Yes and no. To live in the present NOW means always to do the best we can to start right causes NOW. Illogical and impractical as it is, yet most people live in the Future, with their hopes pinned to that Future. On the other hand, some people live with the remembrance of the Past; they are tied to their dead Past. That also is not living NOW. "NOW is the appointed time," do we read in the sacred Books. NOW we must do everything which is to be done; NOW is the very wonderful and only moment for us to live in – a moment which very often is not at all understood by some, even of the great philosophers. They entirely disregard the NOW. They claim that NOW does not exist because everything continually changes, is in a condition of perpetual becoming, and that therefore it can never be NOW, but is either the Past or the Future. If that were really so, we could never use constructively the laws of Cause and Effect, as the Future would be always beyond our control. Therefore we would never be able consciously to build and direct our lives; we would always be slaves of Fate. In living NOW, in performing NOW our duties as they come to us, we place ourselves in the following position. We are, so to speak, standing on a line of demarcation, on one side of us the Past, on the other side the Future, and in front of us the Present. In the Past we have experience, in the Future all possibilities, but NOW is the time for us to act, to plant the good seed, to start positive causes, taking advantage of lessons of the Past so as to create the Future we desire. Some day TOMORROW will become TODAY, the Future will become Present, as time is moving along. We alone are immovable in that ever present NOW. Events are passing before our eyes as a film on a screen. It is the film of our own life which we witness NOW. We are both the audience and the actors, and our state of consciousness is the screen on

LESSON-FIVE

which we perceive everything. NOW is so marvelous because we perform in it simultaneously two actions; we reap the Past and sow the Future. These two actions we can perform continually only NOW. That is why NOW is so important and why NOW holds for us the key to our destiny. The Past cannot be changed; we have to take it as it is. But our Future is completely in our hands, and, if we start the right causes, should never occasion us any worry, as it will take care of itself because of the law of Cause and Effect. When Jesus said: "Take therefore no thought for the morrow, for the morrow will take thought for the things of itself; sufficient unto the day is the evil thereof," He meant that we must NOW do the right thing and then the Future will take care of itself because of the law. It is unavoidable and yet we realize it so little that we continually worry about the Future. Whenever we do anything, we wonder, "How will it come out?" Why should we worry? If we do the right thing, leave it alone and it will come out all right, through the operation of the law of Cause and Effect. Worry is a leak through which energy is wastefully dissipated in the unknown void of the Future instead of being constructively applied in the Present. We can perform real action only on the plane on which we are living NOW in body, mind, and Soul. For the Great Principle, there is only one plane, that of the EVER PRESENT NOW. There is no Past or Future for the Absolute, because It is all-inclusive, and when we reach the highest state of consciousness there will be the most complete sense of the EVER PRESENT NOW, as Past and Future will be One with it. In the Bhagavad-Gita, Krishna is recorded as saying: "Do not think about the fruit of your action; but perform action." That is the same as when Jesus told us not to worry about the next day. Do the right thing today and the next day will take care of itself. That does not mean that we should cease planning. Naturally we should plan things; but when we plan them as well as we can, when we have prepared the seed, if we have prepared a good seed and planted it rightly, it will grow well. Never worry about the result; there is the law back of it. That is why we must be satisfied with today and not try to imagine or make certain calculations that it will work out this or that way. Usually our calculations will be upset because in worrying about the Future we do not give enough attention to the Present. We cannot have the Great Law operating in the Future, the Great Law being a Law of the ever present NOW. Neither the Past nor the Future can exist for that Great Law, because, like the Great Principle Itself, it is an all-embracing Law, and is therefore always operating NOW.

卐 We make certain mistakes periodically, and then say, "Next time I am not going to do that," but when next time comes we do it again. Why? Because of that law of Cause and Effect. Each time we make a mistake we start a new cause for that mistake to be repeated, and usually, if we watch these periodical mistakes, we can see that we make them at certain times or in meeting a certain kind of people, or on being confronted with certain similar conditions. So whenever we feel that moment approaching and the ground begins to be slippery, there we have to watch, and, being determined not to yield to that mistake again, we will, through the conscious application of that law of Cause and Effect, destroy the negative causes and stop the repetition of the negative effects. Instead, we have started a positive cause which will some day culminate in a positive effect. If we keep to that decision to overcome imperfections, the law will carry us through with harmonious results, and we will be able to correct by and by all our mistakes. They will never occur again because we are setting up new causes, harmonious causes, which will be then continually expressed in corresponding new effects.

卐 On our life paths we very often stumble, we may even fall, yet we should never worry about our stumbling or our falling. We should always bear in mind that it does not matter so much that we have fallen over an obstacle. The important fact is that we are on the other side of the obstacle, that we have advanced in spite of it. This is the main point to be always remembered by us, and then the fall itself will not appear to be so hard.

卐 The law of Cause and Effect, in its present aspect of a transitory, material law, is not harmful to us if we know how to use it properly. If we only do the right thing we can use it in such a way that it will always work with positive results. That law explains also what is called Reincarnation. Why do some individuals come to the Earth to suffer and others to enjoy? If for some reason they could not get all they deserved for their good or evil deeds in one incarnation, in one life on Earth, then they must come back to this plane again in order to get it in another life. In other words, they come to this Earth as children go to school; it is indeed the School of Life, where all lessons must be learned and all mistakes corrected. Then only are we ready for some higher and greater work. This explanation is the only logical one which completely does away with that seeming injustice in the destiny of human beings. In any case, it certainly is more acceptable than the theory of eternal bliss and eternal punishment.

卐 This last law of Cause and Effect closes the cycle of the Seven Laws. Two more Laws will be given, making nine, the Law of Love and the Law of Evolution. These Laws, although direct emanations from, and comprehended in, the first of the Laws of the Absolute, are given separately, at the end of this lesson on Laws, in order to emphasize the fact that no matter how strong the Negative, with its transitory laws, may appear to us, the Positive, with its Eternal Laws, is nevertheless supreme. It is the Beginning and the End of everything.

THE LAW OF LOVE: NO MATTER UNDER WHAT CIRCUMSTANCES, ALWAYS MEET EVERYTHING AND EVERYBODY WITH LOVE.

All great teachers of Humanity have always had their teachings based on Love. They loved human beings, and they taught human begins how to love. People usually see in those teachings only the emotional, the altruistic, the ideal, yet how few realize the immense practical value and the real science back of them. Let us analyze now, from the scientific point of view, why the continual application of that Law is one of the most important means for our evolution. We have an immutable Law with says "Everything is Vibration," and therefore Love also is a certain kind of vibration. But so is hatred, jealousy, etc. Suppose an individual sends to us a negative thought vibration of hatred or jealousy. That unit of negative vibrations penetrates into us, and because of the Law of Vibration, arouses in us the corresponding unit of negative vibrations. Having in us two units of negative vibrations, we feel uncomfortable, and we throw them back to the individual who first sent to us the thought of hatred or jealousy. Again because of the Law of Vibration, they arouse in that individual two corresponding negative vibrations. He in his turn, disliking to feel four units of negative thought vibrating within him, throws them back at us. Receiving this time four negative units, which arouse within us a corresponding four, we send back eight. He gets eight, and sends back to us sixteen. We, on our side, return him thirty-two, etc., the number of units of negative vibrations exchanged increasing thus in geometrical progression. When both sides have reached the limit of endurance in that direction they explode; that is, they suddenly throw off all the negative vibrations accumulated in each one of them, and that explosion means fight. The fight may be with acts, with words, with looks, or even with thoughts. In any case, it is a fight, which results in injury to both sides. That is the ordinary way, among human beings, of eliminating their negative vibrations – certainly not a practical way, after all, because it always weakens both parties, and sometimes injures them beyond repair. That proves that retaliation, as stated in the law of Moses, which says "An eye for an eye and a tooth for a tooth," and which is so generally accepted by human beings, is not the best method of solving that problem. Now, whenever we apply the Law of Love in a similar case, we obtain there entirely different results. An individual may send to us negative vibrations, thoughts of hatred and jealousy. According to the Law of Vibrations, they will arouse in us the corresponding negative vibrations. Yet if we remember the Law of Love, we can meet those negative vibrations with Love, consciously brought forth within us. As the Positive always destroys the Negative, which has no power over it, the positive vibrations always destroy the negative vibrations sent from that individual. After they have destroyed these negative vibrations, they reach the individual himself, and arouse within him the corresponding vibrations of love. Though surprised at the way we retaliated, the individual may send us another discharge of negative vibrations, which we meet again in the same way. And again the positive vibrations of Love proceeding from us will do their pacifying work within the other individual. He may send a few more discharges of negative vibrations, the number of which will depend on the strength of the negative passion which is governing him at that time. But we, meeting them always with Love, finally destroy all reserves of the negative vibrations which the individual possesses at that moment. And the individual, because of the Law of Love, begins to feel in their stead peace and harmony, and sometimes even love. All the negative seems as if wiped out, and replaced by the positive. Often the individual, out of stubbornness, does not want to admit it, because he thinks that by so doing he acknowledges, defeat; but in reality there was no defeat whatsoever, on either side. On the contrary, Love carried the victory to both.

The above cited example shows how infinitely superior and more practical is Love than retaliation, yet how few people realize its practicability and its universal use. They consider it a weakness, a lack of manliness, not to strike back when they are struck. On the contrary, it is much more difficult, and requires greater self control and more developed willpower, to stand those continual attacks of negative vibrations, and to meet and overcome them by vibrations of Love. The more we apply that Law of Love in our lives, the stronger we become on our positive side, and the greater is the harmony within us, until finally we reach a condition of such harmony that no negative vibrations of any kind can ever touch us more because there is no longer in us a response to anything negative. Then only everything positive will come to us. Each human being will some day have to learn that Law of Love, because it is the only way, the quickest and easiest, to do away with wars, revolutions, strikes, domestic troubles, and all kinds of disagreements and misunderstandings among human beings. Then peace will be established on this Earth, not as something imposed from without by a stronger nation, but as something from within, an inherent part of each human being. And as nations are made up of individuals, when the individual will be able to express peace and good will toward other men, nations will then manifest on a large scale what each citizen does on a small scale. Then the whole Human Family will be at peace, and peace will reign on this Earth. How true, how scientific, ring down to us through the centuries those loving words of the One Who was Love, "LOVE YOUR ENEMIES, BLESS THEM THAT HATE YOU,

SCIENCE-OF-BEING

DO GOOD TO THEM THAT DESPITEFULLY USE YOU."

Those who have attained the highest on the path of Love, when they reach that condition where nothing but love comes to them from everywhere and from everybody, are then ready for the final test of Love. Jealousy, hatred, malice, all evil passions, are thrown at them again, but this time not to awaken within them the corresponding characteristics which no longer vibrate with them. All negative, all evil, comes to them for liberation from its own self for transmutation into good. The Life Energy, pure and harmonious, imprisoned as in a shell in every negative act, thought, or emotion, is irresistibly attracted toward those who are the luminaries of Love. Unconsciously it feels that only they are great enough to pierce with the arrows of Love that negative shell around it, to liberate it and thus transmute evil into good. There is no higher and greater work to perform on this plane than the transmutation of evil into good, and those who are able to do it justly deserve to be called the Saviours of the World. It is usually with their lives that they pay the price for that transmutation, for that service they render to Humanity. But is there an effort too great, a price too high, to pay for the liberation of Humanity from the bonds of Evil? Human hatred, jealousy, and all the other evil passions, like a great wave, lifted Jesus to the Cross. As a deadly arrow, they transfixed the human body of Krishna and caused His mortal self to die. They persecuted Buddha, and every other lesser teacher who ever taught Humanity the Law of Love. As in the days of old, so in modern times the same fact repeats itself. It is the age-old Evil which comes continually for liberation from its own negative qualities. And Love, gentle yet strong, presses to its heart those thorny branches of Evil, and with its warmth, its tenderness, makes them burst forth into beautiful blossoms of Love.

# LESSON·FIVE

THE LAW OF EVOLUTION: ALL VIBRATIONS TEND TO RISE UPWARD IN THE SCALE OF ETERNAL HARMONY.

The Law of Evolution, that saving ray of the Great Law, expresses itself on the three planes, the physical, the mental, and the Spiritual. When on the Spiritual plane, it appears as Eternal Unfoldment. When seen through the physical or mental lens, its evolutionary action is called Progress. This wind which whirls the dust from the ground and carries it up into the air, is governed by that Law. It proceeds in spirals, the spiral being the form through which the Law operates. The cyclone on dry land, the typhoon on the sea, are governed by the same Law. Whenever left to themselves to operate normally, all vibrations tend naturally to rise upward. It is only through conscious or unconscious perversion that this upward tendency can be reversed. Evil itself is nothing but the reversed upward movement of good. Positive vibrations, whenever reversed in their ever ascending and unfolding course, become negative, and assume then all those characteristics which are called "evil." If it were not for the Law of Evolution, the laws of Rhythm and Polarity would have kept Humanity in their clutches eternally. Yet no matter how much those laws, especially the law of Rhythm, try to throw us back to the point from which we started, they do not succeed because of that Law of Evolution. There is always a little gain on the side of the Positive, due to the continual operation of that eternal Helpmate of ours. We call it HOPE, as it always carries us beyond our own human selves, remains with us, sustains and uplifts us, when everything else seems to have deserted us. It is like the last string of that great Lyre called Human Life, which, when the rest are broken, still strikes into our hearts new courage to continue the struggle and to win our fight. Being a Law and an eternal one, it is not only Hope that the Law of Evolution brings to us, but also the assurance that no matter what may happen, SUCCESS and TRIUMPH are ours eventually.

QVESTIONS & ANSWERS

LESSON FIVE

1. QUES. How many laws govern the Universe in the Absolute?
   ANS.   One Universal, All-Inclusive Law called the Great Law.

2. QUES. How many laws govern this World in the present state of human consciousness?
   ANS.   Seven Laws, of which three are immutable, eternal, Laws of the Absolute, and four are transitory, mutable, laws of the Relative.

3. QUES. Why are there three Laws of the Absolute?
   ANS.   Because of the Triune State of the present human consciousness, through which the One Universal Great Law appears in three aspects.

4. QUES. What are the three Laws of the Absolute?
   ANS.   First: Life, Mind, Truth, Love, Spirit, is All in All. Second: The Same Law governs always everything, everywhere, in the same way, from the greatest star to the smallest electron. Third: Everything is Vibration.

5. QUES. What does the first of the Laws of the Absolute mean?
   ANS.   It means the All-ness of the Great Principle

6. QUES. What does the second of the Laws of the Absolute stand for?
   ANS.   It stands for the Universality of the Great Law.

7. QUES. What does the third of the Laws of the Absolute mean?
   ANS.   It means Infinite and Eternal Activity.

8. QUES. What attitude has one to take in regard to those Laws of the Absolute?
   ANS.   One has to attune, to harmonize, oneself with them.

9. QUES. What practical result does that bring?
   ANS.   An ever-increasing sense of freedom and actual power.

ᒧ LESSON-FIVE

10. **QUES.** What results are brought about by the transgression those laws?

    ANS. Disharmony and loss of all power.

11. **QUES.** Are those Laws of the Absolute inferior to the Great Principle Itself?

    ANS. No, because they are an integral part of the Great Principle, and are the means by which It governs the Universe.

12. **QUES.** What are the four laws of the Relative?

    ANS. They are the laws of Polarity, of Rhythm, of Gender and of Cause and Effect.

13. **QUES.** Why are they called transitory laws?

    ANS. Because they were brought into existence by Mind (Lucifer) himself, and must therefore be also destroyed by Mind.

14. **QUES.** How did they first come into existence?

    ANS. Mind (Lucifer) claiming to be a power by himself, constituted a seeming power aside from All Power. Thus was the law of Polarity brought into existence. Out of the law of Polarity grew all the other laws of the Relative.

15. **QUES.** What power have those laws nowadays?

    ANS. They rule Humanity with a rod of iron, and try to stop all progress.

16. **QUES.** What attitude should one have towards those laws?

    ANS. One should learn how to master them.

17. **QUES.** What will be the practical result of mastering those laws?

    ANS. Freedom, power and dominion over all.

18. **QUES.** By what means can that be achieved?

    ANS. By actually living the Laws of the Absolute. Their power will overcome all the limitations imposed by the laws of the Relative.

SCIENCE-OF-BEING

19. QUES.   How does the law of Polarity read?

    ANS.   "Everything in this World in the present state of human consciousness appears to have two poles, the positive and negative poles."

20. QUES.   What does the law of Polarity mean?

    ANS.   It means perpetual disharmony due to the continual fight of the two principles, the Positive and the Negative.

21. QUES.   How does one overcome it?

    ANS.   By always casting one's weight in the scale of the Positive.

22. QUES.   How can one enforce positive statements?

    ANS.   By backing them up with the following words: "With the help of the God" or "With the help of the Great Law."

23. QUES.   Why are those words so powerful?

    ANS.   Because neither God nor His Great Law have any opposites.

24. QUES.   Has the Negative any power over the Positive?

    ANS.   In reality it has not, because its non-existence, but in the present state of human consciousness it has to the extent that one concedes that power to it.

25. QUES.   Why has the Negative such power over human beings?

    ANS.   Because they believe in it and utterly fear it.

26. QUES.   How can that power be destroyed?

    ANS.   First, by discovering it; second by knowing that it is not dangerous; and finally, by realizing that it has no existence or root in the Absolute.

27. QUES.   What statement did Krishna make about the law of Polarity?

    ANS.   That God is above it.

28. QUES.   What was the comment of Jesus concerning it?

    ANS.   That the Law of God is the Only Power.

LESSON-FIVE

29. QUES.   Why is it difficult to keep a secret?
    ANS.   Because of the law of Polarity.

30. QUES.   Why is there an inevitable reaction to each action?
    ANS.   Because of the law of Polarity.

31. QUES.   What are the causes of indecision?
    ANS.   The law of Polarity.

32. QUES.   How does the law of Rhythm read?
    ANS.   "Everything in this World in the present state of human consciousness inhales and exhales, goes up and down by compensated oscillations."

33. QUES.   What is the operation of the law of Rhythm on the largest known scale?
    ANS.   In the progress and retrogression of Humanity.

34. QUES.   How does it effect individual nations?
    ANS.   They rise and fall, to rise and fall again, repeatedly, until they have learned how to overcome that law.

35. QUES.   How does the law affect individuals?
    ANS.   By bringing into their life periods of success alternating with periods of failure.

36. QUES.   How can that law be overcome in individual life?
    ANS.   By taking all possible advantages of its ascending forward movement, and by being determined not to be carried away during its backward and downward movement.

37. QUES.   Should one keep to the matter one has on hand, even through the backward movement of the law of Rhythm?
    ANS.   Yes, but one should carefully avoid starting anything new during that period, as it is bound to be a failure.

38. QUES.   What is the best general attitude during the backward movement of the law of Rhythm?

ANS.   Optimism, coupled with increased activity.

39. QUES. What changes are brought about in one's life by mastering the law of Rhythm?

      ANS.   Success without periodical failures.

40. QUES. Have those who have achieved success in their life mastered the law of Rhythm?

      ANS.   Yes.

41. QUES. Does the law of Rhythm manifest itself also on the physical plane?

      ANS.   Yes, throughout all Nature. Its operation is especially noticeable in a body of water during a storm.

42. QUES. What does the Biblical story of the dream of the Pharaoh, about the seven cows, explained by Joseph, refer to?

      ANS.   To the law of Rhythm

43. QUES. What is the law of Gender?

      ANS.   An aspect of the law of Polarity.

44. QUES. How does it read?

      ANS.   "Everything in this World in present state of human consciousness has two genders, the male and female gender."

45. QUES. How does it operate?

      ANS.   Through the influence of one gender upon the other.

46. QUES. What is the real purpose of marriage?

      ANS.   The building up of character by mutual development of complementary characteristics.

47. QUES. According to the law of Gender, what are human beings?

      ANS.   They are half-individuals, who seek completion through marriage.

48. QUES. Do men and women already possess, in a latent state, their

complementary qualities?

ANS. Yes. Each man possesses latent female qualities, and each woman latent male qualities.

49. QUES. What happens to two individuals who worked out their mutual completion?

ANS. They become independent strong, and more loving, because of their inner completion.

50. QUES. Which is the easiest way to work out that completion?

ANS. Through marriage based on mutual love.

51. QUES. If the love is on one side only, can the problem of completion be worked out?

ANS. Yes, but with much greater difficulty.

52. QUES. What chance for completion have those who married only for worldly considerations?

ANS. None whatsoever. Therefore the sooner they part, the better it is for them.

53. QUES. Is completion worked out in some other way?

ANS. Yes. In general, through association with other individuals, be it men or women.

54. QUES. Does it also affect children?

ANS. Yes. That is why co-education is desirable.

55. QUES. How does the law of Gender express itself through the human Mind?

ANS. Through the Self-consciousness, the male, and the Sub-consciousness, the female of the human Mind.

56. QUES. Does every individual, be it man or woman, have the two genders in their respective minds?

ANS. Yes.

57. QUES. What is the law of "Cause and Effect" and how does it read?

ANS. "Every effect has its cause and every cause has its effect."

58. QUES. Has the law of Cause and Effect any connection with the Laws of the Absolute?

    ANS. Yes. It has its roots in the Absolute, but, Cause and Effect being instantaneous and simultaneous there, its operation is entirely different form its mode of expression as a transitory law.

59. QUES. Why does it express itself differently as a transitory law?

    ANS. Because of our present limited concept of Time and Space.

60. QUES. How does that law affect human beings?

    ANS. It shapes their destiny.

61. QUES. Can man himself change his destiny?

    ANS. Yes, by continually starting positive causes, which will culminate in positive effects.

62. QUES. Has one control over the Past and the Future?

    ANS. None over the Past, all over the Future.

63. QUES. Of what use is the past?

    ANS. It stands as a lesson to us for the Present.

64. QUES. Which is the most important time on which to center all one's thoughts and energies?

    ANS. The ever-present NOW.

65. QUES. Why is that NOW so important?

    ANS. Because it stands for the Absolute, Which includes in Itself the Past, Present, and Future.

66. QUES. What actions does one continually perform in the ever-present NOW?

    ANS. One reaps the Past, and sows the Future.

67. QUES. Can the effect of a cause once started be avoided?

    ANS. No. The law itself prevents it.

LESSON-FIVE

68. QUES. What is the operation of the law of Cause and Effect in what is called reincarnation?

ANS. In their successive reincarnations human beings reap the effects of causes they started in previous ones.

69. QUES. Does that explain why some human beings are born with all kinds of limitations, and others with all advantages, some to suffer, other to enjoy?

ANS. Yes. It is all due to the operation of the law of Cause and Effect, which follows human beings through their successive lives, and exacts from them the last farthing.

70. QUES. Can prayer modify the operation of that law?

ANS. No. There is no pleading with the law. But prayer can give one strength to start positive causes in spite of negative effects, and thus change the Future.

71. QUES. How did Jesus formulate the law?

ANS. "With what measure ye mete, it shall be measured to you again."

72. QUES. What are the practical advantages of the knowledge of that law?

ANS. It does away with worries by enabling one to control one's Future in starting positive causes, which because of that law are bound to culminate in corresponding positive effects.

73. QUES. Is the cycle of the Seven Laws closed by that law of Cause and Effect?

ANS. Yes.

74. QUES. What is the Law of Love and the Law of Evolution?

ANS. Two divine rays of the Great Law sent down to Earth to help humanity.

75. QUES. How does the Law of Love read?

ANS. "No matter under what circumstances, always meet everything and everybody with Love."

76. QUES. What is the practical advantage of that Law?

ANS.   It destroys the Negative and strengthens the Positive as well within as without the individual who uses it.

77. QUES. Can it overcome all Negative?
      ANS.   Yes, because Love is that Infinite, Universal Power which has no equal.
            Love is both the Law and the fulfillment of the Law.

78. QUES. Why does the Negative still come to those who have risen to the highest in the Positive?
      ANS.   Because in those instances it seeks transmutation, release from its own negative condition, which can be achieved only through the Law of Love.

79. QUES. What is the Law of Evolution?
      ANS.   It is the last string of the great Lyre of human life, and is also called Hope.

80. QUES. How does it read?
      ANS.   "All vibrations tend to rise upward in the scale of Eternal Harmony."

81. QUES. What is its practical value in human life?
      ANS.   It always lifts those who are fallen, and gives hope to those who are discouraged. Being a ray of the Great Law, it continually opposes itself to the operation of the law of Polarity and Rhythm, and thus counteracts, in a certain measure their negative effects.

82. QUES. What is Evil?
      ANS.   Evil is but the negation of the Law of Evolution. It is the reversed, backward movement of positive vibrations.

LESSON SIX

SCIENCE-OF-BEING
SIXTH-DAY

LESSON - SIX
MIND-FORCE
THEORY-&-DEMONSTRATION

CREATION - MAMMALS-&-MAN

ELEMENT - FIRE

COLOR - - GREEN-YELLOW

SCIENCE·OF·BEING
SIXTH·DAY

·I·AM ALL POWER·

WITH·WHAT·POWER

THEN·ART·THOU

FIGHTING ME

LESSON · SIX
MIND·FORCE

N this present stage of Evolution it becomes vitally important for Humanity to have a thorough knowledge of the Mind, and of the laws that govern it. Evil – that is, the conscious or unconscious violation of the Laws of the Absolute, due to the reversal of the natural ascending movement of all vibrations – originated in Mind. Mind, from its mental plan, is sending its perverted vibrations into the physical, or magnetic, plane. It is Mind which,

SCIENCE-OF-BEING

when misused, debases Life, and it is the problem of Mind to regenerate Life, through the proper use of Knowledge. It is on the plane of Mind that all mistakes must be corrected, that all evil must be transmuted into good, because it is on this plane that the first negative vibrations started, and therefore must also die away. Mind has a higher rate of vibration, and hence greater power, in a way, than Life. Being aware of its own existence, it can consciously concentrate and direct its own powers wherever it wishes. When Self-Consciousness enters the ordinary Magnetic Vibrations it raises them to a certain height and changes the whole of their nature, making them conscious of their own existence. At that point they cease to be called Life Energy, and are operating under the name of Mind Force. In other words, the first manifestation of Self-conscious Magnetic Vibrations is called Mental Vibrations, whose various combinations constitute thoughts. As for the Magnetic Force within the body, the solar plexus is acting as a distributing agent for it. With the Mind Force, it is the brain which performs this office. Ideas are formed in Mind, which, working through the brain, translates those ideas into thought, and conveys them to a certain gland located at about the center of the forehead, whence they are projected into Space as Mental Vibrations. This gland is called the Pituitary Body, or Telepathic Apparatus, and its function is to send out and receive simultaneously Mental Vibrations. The Ancients, especially the Hindus, knew this function of the Pituitary Body, which they called the Bump of Wisdom, or the Eye of Siva (Mind, Lucifer). Very often their divinities and saints were represented in painting and sculpture with that Bump of Wisdom, a glowing precious stone sometimes marking its place. The Pituitary body, or Telepathic Apparatus, is a most wonderfully constructed sending and receiving station for Mental Vibrations. It is infinitely delicate and sensitive, so that it can perceive the slightest vibrations, at the greatest distance, and at the same time it is strong enough to send out vibrations of a power which has no equal on this material plane. The wireless stations which send their messages throughout the world operate on the same principle as the Pituitary Body. Only this Telepathic Apparatus, when developed, is incomparably more effective than the best wireless station. The ordinary

LESSON-SIX

Mental Vibrations proceed from the Telepathic Apparatus in so-called spheric waves – that is, like rays of light darting from a central point, and forming around that point an ever increasing sphere whose boundaries are restricted only by the magnetic attraction of the Earth, thus creating a kind of mental atmosphere surrounding this globe. So it is with all vibrations, because they are all governed in the same way by the Great Law. That peculiarity of vibrations in general explains why the ordinary thought is perceptible only at a short distance. Every thought starting from the Telepathic Apparatus is sent in innumerable mental rays, in all directions from it. Each mental message has its particular vibratory rate which, when it impinges upon the Telepathic Apparatus of another individual, is immediately translated into the original thought just as the dots and dashes of the Morse Code are translated into the words of the message by the wireless operator. A certain amount of energy is used for every individual thought. That energy is embodied in each mental ray of a thought, and manifests itself also as the attraction which holds those rays together, thus forming the above mentioned mental sphere. When starting from the Telepathic Apparatus, that sphere of Mental Vibrations is small, but its size increases almost instantaneously, because of the forward movement of the Primal Energy embodied in its component rays. Though the amount or original energy in each thought is not increased, yet the size of each mental vibratory sphere grows to almost unlimited proportions, and the same amount of energy has to cover this ever increasing area, thus weakening the Mental Vibrations to such an extent that they become almost imperceptible. This is why, when near to a center of such ordinary mental activity, one can easily perceive it – a perception which is completely lost at a certain distance, for the reasons stated above. The mental atmosphere surrounding this Earth is made of infinite varieties of these ordinary Mental Vibrations, which are called "THOUGHT DUST." They are imperceptible, because they are so diluted. Yet even that "thought dust" becomes a valuable substance when placed in contact with the concentrated thought. It is then the very element which makes that second kind of thought grow and increase in power during its projection through Space. In order to make a thought strong, and enable it to reach, as rays of light sent from a projector, any individual, no matter how far removed he may be, the spheric vibrations of the ordinary thought must be concentrated into a single ray, made one-pointed, thus sending all their power in one direction instead of letting it radiate in all directions. The way to proceed is as follows: First make the mental contact with Universal Life Energy, as indicated in Lesson II. When the Life Force is felt to flow, take a simple thought, a concrete object being preferable to an abstract one, at least for beginners. For instance, take a flower, a carnation. Then with a conscious, sustained effort of will power, concentrate the mind on that thought of the carnation. Those who do not know much about the mastery of Mind will find it rather difficult at first to do this. All kinds of extraneous thoughts will all the time flash through their minds and thus divert their attention from the original thought of the carnation. One has to watch that mind continually, and by the constant exercise of will power bring it back to the thought on which it is to be concentrated. By and by the mind, so restless and difficult to curb in the beginning, will become more docile and obedient. Concentration is a science in itself, and can be attained only through patience, perseverance, and the continual exercise of will power. When the mind has been so trained that it can remain concentrated for any length of time on a certain object, be it concrete or abstract, then the work of concentration has been properly carried out. The mental image of the carnation, mentioned above, must become so real, so tangible, that one should be able to see it, to feel it, to smell it, mentally, just as if it were an actual flower. When that is achieved, the next step is to be taken. Still holding before the mental eye the concentrated thought of the carnation, inhale deeply, thus lifting the diaphragm and expanding the solar plexus. Having reached the climax of inhalation, think for one instant about the person to whom that concentrated thought is to be sent. That quick thought is nothing but an ordinary thought which does not interfere with the concentrated one, and which can be sent out from the Telepathic Apparatus without diverting the mind from the concentrated thought. The ordinary thought, through its spheric expansion, will instantaneously reach the limits of this Earth, and will somewhere contact the person to whom the concentrated thought of the carnation is to be sent. That contact, once established, connects that person with the operator by an invisible mental line. After that, exhale, and in that moment let the concentrated thought of the carnation go. The exhalation contracts the solar plexus, which then sends through the spinal nerve and brain to the Pituitary Body the Life Force which is needed to vitalize and propel the concentrated thought. In a moment of strong desires or passion the whole process, including concentration, is done automatically, which accounts for the heavy breathing during such times. That is why thoughts sent in those moments carry with them such constructive or destructive powers. The one-pointed thought, filled with Life Energy, will dart like lightening from the Pituitary Body into Space, and because of the physical law which says "all elements choose the path of least resistance," it will follow the invisible mental line already established between the two parties by the ordinary thought. The concentrated, one-pointed thought will reach the person, no matter how far away he may be, and will strike his Telepathic Apparatus. If the individual is not concentrating his mind upon some other thought at that time, he will become conscious of the thought of the carnation. The law of Gender, explained in the fifth lesson, is continually operating also in the human mind. According to that law of human beings, both men and women, have each of them their minds manifesting the two genders, the male and the female. The Self-consciousness belongs to the male gender, and the Sub-consciousness to the female gender. All thought emanating from the Self-consciousness therefore belongs to the male gender. The one-pointed thought proceeding from the Telepathic Apparatus of an individual is naturally attracted to, and strikes, the corresponding Apparatus in another individual, which acts like a wireless receiving station. This is the first action of the one-pointed thought. After the concentrated thought of the carnation has reached the other person's Telepathic Apparatus, and produced there its impression, exactly as in the receiving station of the wireless, it does not stay there. It penetrates into the Sub-consciousness, the female mental self of the individual, and there it acts like a seed planted in the ground. It is important to note, in regard to the reception of the mental message by the Telepathic Apparatus,

SCIENCE-OF-BEING

that all thoughts are usually recorded exactly as they are received, without any increase or decrease, just as in the case of wireless messages. But when the concentrated thought of the carnation has penetrated into the other individual's Sub-consciousness, it begins to grow there like an ordinary seed thrown into the soil. The more Life Energy there was conveyed into the one-pointed thought during the exhalation and contraction of the solar plexus, the more vital that seed will become, and the stronger the growth of the mental plant springing from that seed will be. There the law of Gender has its full sway. The Sub-consciousness, the female of the mental Self, exercises the function of its gender, increasing and multiplying by many times the seed thrown into it. It is almost incredible how much the Sub-consciousness can develop and increase a strong thought seed thrown into it. In its turn, the thought seed acts like an ordinary seed. It puts forth a sprout, and sends down a root. The root penetrates deeper and deeper into the soil of the Sub-consciousness, and the sprout grows up through it into the Self-consciousness of the individual, who at that moment becomes aware of that thought planted in his Sub-consciousness. Then the individual again begins to entertain the same thought, but in a different way. It is no longer a casual thought, forgotten in the moment. Continual thinking of it takes the place of causal thought, as from the Sub-consciousness similar thoughts are all the time being sent into the Self-consciousness of the individual. The Sub-consciousness is yielding the harvest which the Self-consciousness reaps. In the aforesaid instance of the concentrated thought of the carnation, that thought seed, thrown into the field of the Sub-consciousness of the person to whom that thought was sent, will grow there and develop in the manner just explained. Then that individual will become conscious of that thought of the carnation in a most unusual way. He will no longer think of one carnation, but of a whole field of them, and of every kind. For some time his whole mind will be occupied by carnations, and the richer the harvest, the longer he will think of them. That female quality of the Sub-consciousness explains the necessity of guarding against the intrusion into it of undesirable thoughts. The Self-consciousness can, with comparative ease, destroy any undesirable thoughts merely by denying them, so long as they have not yet

penetrated into the Sub-consciousness. But once penetrated there, they become too deeply rooted to be easily removed. That is why one must be an alert sentinel at this mental door. Chronic troubles of any kind are usually due to that very reason; and until the disharmonious mental growth is extracted with all its roots, no permanent cure can be obtained. From what has been said above, it is evident that the more Life Energy there is embodied in the thought, the stronger the results will be. That explains why some individuals, devoid of any oratorical talent or harmony of speech, are nevertheless able to produce a deep impression on their audiences, while on the other hand some individuals seemingly endowed with all qualities to captivate their listeners, even if they please their audiences for the time being do not impress them lastingly. Lack of vitality is the cause of it. They have not sufficient life energy within themselves, or don't know how to contact it outside themselves, in order to produce on the public an abiding impression. As a general rule, simple, short thoughts give better results than long, complicated ones, because of that peculiarity of the Sub-consciousness, of breaking up into their component parts all such compounded thoughts. A complex thought being thus divided, its strength is proportionally lessened. The Sub-consciousness, being below the Self-conscious status, rears and develops without discrimination any kind of thought, the negative as well as the positive. It is the field in which wheat and tares are growing together, until the day of harvest, when the Self-consciousness makes a selection and throws away the tares, keeping the wheat. In that scientific mental work, every action is based upon and governed by a mental law. Therefore there is no need to worry or doubt that proper results will be obtained, as long as the mental law is rightly applied. It is just as exact in its results as is the solution of a mathematical problem according to the laws of mathematics. That second operation of the same thought is a very important one in Mental Science, because of the extraordinary results obtained through it.

卐 Last comes the third operation of the same thought. Of all three, it is the least known, and at first sight, seems the least important. Yet it is of the greatest importance, especially to the operator, because it concerns him directly and most vitally. After the thought has accomplished its procreative function in the Sub-consciousness, it does not remain there. It proceeds further, and again like a ray it darts into Space. There that concentrated, one-pointed thought, full of Life Energy, proceeds at an incredible speed through Space, and goes as far as the Earth magnetic attraction permits it. The more Life Force there was embodied in that thought, the further it will go, and the stronger power of attraction it will develop. Because of that inherent quality of attraction, that living, concentrated mental ray, flashing through Space which is filled with "thought dust," attracts to it loose particles of the ordinary spheric thought vibrations, the product of thinking Humanity. Thought particles of the same rate of vibration, of the same kind and character, are attracted to that mental magnet which is the one-pointed thought. And that thought, rushing through Space, thus grows continually bigger and stronger. When the propulsive power embodied in the thought at the moment of its start from the Telepathic Apparatus has finally been neutralized by the Earth attraction, the one-pointed thought-ray is then compelled by that physical law to turn back, and return to its starting point. Like an ordinary projectile, it describes its course in an ellipse. It acts like a boomerang, that peculiarly shaped weapon made of light wood curved in a certain way, which the Australian natives use especially to hunt birds. Thrown into the air, after it has reached its mark the boomerang returns to the thrower. The one-pointed thought is indeed a boomerang. It finally always returns to the one who sent it. And on its backward course the concentrated thought, passing always through the "thought dust" of this planet, still grows and grows, so that when it finally comes back to the one that first sent it, it is usually not recognized, because it has become so big. It is indeed difficult to recognize, in the strong, lusty, thought-fellow, the original thought-child which was sent into the World. And because of that change, very often it is refused admission by its own parent. No thought, no feeling, no action, good or evil, is ever lost. Soon or late it will come back. It is unavoidable, because it is a law, which is often called the law of Retribution. It is considered a moral law, the operation of Divine Justice, yet in reality it is nothing but a physical law, which no man living in a physical body can

ever avoid, because it is a law of Nature. When human beings will know that to be a law with which no avoidance, pleading, or compromise is possible, they will, out of self-protection, cease to send unkind thoughts or feelings, or perform evil actions, because they will know that soon or late they will have to encounter the consequences. And the shock will be great, because concentrated thoughts always come back vastly increased. This mental law explains that statement of Jesus which created so much discussion among all Christian theologians, and which was never settled by them in a satisfactory way. Jesus said, "WITH WHAT MEASURE YE METE, IT SHALL BE MEASURED TO YOU AGAIN," and He added also, "THAT THE MEASURE WOULD BE FULL, PRESSED DOWN AND RUNNING OVER."

卐 Almost everyone has had the experience in life that kind thoughts or good actions which they continually bestowed upon some individuals, were not at all appreciated, and seemed to be entirely wasted. Ingratitude was often the only return for such kindness, which naturally caused great disappointment. On the other hand, for no apparent reason, complete strangers with whom one was later thrown in contact began to show unexpected kindness in thought and deed. Naturally, an unconscious comparison between the two cases arises in one's mind, and the question presents itself of why those to whom good was done did not respond, while others to whom nothing was given became channels for good to be expressed. And because that good came from strangers, it made one feel almost uncomfortable, so that one was even tempted to refuse it. That must never be done, however, because it means to refuse admission to one's own thoughts or actions. Those kind thoughts or deeds which were considered lost are thus coming back to their author, and vastly increased, for the reasons explained above. Good thoughts are to be received with joy, and evil thoughts with love, so as to transmute their nature from negative to positive. No matter how much one may try to prevent those thoughts from coming back, they will continually return until they gain admission.

卐 The concentrated thought, when filled with Life Energy, possesses a tremendous creative power. As the law of Attraction is continually operating

SCIENCE·OF·BEING

through it, it gradually attracts all the elements necessary to bring that thought into actual manifestation on this material plane. Thus all human desires can be scientifically realized in one's life, if they are not contrary to the Universal Laws. The following method can be used to secure the desired success. After the mental contact with the Universal Life Energy is made, concentrate the thought, as explained previously, on the desired object. Make it so real, mentally, that it will seem to be an actual fact. Repeat this as often as possible, and at the same time use constant effort to come into material contact with the desired object, which will then finally grow into one's life. Life Energy, with its unlimited power of Attraction, will attract to the mental concept of the concentrated thought the material elements for its expression. Never doubt, or fear that it will not be so, because fear or doubt will prevent the realization of one's desires. Remember that, in conjunction with the mental law, is continually operating the Law of Attraction. All one needs to do is to perform one's part properly, and leave the rest to the law of Cause and Effect, the continual operation of which will bring about the desired results. Thus worry, that great enemy of all unfoldment, will also be destroyed. As an artist, before painting a picture, must have it already created in his mind, so it is in life. First must be created, by the concentrated thought, the mental image of the thing one desires. Repeatedly dwelling on it increases its powers in every direction, and condenses them until, like invisible vapors which, when condensed, appear suddenly as a visible drop, they burst forth in a material realization. The more Life Force there is used in the concentrated thought, the stronger are those powers manifested in it. By continual contact, through the mental method, with Universal Life Energy, that power is developed to an ever increasing degree. Thus every human being can by and by have all his desires realized, if he will persevere long enough in constructive work in that direction on the two planes, the mental and the physical. With Mental Vibrations, as with everything else, perseverance is one of the important factors of Success. Therefore the cardinal point to be remembered is that in order to obtain Success, mental activities must be combined with actual driving and working in the same direction also on the material plane.

LESSON-SIX

The reason why our creative thoughts and desires are not immediately realized is because of our present material state of consciousness, which must translate everything into its own terms to make it tangible. In other words, physical effort and work are necessary to materialize it in ones' life. When our state of consciousness will have risen to the plane of Mind, every thought will be a creation by itself, and just as real and tangible to those living on that plane as are material things to us now. Then the whole World will be a mental World, in which Humanity will live unrestricted by the physical, material limitations which now bind them. Yet even that is not a perfect condition, as the human mind is still full of its own limitations. It is Lucifer, who is still an exile from Heaven, and who therefore cannot grasp such concepts as Infinity and Eternity. Only when Love, the Christ element in each human being, will have purified the human mind, and restored Lucifer, the fallen one, to his original status of eternal perfection, will Mind break all its limitations, and be reunited with the Infinite and Eternal. That last step will be called the Spiritual State of Consciousness. And when Humanity will have reached it, they will realize that the Realm of Spirit is all there is.

The power of concentrated thought has a special application in healing all kinds of troubles, physical, mental, and emotional. These, in the form commonly called diseases, are like parasites preying on their victim. They clog the normal functions of the body, which becomes sluggish or temporarily abortive, although their fundamental natures remain the same. Such mental parasites appear to be negative through and through, yet that is not the case. Even mental germs of diseases, or evil thoughts, could have no actual power if it were not for the Life Energy which animates them. In those instances perfect Life Energy is clothed with negative thought films, which hold it imprisoned. It is like a soap bubble which, although it may appear to be a homogeneous mass throughout, is nothing but a tiny film separating the air within from the air without. A slight touch breaks the film, and the soap bubble is no more. So it is with diseases and all other kinds of negative thoughts growing in the field of the Sub-consciousness. They are but bubbles of evil, and are destroyed by the strong contact of a concentrated, positive thought. The bubble of evil then bursts, and Life Energy, pure and perfect, is liberated from it, to become one with the concentrated thought, thus increasing that thought's healing power. The negative is destroyed in that way, by the proper use of mental laws.

卐 Whenever a case of negative condition is handled, the first thing to do is to make the mental contact with Universal Life Energy, and let the magnetic current flow into the body of the patient until the point of saturation is reached. The next step is to deny silently the fear of the trouble which is besetting the patient. Negation of anything on the mental plane means death to the thing which is denied. As the fear of any kind of trouble is the power by which that trouble has hold of an individual, it is therefore essential first to deny and thus destroy that fear. That fear once destroyed, the elimination of the trouble itself is a comparatively easy task. There is another reason why it is preferable to deny the fear of a trouble rather than to deny the trouble itself. A silent denial of the negative condition itself is usually not very favorably accepted by the patient's mind. To deny a violent headache, which appears so real to the one who has it, will result only in stirring up a silent mental protest in the mind of the patient. "My head is splitting, and you try to assure me that there is no headache," is the retort of the mind to such a denial. On the other hand, the denial of the fear of the same negative condition will produce opposite results in the mind of the patient, which will say, "It is true that my head aches terribly, but I do not fear it; I am brave enough to face it, and to try to overcome it." Such a method of procedure always works better, because of the peculiar psychology of the mind of the individual. Everyone likes to be called brave, and even the human mind is not an exception to that general rule. Mental denials should never be made in an aggressive tone, for two reasons. First, it would antagonize the patient's mental self; secondly, it would show that the operator himself is making a reality out of that trouble which he tries to remove. Those who are conscious of their own power are always calm and dignified, and never aggressive, because aggressiveness is due to latent fear, and is therefore weakness, not strength. Neither must the denial be too often repeated, as otherwise it may produce just the opposite result from the desired one. By too many repetitions of the denial, unfortunately the trouble itself, which one is supposed to destroy, is being emphasized, because the patient's mind is continually dwelling on it, with the result that the trouble one wishes to overcome has been greatly increased in the patient's mind. A strong, calm, dignified, denial produces the best results. The only consideration Jesus ever showed to evil was to say, "Get thee behind me, Satan!" He knew the law, and scientifically applied it all the time, because He was the greatest scientist the world has ever known. After the denial of the fear of the trouble, the operator must realize within his own mind the opposite Positive Reality. There, all the science and knowledge derived from the previous lessons must be properly utilized. The basic, eternal Truth to be realized is that man is the eternal and perfect manifestation of the Absolute, and is in direct and constant relation with It. That realization of Eternal Harmony is often called the "DECLARATION OF TRUTH." It is indeed a declaration of Truth, the stating of those Eternal Verities. It is just the opposite of what are commonly called suggestions. There the operator, by the use of the mental laws, merely suggest to the patient a certain thought. That thought may or may not be true, yet the Self-consciousness may accept it because of ignorance, and the Sub-consciousness develop it, being without the power of discrimination between good and evil. Such a method is reprehensible, because it is not based on a Universal Law, but on personal will power. The statements of the Positive Reality are like harmonious notes, which are caught by the mental strings of the patient in responsive vibrations to the original sound, because each individual possess within himself those latent strings of perfection, WHICH ARE HIS OWN BY BIRTHRIGHT, being a part of his eternal nature. It is the awakening of an individual to his own eternal, perfect status, and the more the individual becomes conscious of it, the greater is the victory on the side of the positive. The thoughts of health and harmony sent by the operator to his patient are both healing vibrations and seeds of health. The operator must never make a reality out of the trouble he wishes to overcome in this patient. Though performing all that mental work within his own mind according to the rules stated in the beginning of this lesson, he does it only for the patient. The operator's own knowledge of the unreality of all negative must be so strong that he does not need to deny for himself even the fear of its existence. All the operator needs to do is to change the patient's way of thinking, by destroying those negative bubbles of evil in all its manifold aspects. Once the field of the Sub-consciousness of the patient is weeded of all mental tares, the wheat – that is, the normal, positive, thoughts – will grow and manifest itself in the activities of the person. Then the patient is healed. In severe chronic cases, after several successful mental treatments, the individual often has a sudden relapse. Negative physical and mental developments may become so pronounced that the patient feels he cannot stand it any longer. He feels as if all the powers of evil were loosed upon him, depriving him even of the hope of a possible recovery. It is a condition so painful that many cannot bear it, and request the operator to stop the treatment, as they seem to be growing worse all the time. Yet it is a good sign, after all. It is called "MENTAL CHEMICALIZATION," or uprooting of the negative thoughts from the Sub-consciousness of the individual. When a plant of the negative feels its last hour has come, it clings with all its power, through its roots, to the soil of the Sub-consciousness. Naturally then, the process of eradication from the Sub-consciousness is, like every extraction, a very painful operation, the more so because it is mental instead of physical. In such a case the operator must explain to the patient the causes of that reaction, and show him the advantage of carrying that operation to the very end. In some cases the negative in the patient seems to be so strong that it is felt, even by the operator himself, as a great pressure which he is unable to lift. In such a case the mental treatment must be stopped for a while and the whole work left exclusively to the Magnetic Force. After a little while the Life Energy of the Universe, flowing through the operator to the patient, will, with its wonderful basic qualities of harmony, restore harmony within the operator, who will then be able to resume the mental work.

卐 As with the magnetic treatments, so also with the mental ones. It is impossible to tell how long a patient should be treated. Each case must be handled individually, and as there are no two cases alike, it is left to each individual's intuitive powers to know when to stop. A fairly good indication

LeSSON-SIX

that the treatment is successfully completed is a certain sense of relief and harmony which then pervades the operator. Mental treatments may last from five minutes to several hours, in some exceptionally acute cases. Whenever possible they ought to be combined with magnetic treatments, because in that way the negative conditions are simultaneously attacked and destroyed in both the body and the mind of the patient, thus bringing better and quicker results.

卐 No mental treatment of any kind should be given to people without their knowledge and their special consent. The following exceptions may be considered: First, in treating insane people, whose minds are not capable of determining whether they wish to be treated or not. Second, in cases where people, through accident or for any other reason, were rendered unconscious. Third, intoxicated persons whose powers of discrimination are temporarily in abeyance. When handling such cases, the operator must be very careful to protect himself from mental transmissions of the physical condition of the patient, as otherwise the patient will be disintoxicated at the expense of the operator, who will in his turn become intoxicated. The fourth instance of mental treatment without the consent of the individual is in the case of small children, who are not yet sufficiently developed in their conscious status to make their own choice. In such cases the consent of the parents, especially of the mother, is absolutely necessary. Without that consent no successful treatment could be given to a child, because the mother thought acts upon a child as the protecting cloak. Therefore not only the consent of the mother is required, but she must be included in the treatment in order to reach her child properly.

卐 As a general rule, it is advisable always to protect oneself mentally, when treating, from the possible transfer of the negative condition of the patient to the operator. Also when in a crowd, or among people whose thoughts are not harmonious, that self protection is necessary. It is achieved by mentally denying the possibility of transfer of such condition from one individual to another. It is like surrounding one's self with a mental wall which, if properly built, is strong enough to repel any such negative intrusions. Yet when building

195

that mental wall of self protection, one must be very careful not to entertain any fear or doubt of its efficacy. One must remember that ONE IS A LAW TO ONE'S SELF ON THE PLANE OF MIND, and doubts and fears are cracks in that mental wall of self protection, through which that from which it is desired to be protected can penetrate.

卐 Though the wall of mental protection is a good bulwark against the ordinary mental intruder, it is not sufficient when dealing with so-called mental malpractices – that is, the use of mental forces by some individual for evil ends. There the only complete self protection is vibrations of Love. These being all powerful, perfect in every way, pervading the three planes, the physical, the mental, and the Spiritual, they form around one a sphere of Love which, like a diamond armor, repels and destroys every negative vibration launched against it. That important point must always be remembered, THAT LOVE IS THE ONLY SAFE PROTECTION WE HAVE.

卐 Whenever Mental Vibrations are used on one's own self, be it for healing, business, mental self-development, or any other purpose, the same process is employed as described in the beginning of this lesson, with the sole difference that the concentrated thought must be, so to say, inhaled together with the air when the diaphragm is lifted and the solar plexus expanded. Thus the concentrated thought will be thrown by the Self-consciousness of the operator directly into his own Sub-consciousness, where the process of multiplication and development is the same as when that concentrated thought is thrown into the Sub-consciousness of another individual. Needless to say, the ordinary thought necessary to establish a connection between two parties is not to be used here. It is exactly the process used when one is trying to learn something by heart. To memorize properly means to plant one's own thought seeds in the ground of one's own Sub-consciousness, where they will in due time yield a harvest. To remember is nothing but the ability to contact at will one's own Sub-consciousness, where all impressions are stored. When treating oneself mentally, it is always advisable to start with the magnetic treatment, because of extraordinary harmonizing effect of the Magnetic Vibrations.

LESSON~SIX

When treating patients at a distance, the ordinary Mental Vibrations do not imply by themselves a magnetic treatment. In order to combine the two, the following method is to be used. Concentrate the mind on the patient in such a way as to think of him as present. Make the mental image of the patient so real and tangible that he appears to be actually present, in the physical body. The mental image of the patient thus created will be the reflection of his physical self, and each mental cell of that reflection of his body will be connected by invisible Mental Vibrations with the corresponding cell of the physical body of the patient. As there are about fifty billion cells in the human body, each of which vibrates independently of the others, the mental image of the patient will therefore have at least fifty billion mental lines through which will flow the magnetic current directed to that mental image by the operator. In order to increase the flow of the magnetic current to the mental image created by the operator, it is advisable not only to direct one's hands, as indicated in the magnetic treatment, toward the mental image, but also to use (especially for beginners) either a chair or some other convenient material object, which must be imagined to be the body of the patient, and on which the hands of the operator may rest. The magnetic current sent into that material object will, because of the mental image of the patient intimately connected with the object, be transmitted from it to the patient in the manner previously stated. During such absent treatments, another feature can be taken advantage of, which it is not advisable to employ in present treatments. Audible treatment can be applied. The sound vibrations of the spoken words will also strike the mental image of the patient, and from there will be conveyed, together with the magnetic current, to the patient himself, thus increasing the power of the Magnetic Vibrations. When properly executed, such combined absent treatments secure most powerful results. In fact, they are much stronger than the ordinary treatments, with the patient actually present, because the patient's negative condition produces no impression on the operator, and therefore has no effect on him, on account of the distance which separates the two. Usually the patient, on the other end of the mental line, feels the presence of the operator, as vividly, as tangibly and closely, as if he were actually there, in his physical body. In some instances the patient may even see the operator and talk with him, and be convinced that the operator really came to him, although the operator may be, at that time, a thousand miles away. That peculiar mental and magnetic phenomenon, based on the law of Vibration, explains how sometimes the same individual is seen by people at the same time in several different places. For some reason, those people were thinking very strongly about the one who appeared to them in what is called his "astral body." Through one of his rays they perceived the whole individual, as through a ray of the sun we can see the sun itself. And as each individual radiates innumerable rays, many people can therefore simultaneously perceive that individual across Space in various places. All that is necessary is that they shall be "en rapport" with him – in other words, they should be magnetically and mentally attuned.

There is another form of mental force which is much used nowadays, and which is called hypnotism and suggestion. Suggestion includes also auto-suggestion. Those methods are all fundamentally immoral, and therefore reprehensible. They violate one of the basic rights and privileges of every human being, the right of self-determination. They are based exclusively on Will Power, and their method consists in using that Will Power in connection with thoughts in order to subjugate the other individual's will power. If abused, they utterly destroy the character of the subject, and even when used with moderation, they still always neutralize his individuality. Even auto-suggestion works destructively, in the respect that by continual repetition of the same thought, the mind of the individual becomes numbed, mentally frozen, almost lifeless, acting like an automaton. This shows how unscientific such methods are since they can produce such negative results. Hypnotism, suggestion and auto-suggestion, instead of building up the character destroy it, and make their victims helpless puppets in the hands of the outrager. Many crimes and evil actions have been performed by different people and were attributed solely to them, when in reality they were nothing but channels through which was operating the hidden mental power of some other individual. Under no consideration should anyone ever use that power, even for healing purposes, nor should one ever let oneself be hypnotized, even if

LESSON~SIX

only for the sake of an experiment. In every instance, a mental and moral loss will be the result of it, and even the operator himself cannot escape the penalty for violating such fundamental laws. Soon or late, as a result of the reaction of his own destructive thoughts and activities, in accordance with the operation of the mental laws, he himself will lose all will power, will have his mental and moral forces almost entirely obliterated, and will die a physical, mental and moral wreck. No one should ever expect to be able to escape such penalty, because there is no compromise with the laws of Nature.

卐 On the other hand, the scientific mental treatment, as was stated previously, consists in affirming Eternal Verities, without any desire to force them upon one. The mental laws will take care that a result shall be obtained. The personal responsibility of the operator is thrown entirely upon the laws themselves, and the laws take good care that everything shall be carried out properly. That scientific method of mental treatment is the stimulation of the individual and his awakening to his true status. The suggestion method, on the contrary, thickens the veil of the individual consciousness, and paralyzes its activities.

卐 Humanity of today passes through a great crisis. The development of man's latent forces, the power of the liberated thought, bring about fundamental changes in human nature. The ordinary means by which the outside world is contacted are no longer sufficient. New ways are sought – and found. Until today human beings have been conscious of only five senses, channels through which impressions are conveyed to them or from them. As Humanity is now approaching the sixth period of its evolution, called allegorically in the Bible the sixth day of creation, a new sense, the sixth sense, is being developed. That new channel through which impressions are conveyed is called "Intuition." Intuition is that something which so often speaks within us, and seems to tell us what to do, and what not to do. It is not the voice of our conscience, which is heard only when we have done something wrong. It is a "still, small voice," called often the voice of God, of Divinity, but which after all is only our own higher Self, called the Super-consciousness, of which our Self-consciousness becomes aware. Our higher Self knows everything. It is not limited by Time or Space, and does not need Reason to aid its mental work. It knows, because it embraces simultaneously the cause and the effect, the past, present and future. Whenever we listen to that small voice of Intuition, and follow its advice, we obtain positive results, though sometimes that voice seems to speak against our own reason. After all, it is but a seeming contradiction of our reason, due to the present limitation of that faculty. In order to develop Intuition, we must train ourselves to differentiate between the voice of our own desires, and that of our Super-consciousness. There is an easy way to discriminate between the two. Whenever Intuition speaks to us, there is felt a peculiar sense of peace and harmony, though it may happen in a moment of most disharmonious conditions. On the other hand, when our desires speak within us, a sensation of restlessness comes upon us. Therefore listen to the voice of peace and wisdom which will lead one into Harmony, and discard the aggressive clamor of desires, as no good will come out of it. The more one listens to Intuition, the more is Intuition developed, and the surer and wiser become all our actions. Thus human beings, in developing within themselves that Divine Ray of Intuition, will manifest Wisdom, will become six-pointed stars, stars of wisdom, and will bring about the Dawn of the New Day, the Day of Peace, of Harmony and Power.

QVESTIONS & ANSWERS

LESSON SIX

1. QUES.   What is one of the great problems of today?
   ANS.   To educate one's mind to regenerate itself.

2. QUES.   How is it done?
   ANS.   By raising the vibrations of Mind to those of Truth and Love.

3. QUES.   How did the first mistake originate?
   ANS.   It originated through Mind, and through Mind it must be destroyed.

4. QUES.   How does Mind express itself in our present state of consciousness?
   ANS.   Through Mental Vibrations, combined units of which are called thoughts.

5. QUES.   What are Mental Vibrations?
   ANS.   The first manifestation of Self-conscious Magnetic Vibrations.

6. QUES.   What role does the brain play in the thinking process?
   ANS.   It acts as a transmitting station.

7. QUES.   What is the Telepathic Apparatus?
   ANS.   It is the Pituitary Body, located in the front part of our brain, which sends out into Space Mental Vibrations, in the form of thoughts.

8. QUES.   Does the Telepathic Apparatus also receive mental messages?
   ANS.   Yes. It is both a sending and receiving station.

9. QUES.   How does the ordinary thought proceed?
   ANS.   In spheric mental waves emanating from the Telepathic Apparatus.

10. QUES.   Is the ordinary thought perceptible at a long distance?
    ANS.   No, because it becomes too diluted.

11. QUES. What is thought dust?
    ANS. Loose particles of ordinary thoughts, floating in Space and surrounding the Earth like a cloud.

12. QUES. How is the thought made strong and perceptible at any distance?
    ANS. By concentrating it, making it ONE POINTED.

13. QUES. How is this done?
    ANS. Through an effort of will power the Spheric Mental Vibrations are focused in one point.

14. QUES. How is a concentrated thought sent at a distance?
    ANS. By using the Life Energy stored in the solar plexus to propel that thought.

15. QUES. What will be the guiding line which will bring that thought to its destination?
    ANS. Invisible mental lines previously established by the ordinary thought between the sender and the receiver.

16. QUES. To what gender does thought belong in general?
    ANS. Every thought passing through the Self-consciousness, which is of the male gender, assumes that gender.

17. QUES. How many genders are there in Mind?
    ANS. Two; the male, represented by the Self-consciousness, and the female, represented by the Sub-consciousness.

18. QUES. Has every individual the two genders in their receptive minds?
    ANS. Yes, without distinction of sex.

19. QUES. What is the first operation of the concentrated thought send through space?
    ANS. It strikes the Telepathic Apparatus of the receiving individual, is from there conveyed to the brain, and the individual becomes conscious of it.

LESSON-SIX

20. **QUES.** What is the second operation of the same concentrated thought?
    ANS. After having contacted the Telepathic Apparatus, it sinks into the Sub-consciousness of the receiving individual.

21. **QUES.** What does it do there?
    ANS. It grows like an ordinary seed thrown into the soil.

22. **QUES.** What is the main quality of the Sub-consciousness.
    ANS. It increases and multiples every thought seed thrown into it.

23. **QUES.** Does the Sub-consciousness possess the power of discrimination?
    ANS. No. Being below the Self-conscious state, it does not know how to differentiate between the positive and the negative, and rears the wrong as well as the right.

24. **QUES.** When does the Self-consciousness become aware of the thought seed thrown   in its own Sub-consciousness?
    ANS. When the thought seed becoming a thought plant, penetrates into the Self-consciousness.

25. **QUES.** Why is it difficult to eradicate a thought from the Sub-consciousness?
    ANS. Because it has rooted itself there.

26. **QUES.** What is the next operation of the concentrated thought?
    ANS. It leaves the receiving individual and proceeds again into Space.

27. **QUES.** How does it act there?
    ANS. Like a torpedo it rushes through Space, attracting to it loose particles of thought dust of corresponding rates of vibration.

28. **QUES.** Why does it attract those thought particles?
    ANS. Because of the magnetic power of attraction of the Life Energy with which the concentrated thought is charged.

29. **QUES.** What is the result of that attraction?

ANS.   The concentrated thought grows bigger and stronger.

30. QUES. How far does it proceed into Space?
      ANS.   As far as the Earth's attraction permits it.

31. QUES. What then happens to the thought?
      ANS.   Like a boomerang, it returns to its point of departure.

32. QUES. What laws govern the operation of the thought?
      ANS.   The same laws acting on the mental plane which govern physical bodies on the physical plane.

33. QUES. Does the concentrated thought return direct to its starting point?
      ANS.   If it was sent into Space without any definite destination, it returns directly. If it was sent to another individual, in returning it uses some individual as a transmitting station.

34. QUES. Why is it transmitting station needed in the latter case?
      ANS.   Because of the law of Polarity.

35. QUES. Why is the concentrated thought often not recognized on its return?
      ANS.   Because it has grown so big.

36. QUES. Is any thought, feeling, or action, good or evil, ever lost?
      ANS.   No. It always comes back to its author, vastly increased.

37. QUES. Is there any possible way to avoid that coming back?
      ANS.   No, because it is due to the operation of the law, and one reaps what one has sown.

38. QUES. What does the third operation of the concentrated thought explain?
      ANS.   That saying of Jesus, "With what measure ye mete it shall be measured to you again – a measure full, pressed down, and RUNNING OVER."

LESSON-SIX

39. QUES. What is the difference between a creative thought, and simply a thought?

    ANS. The creative thought is charged to the full with Magnetic Life Energy. The ordinary thought, on the contrary, has only a very limited amount of Life Energy.

40. QUES. What power does the creative thought possess?

    ANS. It attracts to us all things which we may desire.

41. QUES. Can we have all our desires thus realized?

    ANS. Yes, if they are not contrary to the Universal Laws.

42. QUES. Which is the best method of securing the desired success?

    ANS. Make the mental contact with Universal Life Energy. Make the desired object real mentally. Repeat this as often as possible, and the desired object will come into one's life through the power of attraction of the creative thought.

43. QUES. Is it also necessary to use physical effort to bring about the desired success?

    ANS. Yes, because of our present state of consciousness, which makes it necessary to translate everything also into Matter in order to materialize it in ones' life.

44. QUES. When will thought become an actual direct creation?

    ANS. When Lucifer, the fallen Mind, will be restored to his original status of Eternal Perfection.

45. QUES. What will that last step be called?

    ANS. The Spiritual State of Consciousness, Heaven, or the Realm of Harmony.

46. QUES. What are diseases?

    ANS. They are mental parasites, preying on the Sub-consciousness of the individual, and manifesting themselves to him in the form of ailments.

47. QUES. Are those mental parasites negative through and through?

ANS.   No. They are but thin films of negative vibrations imprisoning the positive Life Energy within them.

48.   QUES.   How can they be destroyed?

      ANS.   By concentrated positive Mental Vibrations, which will pierce them like an arrow.

49.   QUES.   What is the best way to treat diseases mentally?

      ANS.   First, deny the fear of the disease; next, mentally realize the positive truth back of that denial.

50.   QUES.   How many times should the denial of a fear be repeated?

      ANS.   One short denial, with authority and force, is sufficient.

51.   QUES.   What positive statements should be used in order to bring about the healing?

      ANS.   All knowledge concerning Man's eternal and direct relation with the Absolute, and his perfect status in the Realm of Eternal Harmony, should be realized in treating the patient mentally.

52.   QUES.   What are the effects of the positive work of the concentrated thought?

      ANS.   It awakens within the patient the conscious realization of his eternal perfect status and thus heals him.

53.   QUES.   Is it necessary to picture mentally the body of a patient as perfect?

      ANS.   No. All that is needed is the realization that the fundamental vibrations of the body of the patient, representing the activities of his soul are basically harmonious.

54.   QUES.   Is it necessary, when treating the patient mentally, to treat him also magnetically at the same time?

      ANS.   It is advisable, whenever possible, to combine the two treatments, for the following reasons: First, because of the extraordinary harmonizing effect of the Magnetic Life Force on both operator and subject; and secondly, because the negative is thus attacked from two sides – from the outside magnetically, and from the inside mentally.

LESSON-SIX

55. QUES. What is the best attitude for the operator to take during mental healing?

    ANS. An attitude of love and compassion.

56. QUES. What is mental chemicalization?

    ANS. It is the reaction of the Negative to the mental influence of the Positive. The bubble of the Negative inflates to the limit before bursting.

57. QUES. What is to be done in case of mental chemicalization?

    ANS. Explain to the patient the causes of it, and persevere in the treatment to the end.

58. QUES. How long should one treat mentally?

    ANS. No, definite rule can be given, the operator must sense within himself when to stop. As a general rule, from five to fifteen minutes is quite sufficient; in exceptionally acute cases treatments may last several hours.

59. QUES. Can one treat people mentally without their special consent for it?

    ANS. No, except in the following instances: First, when treating insane people; secondly, when treating people rendered unconscious; third, intoxicated people; fourth, children.

60. QUES. How should children be treated?

    ANS. By including the mother also in the treatment.

61. QUES. Is it advisable to protect oneself mentally when treating patients, or when mingling with different people?

    ANS. Yes, in order to prevent the penetration of undesirable thought seeds into one's sub-conscious mind.

62. QUES. How is that protection established?

    ANS. By building around oneself a mental wall.

63. QUES. Does mental protection secure one complete safety?

    ANS. No. Only Love Vibrations give one complete protection,

because they form around an individual a complete sphere of vibrations which nothing negative can pierce through. Love is the only safe protection we have.

64. QUES. What process is to be used in mental self healing?
    ANS. The same method as is used in healing others, except that instead of sending the concentrated thought to another individual, it is allowed to sink into one's own Sub-consciousness.

65. QUES. Can magnetic and mental treatments be combined when treating a patient at a distance?
    ANS. Yes.

66. QUES. What is the method of procedure?
    ANS. Create through mental concentration the image of the patient. Then treat that image both magnetically and mentally as if it were actually the patient himself.

67. QUES. Through what means will the Magnetic and Mental Forces be conveyed from the image to the patient himself?
    ANS. Through billions of mental lines connecting the two.

68. QUES. Is it advisable to use audible mental treatment in such cases?
    ANS. Yes.

69. QUES. What is the difference between the scientific method of mental treatment, and hypnotism, suggestion, and auto-suggestion?
    ANS. The first awakens the individual to his true, perfect, and eternal status. The second, third and fourth, paralyze the expression of individuality by substituting new beliefs for old ones.

70. QUES. Are hypnotism, suggestion, and auto-suggestion dangerous?
    ANS. Yes, they are one of the most dangerous and most immoral abuses of Mental Force.

71. QUES. Should hypnotism, suggestion, or auto-suggestion be used in therapeutics?
    ANS. No, under no consideration.

LESSON-SIX

72. QUES.   What is the penalty for the abuse of Mental Force?
    ANS.   The complete loss of it.

73. QUES.   What is the sixth sense?
    ANS.   It is Intuition.

74. QUES.   How does Intuition express itself?
    ANS.   Through an inner voice which is continually speaking to us.

75. QUES.   What is the practical value of Intuition?
    ANS.   It enables one to sense Truth independently of the reasoning powers.

76. QUES.   What is the sign by which the voice of Intuition can be distinguished from other inner voices?
    ANS.   Whenever Intuition speaks to us, a peculiar sense of peace and harmony is felt.

77. QUES.   How can Intuition be developed?
    ANS.   By continually listening to its voice, and co-ordinating our reason with it.

78. QUES.   What are the practical results obtained by developing Intuition?
    ANS.   Man will become six-pointed that means, perfectly balanced.

79. QUES.   What effect would that have on Humanity's Evolution?
    ANS.   It would bring about the dawn of the New Day, the Day of Peace, of Harmony, and of Power.

SCIENCE·OF·BEING

LESSON SEVEN

SCIENCE·OF·BEING
SEVENTH·DAY

LESSON·SEVEN
SPIRITVAL·POWER
THEORY
PVRIFICATION·BY·FIRE
'I·AM·THE·FIRE·THAT·BVRNS·AWAY·ALL·DROSS,
LEAVING·BEHIND·THE·SHINING·MIRROR·OF·THE·SOVL'
INITIATION·-
THE·SPIRITVAL·MAN·

CREATION · THE·ABSOLVTE·IS
REVEALED·
ELEMENT · AIR·· (ETHER)
COLOR · · WHITE·SILVER

SCIENCE·OF·BEING
SEVENTH·DAY

LESSON·SEVEN
SPIRITUAL·POWER

SPIRITUAL Power is obtained only by those who honestly and unselfishly live a life of Activity, Intelligence, Truth, and Love. As it was explained in the First Lesson, they are bound to reach Spirit, the culminant point of the Life Pyramid, not only because they want to be Spiritual, but because in living their daily life according to the Laws of the Absolute they cannot help reaching Spirit through the operation of the very laws they live.

SCIENCE-OF-BEING

᭰ First a few glimpses of that Spiritual Power will come to them. They will, during their silence and in contacting the Universal Life Energy, rise higher and higher until finally they will reach Spiritual Vibrations, which are the highest we know of in our present state of consciousness. Very often high mental vibrations are taken for Spiritual ones, but whoever has experienced Spiritual Vibrations can never confuse the two. When mental vibrations rise very high, they become not only very powerful but also very soothing and harmonious because of their approach to the Spiritual Plane. Still they are not yet Spiritual.

᭰ Mental vibrations can come very close to Perfection, but they cannot yet enter the Gates of Perfection because of the peculiar condition in which the human Mind is now. Mind, Lucifer, is still an exile from Heaven; he has not the right to return to his Eternal Home until he has learned the lesson of Love, has permeated his own quality with the quality of his Eternal Twin, Love (Christ). Until our Mind is pervaded with absolute Love, that Mind will still remain at the Gates of Heaven and will not enter in. It is only Love, the Christ element within us, which can bear us through the Gates of Heaven into Eternal Harmony. Mind has to give up its work there and let Inspiration and Love take us by the hand and lead us into the Realm of Spirit.

᭰ The previous six lessons were gradually preparing the student for this last Seventh Lesson. There has been a great deal of detail in these lessons; but when one comes to the apex, to Spirit, there everything is simplicity, and because of that wonderful simplicity, the Seventh lesson can be properly received only through Intuition and Inspiration.

᭰ Yet, even in this instance, there is a certain way of procedure to reach Spiritual Vibrations, and the theory of it is the following:

WHEN THE POSITIVE THOUGHT IS ESTABLISHED AND THE MAGNETIC CURRENT FLOWING, RISE HIGHER AND HIGHER THROUGH INSPIRATION INTO THE REALM OF SPIRIT. FORGET PERSONALITY AND KNOW THAT

214

LESSON-SEVEN

YOU ARE NOTHING BY YOURSELF AND EVERYTHING WITH GOD, THE FATHER, THE ABSOLUTE, THE GREAT PRINCIPLE, WHICH CREATES, CONSTITUTES, GOVERNS, SUSTAINS AND CONTAINS ALL. TAKE LONG, DEEP, EVEN BREATHS, AND LET YOUR LAST CONSCIOUS THOUGHT BE THE REALIZATION OF YOUR ONENESS WITH SPIRIT. THERE WILL COME A MOMENT WHEN SUDDENLY AN INFLUX OF EXTRAORDINARY LIGHT WILL BE FELT—A LIVING, CONSCIOUS, LOVING LIGHT. LIGHT WITHIN AND LIGHT WITHOUT. YOU WILL FEEL AS IF MERGED IN AN OCEAN OF LIGHT AND AT THE SAME TIME YOU WILL FEEL THAT LIGHT ALSO WITHIN YOU. THAT IS, YOU WILL REALIZE YOUR COMPLETE ONENESS WITH THAT LIGHT. THUS THE SPIRITUAL VIBRATIONS ARE CONTACTED. YOUR WORK IS DONE—LEAVE THE REST TO THE GREAT LAW. WHEN YOU WILL FEEL THOSE SPIRITUAL VIBRATIONS FADING AWAY, DO NOT TRY TO STOP THEM. SPIRIT CANNOT BE FORCED. LET THEM DISAPPEAR NATURALLY.

To establish the positive thought means to do all the mental work as far as concerns the realization of Man's perfect status, his direct and constant relation with the Great Principle, his author. There all the knowledge obtained, especially in the First Lesson, as well as in the other previous lessons, must be used. In other words, within one's mind must be fully realized Man's Eternal Perfection. Naturally, the contact with the Universal Life Energy must be made first, and the Magnetic Current flowing, during the process of establishing the positive thought. When that is accomplished and the realization of Man's Real Self and his relation to the Absolute is clear in one's mind, then is the time to rise higher. Personality must be entirely forgotten, as well of the patient as of the healer. Mind has completed its work, and it is to higher Powers, to Inspiration and Love, to carry the work further. Through Inspiration coming

SCIENCE·OF·BEING

from our Super-conscious Self must we raise our vibrations into the highest; once started in that direction, our vibrations will carry us higher and higher, because of the Law of Evolution which says: "All vibrations tend naturally to rise upward in the scale of Eternal Harmony." In realizing that all Power comes from the Father, from the Absolute, the Great Principle, Which creates, constitutes, governs, sustains and contains all, we thus identify ourselves more and more with that Power. Our last conscious thought must be to know and to feel that Oneness with the Absolute. Then we must let ourselves go entirely and lose consciousness of all surroundings. Long, deep, even breaths taken at that time will help a great deal to increase our emotional vibrations. And then will come a moment when suddenly a flood of dazzling Light bursts upon us. Not mere physical light is It; It is living; one feels Its pulsations. It is conscious; It seems to know everything. One senses how wise It is. And supremely loving is this Light also. It is like the soft caress of a mother—Love within, Love without. One feels as if merged in an ocean of Light, as if waves of that Light are passing through one and beating at the shores of one's inner self. Light within, Light without. A complete Oneness with that wondrous Power is realized, and yet one's individuality is not dissolved, not lost, in all that Power.

卍 At the same time beautiful music, harmonies of the Spiritual Spheres, are vibrating about us, and evoking echoes from within. Wonderful fragrance penetrates one through and through. Like living waters, like nectar, the drink of gods, come those Vibrations to one's sense of taste; and as a lovely breeze, soft yet penetrating to the very depths of one's being, It expresses Itself through the sense of touch. It is Ecstasy, Infinite Bliss, Heaven brought down to Earth. Thus Spiritual Vibrations are contacted; man becomes consciously One with God. There are no adequate words to express this condition. Once experienced, no one can ever forget it. Christians call it Ecstasy, the Touch of Grace. The Hindus call it Samadhi, Nirvana; the Mohammedans, Paradisic Bliss, the Seventh Heaven. Whenever Spirit is contacted in that highest aspect, healing is instantaneous. Not only healing of physical ills, but also of mental and moral troubles. The Ray of Spirit changes entirely the nature

216

of the individuals; like fire, It cleanses and purifies it, and from a sinner It does make a saint. When Mary Magdalene, a woman of the lowest moral standard, bathed with her tears the feet of the beloved Master, she rose into the highest, she contacted Spiritual Vibrations, and from a harlot she became a sainted woman. When Saul of Tarsus, persecutor of Christians, on his way to Damascus, was struck with the Divine Light, Spiritual Vibrations contacted him and he was first blinded, but when he recovered again his sight, from a persecutor of Christ and his followers, he became St. Paul, one of His greatest Apostles. Whenever an individual is touched by Spiritual Vibrations, by Grace, his whole nature is changed and he becomes another being. No man can tell who will respond to that highest call.

卐 Many surprises may await those who try to bring about this contact with the Divine. Some people, seemingly material through and through, suddenly are able, through Love and Inspiration, to rise into the highest; and some, called spiritual characters, believing themselves to be such, when Spirit comes to them, cannot rise to meet the Holiest, and thus remain shut out from the Greatest there is. It requires the cooperation of the patient with the healer, a sincere cooperation, in order to bring about the highest results. If the patient is not ready, no matter how hard the healer may try, he will not be able to lift him into the Realm of Spirit. Therefore, if one would have that wonderful experience of becoming consciously One with the Absolute, it were better to enter alone into the secret chamber of one's inner consciousness, and there try through Inspiration and Love to reach Spirit. When the Spiritual contact is made, the hands of the healer, if they rest on the shoulders or on any other part of the body of the patient, will be raised unconsciously and held over the patient in a position of blessing. The moment we become One with the Absolute, we are so completely identified with His Nature that we unconsciously do what He does throughout Eternity. "He blesses the Universe which He has begotten." Therefore, we bless the World also and the patient who is there under our care; and through our hands, from all our being, are flowing no longer ordinary Magnetic or Mental Vibrations, but the Vibrations

SCIENCE-OF-BEING

of the Spirit Itself, Whose touch is sacred above all. A condition of such Bliss could not last for any length of time, because under the Divine Ray a human body would be dissolved. Therefore, Spiritual Vibrations stay with us only as long as we can bear them, and gradually, like some lovely strain of music, they begin to fade away. No matter how much we would like them to remain, we are not permitted to ask them to tarry longer. Spirit knows Its own and cannot be governed; we must let these Spiritual Vibrations fade away naturally and be thankful to our Father that we were able to contact Him in his highest Aspect. Our work is done; we must leave the rest to the Great Law.

卐 According to Scientific investigations, Spiritual Vibrations are sent out and received through a certain physical organ located in the upper part of the brain behind the Pituitary Body and called the Pineal Gland. The continual, conscious rising within our own selves of our highest emotional vibrations, stimulates more and more the Pineal Gland, that organ of our Super-consciousness, which is also the most sensitive organ in our body. The Pineal Gland then begins to function with increasing power, and in that way acts as a physical channel through which are contacted Spiritual Vibrations, the highest we know of in our present state of consciousness.

卐 The Super-consciousness is in human beings the direct Spiritual link between them and the Absolute. Through it human consciousness is connected with Cosmic Intelligence. It is the guardian angel referred to in different religions, who day and night beholds the Face of God.

卐 Not always is one successful in contacting Spiritual Vibrations. Favorable conditions must combine into a harmonious cooperation in order to bring about that contact. Nevertheless, we must always try to reach the highest, to rise into the Spiritual Realm, and we must not feel discouraged if we do not succeed each time. Each trial, each effort in that direction will bring us closer and closer to the Source of Spiritual Power. Some day we will reach that Spiritual Power, will become One with It; and in that day, all Power will be ours. It is the Baptism by the Holy Ghost when that Power illumines one.

LESSON-SEVEN

But before reaching that very Highest, before being baptized by the Spirit, one must go first through the Baptism by Fire, the purification necessary for a higher initiation.

卐 About two thousand years ago a Voice Crying in the Wilderness, John, the one who walked before Christ, to prepare the way, baptized Humanity with water. That means he cleansed, regenerated their bodies, their physical, animal natures, to receive properly the teachings of the Saviour of the World.

卐 Today, twenty centuries later, comes to Humanity, the Baptism by Fire; that is, the purification of the human mind through knowledge aflame with Love. It is a step higher, it is a preparation for the coming of One, Who, when He comes to this Earth again, will baptize with the Baptism of Spirit, or the Holy Ghost, those who are already purified by Fire, by the radiant Flame of Love. No man will come unto the Spirit until his body is made clean by water, and his mind pure by fire. That is, no man will be liberated from the bonds of ignorance and fear, and rise into Eternal Freedom, who has not regenerated his body through Life Energy (Magnetic Vibrations), and purified his mind by Truth and Love.

THE TWO ROADS

Great signs are given to Humanity today as in the days of old, yet with eyes open they do not see, and with ears open they do not hear, because their hearts are closed through the pride of their minds.

卐 Human beings have two Roads to walk upon. One is the Human Road, the nature of the other road is Divine; and happiness is the goal of both.

卐 Those who decide to walk the Human Road must always look about for help and assistance from their fellow beings. They bow before the powers of this world, they flatter them, they compromise with their own hearts because they think the end can justify the means. And for a time success is theirs. Yet the more they scheme, the more difficult it becomes to keep in harmony with all; still, they advance because support was promised them by word of mouth by many mighty of this world. At last they reach their goal. With hands extended, ready to grasp it, they say it is their own, when suddenly, beneath their feet the very ground is shattered to pieces and they fall, their goal not achieved! Why such disaster, such terrible deception? Why all this loss of energy, of time, of hope? Because their ignorance made them rely upon that which is the most unreliable thing on earth…upon human beings.

卐 And there are those who walk the Divine Road. No human help do they expect. At first their steps are handicapped. They have to fight ill-will, and apathy, and ignorance, and fear. From time to time some promises by humans are made to them to help them in their work. With gratitude they thank, yet do not build on these, as they rely alone on Laws and Divine Help. They know that human beings, those even of the best, are human still, hence limited in every way, and therefore do they trust themselves to God alone. They know that limitations can never prevent All Power from expressing Itself through endless means. They know that if one human promise wanes, that if one human friend will fail, there are ten more through which the Great Law manifests Itself. And if those ten should also fail, there are many others, countless channels, through which all good will come to them who walk the Divine Road. And by and by, slowly, step after step they climb, overcoming obstacles along the way, until easier and broader turns the path on which they move onward. Strength and joy increase continually; there the goal is in sight, within their reach. They raise their hands and take their own. No man can steal away that prize of theirs, because it is their own by right.

卐 Those are the two Roads which lie before each man on Earth; let every human being pause and ponder well which path is best to take.

卐 One last question, a great question, lies still open for those who wish to know. Why is there Evil in this World? If God is God, why does He tolerate all sin, sorrow, suffering, to be spread broadcast upon this Earth? Why should Man, if son of God, the same in essence as the Spirit, the Great All, why should he need to toil, to strive, to suffer? Old as the World is this question. Most difficult to answer. No direct message could reach us through all these labyrinths of the human mind; therefore from above, through Inspiration, veiled in a legend, must come to suffering Humanity the answer. That answer—closing chapter of this book of Science of Eternal Being—is called "The Dream."

LESSON-SEVEN

THE DREAM

Night! The fragrance of a warm summer night suffuses all Nature. The firmament studded with stars glowing like diamonds, a net of glistening loveliness, through which the dark beauty of night is fading.

卐 Soft, living Light invades the clear atmosphere like golden vapor. It increases steadily, penetrating and covering everything. Bathed in its radiance, there appear glittering diamond peaks, mountains of topaz and amethyst, massive rocks of emerald, gigantic monoliths of sapphire, as steps leading to higher regions. The Light grows in strength, investing all things with color and warmth. These are no rays of a sun rising from behind the hills, but a glowing radiance emanating from everywhere, embracing everything, and increasing like some strain of music: and indeed, there is music in the air. Gentle melodies are trembling, soft harmonies are vibrating, and mysterious echoes answer them.

卐 Set amidst these precious mountains, surrounded by a grove of gigantic trees so lofty that they appear to be talking with the clouds, stands a Palace, large as a city and of wondrous beauty. The walls of it are streams of Light rising from the ground and playing in all the colors of the rainbow. Its flat roofs, towers and domes are golden clouds upon which the glow of the spreading Light is shedding its morning splendor.

卐 And still the Light grows in strength. Through the golden roof of the Palace rises an innumerable procession of Beings, each one seeming more wonderful than the other.

卐 Of almost similar height and size are they, but how different each one! Some are like fiery lava streaming from the crater of a volcano; some are like moonrays made living beings; some like roaring waterfalls with rainbows playing about their heads; some like precious stones become alive. Their wonderful bodies appear in all their unhidden glory: no covering conceals their Eternal beauty. And eyes, such as when the Spirit Itself looks on the World It has created, full of supreme majesty and power, full of Infinite Love, are shining from under their divine brows!

SCIENCE·OF·BEING

卐 Two of these Beings rise with the rest from the depths of the Palace, and like twin stars stand tenderly embraced on the top of the highest tower. More radiant, more wonderful than the others are they. Like a brilliant star is the countenance of one. His body, taller and stronger than that of his Mate, is like a phosphorescent opal. Streams of living Light are flowing through his body and making it shine in iridescent hues. His eyes are lightning; a purple cloud his hair; and when he speaks and when he moves, far away thunder is heard..... Golden and shining is his Companion, his body woven of sun-rays, his hair a glowing flame, his eyes reflecting the glory of Heaven itself; and when he speaks and when he moves, soft harmonies fill the air.

卐 With gestures of adoration they raise their arms in triumphant song—greeting to the Spirit, thanks to the Great Giver. Their brothers follow them in the song; all Nature joins in this hymn of gratitude. Birds and animals, trees and flowers, rocks and clouds, waters and the ground itself, sing the eternal praise of all beings to The One Supreme Being, their Divine Father. Stronger and more wondrous grows the great song, flooding the Universe with praise and love; it rises to a thunder of triumph, and dies away in silence.

卐 Silence!—A limpid breeze moves the air, and each one feels within himself the words, "Live and Love." The Great Spirit, The Father, is communing with His children. Infinite bliss fills every being, and pervades the Universe. The Day of Heaven has begun.

卐 But the triumphant band passes out of sight; the roofs are deserted; and the two, the Heavenly Twins, sink back into the Palace. And there they stand within the great tower in the very midst of it. High, circular walls surround them, but there are no openings in those walls. Deep and mysterious is the material out of which they are built; precious also is it, for its name is Silence. And upon those mighty walls of Silence, towering high up into the free air, are set lofty pillars. Precious also is the material from which they are made, shining in all the colors of the rainbow; their name is Hope. And through these pillars of Hope stretching their slender shafts into the highest air, are sailing golden clouds. Silent they move through the tower of Silence; but the birds with the rustling of their wings, do not dare to fly through because of the sacred Silence.

꘠ Upon these pillars of Hope rests a glorious dome, effulgent as a sun, and Joy is the material out of which the dome is made. And the floor upon which they stand is a transparent crystal, a gigantic lens, and through that lens the whole Universe appears stretched out at their feet. Worlds without number, all stars, sun-systems, chains of planets, all beings, every thing, the greatest and the smallest, can be seen through that crystal. Understanding is the material out of which that floor is made. With their feet firmly established on Understanding, with Silence surrounding them, with Hope towering over them and with Joy crowning them, stand the two, keeping watch over the World.

꘠ And the one whose voice is like thunder speaks to his Mate.

꘠ "Oh! Thou loved One! Thou, radiant Joy of the World! Once more we stand ready to fulfill our charge, to carry out our duties in the eternal scheme—Thou the Love of the World, I the Mind of it. All knowledge, all power are ours. Why then must we every morning adore, greet as our Master, One Whom none has ever seen? Thou art from Eternity, and I am from Eternity, and so are all our brothers. Yet who has ever seen the One Who claims to be our Father and Who is called God? True it is that every morning a Voice speaks within us—but there is none can tell whether it comes not from our very selves. Why should we adore any longer One Who remains a mystery to us? Enough that we should be slaves to an unknown master. Let us free ourselves from the bonds by which we are now bound. All powers, all forces are ours; therefore let us rule the World—we two, the greatest powers of this World."

꘠ The answer came soft-winged, tender as Love itself.

꘠ "Ah! Brother. Why these words of pride, of revolt? Thou knowest — for thy heart tells thee in spite of all—that there is a God, that we have an invisible Father, Who is also our loving Mother, and Who enfolds us, His children, in His Divine embrace. He thinks continually of us. He plans ceaselessly for our joy. For us He pours out into manifestation the endless beauties, the transplendent wonders, from the unmanifest regions of His Heart. And He asks nothing from us but our love. Is it so difficult to love Him Who so loves us? Dismiss these thoughts of rebellion, forget these proud words. Sorrow alone can come from them, my Brother."

卐 Like sudden thunder, like the bursting of crashing floods, came the roaring, shattering outcry.

卐 "What is this Hidden Power that can compel Mind? Mind, the glittering luminary of all the Worlds, is regent in the Universe. No servant's place shall I be satisfied to take. But if thou, oh my gentle Brother! wilt not rule with me, and share my power, then alone shall I command the World."

卐 And with these words, swift as a streak of lightning, he rises from the ground of Understanding, through Silence, through Hope, through radiant Joy, into the open. Higher and still more high, past the precious mountains, he climbs the lambent air, leaving behind a blazing train of phosphorus, until his feet touch the summit of the most aspiring peak, the pinnacle of glittering diamond. Poised on the shining spire, his cry goes out to all the World.

卐 "Spirits of Light! Sons of Eternity! The day of freedom, of liberation, has come to us! Free are ye born, free shall ye live! No more adoration, no more praying to a Master, to a God Whom none has ever seen. From now, ye shall be your own masters. Come all, come all to me, and ye shall be free!"

卐 And from the hidden parts of all the World, myriads of Spirits, Sons of Light, are gathering together. They surround the diamond peak where stands the one whose eyes are lightning, whose countenance is like a blazing star. With words of adoration they shout:

卐 "Hail to thee, Lucifer! Son of the Morning! Hail to thee, Liberator! Our Leader, our Master, our God!"

卐 And he who is proclaimed the master of the hour, called the ruler of the world, looks down upon those prostrate at his feet.

卐 "I am your master, I am your god! Follow me, for I alone can give you freedom; new beauties shall ye discover through me, new powers and forces shall ye wield. Ye shall become more piercingly brilliant than ever ye have been, like flaming diamonds, more scintillating than the blazing suns."

卐 But in the sacred grove, hidden amid the giant trees, with sad eyes and a heavy heart, stands one whose name is Love, words of prayer falling from his lips.

卍 "Father, Beloved one! Beating Heart of all the Universe! Forgive them, for they know not what they do. Him they call God, Lucifer they acknowledge as supreme. Yet he is nothing but Thy child, and all his powers and beauties he has from Thee. True it is he appears supreme, for his feet touch the ground, his head reaches Heaven, and his glory seems to fill all Space, yet they are as deceived as he is himself. It is Thy glory which is still shining through him, and Thy power is taken for his own. Father, forgive them, for they know not what they do. Forgive my Brother, Lucifer, for he is still the dearest to my heart: he also knows not what he does!"

卍 From his piercing height, Lucifer heard the faithful, praying voice—and smiled on him in contempt. But suddenly another Voice, heavy with destiny, gathering in its might the Unmeasured Energy of all the Worlds:

卍 "Lucifer! In Heaven all desires are achievement. Thou wouldst be free—thou shalt be free. Go thou, and all those who worship thee, to that further plane to which ye all belong. These Regions of Eternal Light can bear thee no longer. Your bodies cast shadows in the pure skies. From the Spheres of Light to the outer, utmost void—go!"

卍 Thus the Voice from the Vaulted Silence: and on the moment, a sudden burden as of great heaviness falls on Lucifer and his followers. They are no longer able to offer resistance against its weight, and with a blast of thunder and terror, they fall from the Realms of Light into the somber void.

卍 As they fall darkness grows denser about them, until no spark of Light, no hope is left to them. Far in the utter gloom, still falling, they perceive a fiery region which draws them swiftly to it with irresistible force. And they are cast into an ocean of fire, of smoke, of molten metal, of boiling stone.

卍 He who was the first to fall, is also the first to rise again. And he sees his brothers, his followers, once Spirits of Light, darkened, disgraced, extinguished, thrown into that abode of fire and suffering. And he calls to them:

SCIENCE·OF·BEING

卐 "Rise, my brothers! Rise, ye who are still the Sons of Light! True it is that from the highest Spheres of Bliss, we have been cast into this desolation. Yet all knowledge is still mine, and thus all power, and I shall make for you from this hell a new Heaven, and this new Heaven shall be called Earth."

卐 As he speaks the ages pass, the flaming fields contract, the incandescence blazes with a fainter heat, the fumes and vapors gradually disperse, and a lustrous, glowing planet, cradled in fire and beauty, is born. The lovely Earth appears—green hills and gentle slopes and flowery meadows, singing brooks, clear rivers and the blue sea, mountains and chasms and waterfalls. And through enchanted forests birds of a hundred colors are flying, and in the fields animals are roaming. And Lucifer is pleased with his creation and says:

卐 "And now, my Brothers! Ye shall be the inhabitants of his new Heaven and ye shall be called human beings."

卐 And wonderful beings, lofty of stature, strong and comely, appear on the Earth: they propagate and multiply, and rule the Earth. And Lucifer is their king, their god.

卐 So fair a world seemed a true semblance of Heaven. But the canker of revolt which had cast them from Heaven, still lived with them. And the spirit of jealousy, hatred, and pride begins to manifest itself, and grows, and spreads, until the splendid Earth becomes again a hell. But now they are unable to bear any longer the suffering which infests the Earth, and they find no help or relief from Lucifer. In their deep despair, they remember their Father, and turn to him and pray again to God. And God, their Father, hears the cry of His children, and from His Heart sends down to them His Own Love. And Love comes down from Heaven to Earth, and Love becomes a human being; and Love lives with human beings and teaches human beings how to love.

卐 But Lucifer, incarnate also as a human being, sees the menace to his power, and in a passion of hate and jealousy rises against his Brother and slays his Brother. And God's Love shakes off the burden of the Earth, and Earth is without Love again. So sorrow and terror once more prevail, and the

228

suffering becomes intolerable. Again human beings cry out to God for help. And God, the Father, the loving Mother, hears the cry of His children, and from His Heart sends down to them His Own Love. And Love comes down from Heaven to Earth again and Love becomes a human being; and Love lives with human beings, and teaches them the Law of Love.

卐 But Lucifer, the World's Mind, again incarnate as a human being, rises against his Mate, his Eternal Twin, and causes Him to die, for he sees in Him the great menace to his power. And once again, God's Love returns to the Father, and again the Earth is void of Love.

卐 So through the ages, whenever misery and suffering increase upon the Earth so as to make life intolerable, the children of the Earth call out for a Deliverer. And always Love, gentle and tender-hearted, comes to their call, and tries to save His brothers. But Lucifer ever rises against Him, kills His body, and destroys His work, for Love is the continual menace to his power.

卐 And when for the last time, God's Love came down to Earth, and lived the humble life of a simple mortal, giving to Humanity the greatest lesson that Love ever gave, Lucifer, incarnate as a human being, rose once more against his Brother, betrayed Him and brought Him to His death upon the cross. But He, of Whom the World was not worthy, breathing His last breath, dying as a felon upon the accursed tree, prayed for those who had crucified Him:

卐 "Father, forgive them, for they know now what they do. Father, forgive my brother Lucifer, for he knows not what he does."

卐 These burning words of love struck Lucifer like lightning in his heart, and he went out and made an end to his human self. And rising as a spirit, he beheld the greatness of his brother's Love, and the endless evil of his own age-old sin. He saw the sorrow and the suffering which came through him to all beings; and he felt that cold and stony heart of his melt and soften, and he wept tears of blood, tears of fire. And those tears fell on the Earth and the Earth trembled to its very foundation.

卐 Thus for the first time, after countless ages of revolt, did Lucifer lift up his eyes to God, and words of prayer fell from his lips:

SCIENCE-OF-BEING

卍 "Father! I know the Immensity of my sin, and do not beg for forgiveness for myself. For crimes like mine cannot be atoned. But oh! My Father, forgive them, those who followed me in my fall. Forgive them, for they knew not what they did. No fault was theirs but that they loved me more than Thee, and listened to the magic of my words, the glitter of my Mind, so that Thy Laws were all forgotten. Therefore, I pray Thee, forgive them and take them back to Thee: let them return to those pure Spheres of Light, where Bliss and Harmony and Serenity are. But for myself, if by my eternal damnation I can win their eternal salvation, I am ready to be damned for Eternity."

卍 Then from the Vaulted Silence, a Voice, gathering in its might the Unmeasured Energy of all the Worlds:

卍 "Lucifer, thy sacrifice is accepted—and through thy sacrifice shall the World be saved."

卍 And he, the proud one who had thought himself a god, bent his knees, and with his head touched the dust of the ground.

卍 Like far-off thunder sounded his words: "Father, I thank Thee!"

卍 And once again the Voice:

卍 "Lucifer, thou hast sinned much, but thou hast also loved much. Infinite is thy sin, but infinite also is thy sacrifice; therefore, art thou forgiven. Go into the World, live among the children of the World, and carry to them the Light of Knowledge purified by Love. Thus the veils of self-delusion will be withdrawn one by one, limitations will be removed, suffering conquered, sorrow replaced by Joy. And when the last human fault shall have been destroyed, when all thy brothers will have come back to Me, then only will come thy day of liberation. Thy pinions of inspiration, singed by the fires of hell, will have grown again strong enough to lift thee from this Earth and to bear thee back to Heaven. And there, at the burnished Gates of Heaven, the Portals of Eternal Harmony, shall Love, thy Brother, thine Eternal Mate, be waiting for thee, to lead thee back to Me!"

卍 And Lucifer went into the World. And Lucifer taught the World. And to the

QVESTIONS & ANSWERS

World Lucifer carried the Light of Pure Knowledge, glowing with the flame of Love.

• • •

卐 Night! The fragrance of a warm summer night pervades all things. The firmament blazing with stars, and beyond the stars darkness softly fading away. The radiant Palace, the sacred grove, and above them, the mountains of precious stones. And in the sacred grove whose trees are talking with the clouds, rest in sleep myriads of Beings of Eternal Light. Beneath the loftiest tree, the loftiest king of all the woods, lies one whose countenance is as a God's. He lies in deep slumber; and bending over him, calling him softly with words of Love, stands his Mate, his Twin.

卐 "Brother! Loved one, awake! Arise, my Lucifer! The night is fading fast, and soon the Day of Heaven will begin. Now must we sing again the praises to our Father, and lift our voices in adoration and gratitude to God.

卐 Like far-off thunder came the questioning words from trembling lips, and out of sorrowful eyes a flash of lightning: "Oh! Where am I?"

卐 And the answer: "Thou art in Heaven, Lucifer."

卐 But again the question: "Where have I been these ages? This fall, this suffering through countless years; and always fighting thee, my loved one, destroying thy work and killing thee. Where have I been?"

卐 "Not for a single moment of time hast thou left Heaven, Lucifer. But with thy brothers in the sacred grove, beneath the great trees, hast thou slept the night, instead of with me in the Palace. Lonely was I, my Brother, for I missed thy presence."

卐 "But these sorrows, these nights of darkness that I saw and lived? This suffering, these crimes, this agony? What were they all—whence came they and where have they gone?"

卐 And the answer—burning words of Love—"Beloved! It was nothing but a Dream."

SCIENCE-OF-BEING

LESSON SEVEN

1. **QUES.** What is the most direct and simple way to obtain Spiritual Power?

   ANS. By performing one's ordinary daily actions ENERGETICALLY, INTELLIGENTLY, ACCURATELY, and JOYFULLY.

2. **QUES.** Can Mental Vibrations be raised into Spiritual ones?

   ANS. Not until Mind has learned the lesson of Truth and Love.

3. **QUES.** What is the theory of how to reach Spiritual Vibrations?

   ANS. To become one with Spirit, one must forget personality, and through Inspiration and Love realize the Allness of the Great Principle and one's oneness with It.

4. **QUES.** How are Spiritual Vibrations perceived?

   ANS. Through all the senses, which become so acute that they are able to register the highest vibrations.

5. **QUES.** Is it advisable to deny senses in order to perceive Spiritual Vibrations?

   ANS. Denial of senses will not help; their refinement is needed.

6. **QUES.** Through which physical channel are Spiritual Vibrations most easily contacted?

   ANS. Through the Pineal Gland, located almost in the center of the upper part of the brain, behind the Pituitary Body.

7. **QUES.** What part of our mental self does the Pineal Gland represent?

   ANS. It represents the Super-consciousness, of which it is the organ.

8. **QUES.** What effect do Spiritual Vibrations have on human beings?

   ANS. They entirely change human nature from negative into positive.

9. **QUES.** What is that change called?

   ANS. The Touch of Grace, Samadhi, Nirvana, Paradisic Bliss.

10. **QUES.** Can physical diseases also be healed by Spiritual Vibrations?

    ANS. Yes, and instantaneously.

LESSON-SEVEN

11. QUES. How long can Spiritual Vibrations be contacted?
    ANS.   As long as human beings can stand them. Too long a contact with them would completely dissolve the material body.

12. QUES. Is one always successful in contacting Spiritual Vibrations?
    ANS.   No. Favorable conditions must combine in harmonious co-operation in order to bring about that contact.

13. QUES. What is the Baptism by the Holy Ghost?
    ANS.   It is the illumination through Spiritual Power, the contact with Spiritual Vibrations.

14. QUES. What must precede that highest baptism?
    ANS.   The Baptism by Fire.

15. QUES. What is the Baptism by Fire?
    ANS.   It is the purification of the human mind through knowledge aflame with Love.

16. QUES. When will that Baptism come to Humanity?
    ANS.   It has already come to Humanity, and is baptizing it with its radiant flame.

17. QUES. What preceded the Baptism by Fire?
    ANS.   The Baptism by Water, which purifies the body.

18. QUES. What does the Baptism by Water stand for?
    ANS.   For the regeneration of the body through the use of the Magnetic Life Force.

19. QUES. Can anyone reach the Baptism by Spirit, which means the purification of the soul, without first having the mind purified through the Baptism by Fire, and the body through the Baptism by Water?
    ANS.   No.

20. QUES. What do the three kinds of vibrations, the Magnetic, the Mental, and the Spiritual, stand for?
    ANS.   They stand for the three-fold Baptism, which means the regeneration of human beings on the Three Planes.

21. QUES.   What are the two Roads human beings walk upon in their life?
    ANS.   The Human Road, and the Divine Road.

22. QUES.   What is the difference between them?
    ANS.   The Human Road, relying upon human support, leads to failure. The Divine Road, based exclusively upon the Great Principle and its universal Forces and Laws, leads to success.

23. QUES.   What is the most unreliable thing on Earth?
    ANS.   A human being.

24. QUES.   What is the one power on which to rely completely?
    ANS.   The Power of the Absolute, called also the Great Principle, or God.

25. QUES.   What is the origin of Evil?
    ANS.   The belief in separation from All Power.

26. QUES.   Did that separation ever actually take place?
    ANS.   No. It is nothing but a dream which Humanity is dreaming.

27. QUES.   What does the legend "The Dream" represent?
    ANS.   It represents the tragic History of Mind.

28. QUES.   Who are the two principal characters of that Legend?
    ANS.   Two Brothers, heavenly Twins, Lucifer and Christ.

29. QUES.   What do they stand for?
    ANS.   For Mind and Love respectively.

30. QUES.   Where does the action take place?
    ANS.   In the realm of Eternal Harmony, commonly called Heaven.

31. QUES.   Explain briefly the legend.
    ANS.   In the secrecy of Silence, Lucifer and Christ are performing their eternal duties of keeping watch over the world. Being the first dual manifestation of the Great Principle, they are, as Mind and Love, the two greatest powers of this World. Mind, feeling himself to be the possessor of all knowledge and power, refuses to acknowledge the Source of All Power,

his own Father, the Eternally Unmanifest, called God, and claims that power as his own. He offers to share the power of this World with his twin brother, Love. Christ refuses to give up His God, and warns Lucifer of the great danger of pride. Lucifer, or Mind, then decides to rule the World alone, and to substitute his power for that of God. He sends his call throughout the World. He beguiles those fellow spirits who respond to his call with wonderful promises if they will follow his lead, and they proclaim him their liberator and their god. Having broken away form All Power, Lucifer (Mind), loses the greater part of his power, and falls from his high estate, together with those who followed him. This fall is called the Involution into Matter, which is itself nothing but the product of the involutionary process. Though fallen, Lucifer's pride is still unbroken, and with the remnant of his knowledge and power, he tries to create out of the Hell into which they have been precipitated, out of the boiling, fiery mass of pride, revolt, jealousy and hatred, a new heaven which he calls Earth, and he makes human beings out of his fellow spirits, Mind, in his utter pride, wants to create his own world after the divine pattern. Seemingly successful in the beginning, he ultimately fails completely. Pride, revolt, jealously, hatred, all permeating his creation, make again a Hell out of the Heaven which he thought he had created. His twin brother, Love, comes to the rescue, but Mind, out of jealousy, continually fights the only one who could help him. Through ages that fight goes on, until Love wins, and Mind (Lucifer) acknowledges his defeat. There comes to him the realization of the immensity of his mistake, and he decides to face eternal damnation in order to save Humanity. His sacrifice is accepted, but through his own sacrifice the negative in him is destroyed, and the positive and eternal is brought out. He goes out into the world to learn the lesson of Love, and his mission as Mind is to teach Humanity that All Power comes from God alone. Thus he brings back all human beings to the Realm of Eternal Harmony, called Heaven, and redeems himself also. And when that work has been completed, though seemingly it lasts through countless ages, and is so real to him, he realizes that all that negative and sad experience was nothing but a dream.

卐 Having learned the lesson of Love, Mind becomes one with it, in the Bosom of their Eternal Father, God.

卐 Every human being born to this Earth is experiencing within himself that living dream of Mind. Mind is continually fighting against Love, the Luciferian principle combating the Christ Principle, and when the Christ Principle, Love wins, then Lucifer, the fallen Mind, is redeemed and the liberated individual is awakened to his true status of Eternal Perfection as a Son of God.

IT WAS BVT A DREAM & NOW YOV ARE AWAKE

SCIENCE-OF-BEING

The Commandment of
THE LIGHTBEARERS to the World

"BE MAN"—Express in every act of yours All ENERGY, INTELLIGENCE, TRUTH and LOVE; thus Living only will you live; thus acting only can you build to Freedom, Strength and Happiness in Life. This is your Problem: be this your Foremost Aim.

The Commandment! Throughout the whole of Eternity there will never be another Commandment given. THE LIGHTBEARERS Commandment is that great. The FourSquare is the essence of Truth. It covers the ground so completely, that even God, if He wanted to improve It, He could not do so. It was the foundation of Creation, throughout all Eternity, and will continue so for Eternity. The Infinite Intelligence opened my eyes to see the logical sequence of the Four Corners. If we have faith that the FourSquare is all there is, we are open to the Eternal. If we have no faith, we close the door to the Eternal.

~Eugene Fersen ~

SCIENCE-OF-BEING

13960382R00151

Made in the USA
San Bernardino, CA
11 August 2014